Praise for *Never in My Wildest Dreams*

"The remarkable odyssey of Belva Davis is a compelling testament to tenacity and truth. As a pioneering black journalist, she was determined to tell the stories that mainstream news outlets had ignored for too long—and she devoted her career to ensuring that the voices of all Americans became part of our national conversation. This fiercely honest memoir reveals that her struggle was never easy, but helping change the world never is."

> —**Andrew Young**, Former Ambassador to the United Nations, Chairman of GoodWorks International, LLC

"Risk-averse people do not make good journalists. Belva Davis entered the profession during the 1960s when virtually every good story required risk-taking. Belva has lived on the edge of history over the last fifty years in some of its most dangerous places. And she got the stories, including her own. *Never in My Wildest Dreams* is the chronicle of her march through the second half of the twentieth century as a great black woman journalist."

> —**Howard Dodson**, Director of the Schomburg Center for Research in Black Culture

"Good writing is a combination of two things: good thoughts and good prose. Belva Davis tops that. She gives us tough journalism clothed in the tender lyricism of a true poet who journeys to the depth of the human heart."

> —**Abigail Rosen McGrath**, Founder of Renaissance House

"An engrossing account of triumph over adversity. *Never in My Wildest Dreams* is a valuable contribution to the pre- and post-WWII history of blacks in the Bay Area and a fascinating exploration of the determination that carried Belva Davis far beyond her impoverished childhood and local reporting work to the ranks of the nation's most respected journalists."

> —**Jewelle Taylor Gibbs**, Professor Emerita, University of California at Berkeley

Never in My Wildest Dreams

Never in My Wildest Dreams

A Black Woman's Life in Journalism

BELVA DAVIS

WITH VICKI HADDOCK

foreword by
Bill Cosby

PoliPointPress

Never in My Wildest Dreams:
A Black Woman's Life in Journalism

15 14 13 12 11   1 2 3 4 5

Production management: BookMatters
Book design: BookMatters
Cover design: Charles Kreloff

Library of Congress Cataloging-in-Publication Data
Davis, Belva, 1933–
   A black woman's life in journalism / Belva Davis
with Vicki Haddock.
       p. cm.
   Includes index.
   ISBN 978-1-936227-06-8 (alk. paper)
   1. Davis, Belva, 1933– 2. Journalists—United
States—Biography.   3. Television journalists—
United States—Biography.   4. African American
women journalists—Biography.   I. Haddock, Vicki.
II. Title.
   PN4874.D3565A3   2011
   070.92—dc22   2010048995

Published by:
PoliPointPress, LLC
80 Liberty Ship Way, Suite 22
Sausalito, CA 94965
(415) 339-4100
www.p3books.com

Distributed by Ingram Publisher Services
Printed in the USA

Dedicated to
Bill
Steven
Darolyn
Sterling
Dave
Dava

and all who hold fast to dreams

Contents

Foreword
by Bill Cosby

When we had a houseboat in San Francisco Bay in the late 1960s, Mrs. Cosby and I, we would watch the news on TV. And there would be Belva Davis, out reporting stories and anchoring the newscasts. And my wife looked at me and said, "That's the most relaxed woman I've ever seen at being perfect."

What's important to remember is that those of us who made history, those of us who were among the first of our race to do some particular thing in the United States, disproved fallacies that said our lips wouldn't allow us to pronounce words properly; that our brains wouldn't allow us to write, to speak, to make anyone understand anything; and then, of course, that our color would not only turn off viewers but lead them to turn us off as well. Belva Davis, like tennis star Althea Gibson, like educator and presidential advisor Mary McLeod Bethune, carried it off. She made covering the news look so natural, so easy, that people couldn't believe that it was her job.

Belva Davis was someone who sustained us, who made us proud. We looked forward to seeing her prove the stereotypical ugliness of those days to be wrong. She was the first woman of color that many viewers came to know and trust, and she met that challenge with integrity and dignity and grace.

We had first become acquainted some years earlier, when I was doing standup comedy at clubs like the hungry i in San Francisco, and Belva was a disc jockey on black radio station KDIA in Oakland. I was first her interview subject, then her studio guest on her own radio show, and then her friend. I was happy to take the stage and formally introduce her when she was honored with the International Women's Media Foundation's Lifetime Achievement Award. She has always had energy to burn, whether she's gathering the news or fighting for minority rights or producing a community event.

People should know that Belva Davis is a pure, pure woman—warm and generous. But they also should know that they should be careful if they haven't behaved or been fair or honest. When this lady puts pen to paper, the world had better watch out.

one

...

"What the Hell Are You Niggers Doing in Here?"

I could feel the hostility rising like steam off a cauldron of vitriol: floor delegates and gallery spectators at the Republican National Convention were erupting in catcalls aimed at the press. South of San Francisco, people were sweltering inside the cavernous Cow Palace, which typically hosted rodeos. In July of 1964 it offered ringside seats for the breech birth of a right-wing revolution.

My radio news director, Louis Freeman, and I lacked credentials for the press box—actually we knew that some whites at this convention would find our mere presence offensive. Although Louis was brilliant and had a deep baritone voice and a journalism degree, his first boss had warned Louis he might never become a radio reporter because Negro lips were "too thick to pronounce polysyllabic words." But Louis, whose enunciation was flawless, eventually landed an on-the-hour news slot on KDIA-AM, the Bay Area's premier soul-gospel-jazz station; and he was determined to cover the convention. It was said that the national press was flocking to the GOP confab to "report Armageddon." Louis wanted to be at the crux of the story, relaying to our black listeners all the news that white reporters might deem insignificant. I was the station's intrepid ad traffic manager, a thirty-one-year-old divorced mother of two, who had no journalism training. No question Louis would have preferred a more formidable companion: I'm delicately boned and stand merely five foot one in stockings. But I was an eager volunteer. More to the point, I was his *only* volunteer. And I was, in his words, "a moxie little thing." He had finagled two spectator passes from one of the black delegates—they made up less than 1 percent of convention participants. So there we were, perched in the shadows under the rafters,

1

scribbling notes and recording speeches, mistakenly presuming we had found the safest spot to be.

Day One of the convention had been tense but orderly. GOP organizers had strictly instructed delegates to be on their best behavior for the television cameras, and they had complied.

Day Two would be different. Day Two was starting to spin out of control.

Indeed, the "Party of Lincoln" was ripping apart before our eyes. Arizona senator Barry Goldwater, a flinty firebrand whose ruggedly chiseled face would have rested easy on Mount Rushmore, had tapped into a mother lode of voter anxiety about Communism, crime, and especially civil rights. His followers came prepared to jettison the party's moderate wing, and they were spurred on by Goldwater's fantasy of sawing off the Eastern Seaboard to let it float out to sea. The press noted that he could win the nomination by coalescing the right and attracting fringe groups such as the John Birch Society and the Ku Klux Klan, and reporters were openly questioning whether the party was on the verge of being taken over by extremists.

So when former president Dwight D. Eisenhower stepped into the spotlight at the podium, I leaned forward intently, hoping the avuncular Ike would provide a soothing balm of rationality.

Indeed his speechwriters had crafted a temperate address that gave nods to free enterprise, a denunciation of violent radicals on the left or right, and even benign praise about America's progress on civil rights. But Eisenhower had personally and uncharacteristically inserted a couple of poison-tipped arrows into his script, and he let the first fly straight at the press: "Let us particularly scorn the divisive efforts of those outside our family—including sensation-seeking columnists and commentators—because my friends I assure you, these are people who couldn't care less about the good of our party."

The Cow Palace erupted in jeers, boos, and catcalls. Fists shot up in the air and shook angrily in the direction of the press box and broadcast anchor booths. The convention's contempt for even the most respected reporters of the day was palpable—when professorial John Chancellor of NBC News refused to surrender his floor spot to the dancing "Goldwater Girls," security guards brusquely carted him out, prompting him to wryly sign off with "This is John Chancellor, somewhere in custody."

Eisenhower, meanwhile, wasn't finished. "Let us not be guilty of maudlin sympathy," he bellowed, "for the criminal who, roaming the streets with the switchblade knife and illegal firearm, seeking a helpless prey, suddenly becomes, upon apprehension, a poor, underprivileged person who counts upon the compassion of our society and the laxness or weakness of too many courts to forgive his offense." Without actually uttering the word *Negroes,* the former president spoke in a code that needed no translation for those white Americans who regarded black people as an encroaching threat. Eisenhower, whether he realized it or not, seemed to be granting permission to the whites' prejudice and hatred. I suspect he was unprepared for the deafening applause, cheers, shouts, and honked Klaxons that ensued.

Louis and I warily locked eyes, neither of us willing to outwardly betray a hint of alarm. Next on the agenda were controversial platform amendments on civil rights. We had a job to do.

The satirist H. L. Mencken once observed that a national political convention often is as fascinating as a revival, or a hanging: "One sits through long sessions wishing heartily that all the delegates and alternates were dead and in hell—and then suddenly there comes a show so gaudy and hilarious, so melodramatic and obscene, so unimaginably exhilarating and preposterous, that one lives a gorgeous year in an hour."

Mencken, of course, had the luxury of being white. We did not. For Louis and me, the next hour would indeed feel like a year, but a grotesque one.

First, the entire Republican platform was read aloud—a tedious ploy to delay any ugly debate over amendments until the prime time viewing hour would be past. At 10 p.m. the first amendment was offered, condemning radical zealots such as the KKK and the Birchers. Liberal establishment icon New York governor Nelson Rockefeller, whom Goldwater had defeated for the nomination, rose to speak in the amendment's favor. "These extremists feed on fear, hate and terror," he said, as a cacophony of boos began to rise from the crowd. "They encourage disunity. These are people who have nothing in common with Americanism. The Republican Party must repudiate these people!" Enraged at him, the Goldwater crowd interrupted Rockefeller twenty-two times in five minutes, drowning him out with shrieks, noisemakers, a bass drum, and the rebuking cry, "We want Barry! We want Barry!"

While the Goldwater organization tried to keep its delegates in check on the floor of the Cow Palace, snarling Goldwater fans in the galleries around us were off the leash. The mood turned unmistakably menacing. Even eminent campaign historian Theodore White abandoned the arena for the relative sanity of the trailers outside; he would later write that although no one in the Goldwater organization and few on the delegate floor remotely qualified as kooks, "the kooks dominated the galleries, hating and screaming and reveling in their own frenzy."

Suddenly Louis and I heard a voice yell, "Hey, look at those two up there!" The accuser pointed us out, and several spectators swarmed beneath us. "Hey niggers!" they yelled. "What the hell are you niggers doing in here?"

I could feel the hair rising on the back of my neck as I looked into faces turned scarlet and sweaty by heat and hostility. Louis, in suit and tie and perpetually dignified, turned to me and said with all the nonchalance he could muster, "Well, I think that's enough for today." Methodically we began wrapping up the cords to our bulky tape recorder and packing it and the rest of our equipment into suitcases. As we began our descent down the ramps of the Cow Palace, a self-appointed posse dangled over the railings, taunting. "Niggers!" "Get out of here, boy!" "You too, nigger bitch." "Go on, get out!" "I'm gonna kill your ass."

I stared straight ahead, putting one foot in front of the other like a soldier who would not be deterred from a mission. The throng began tossing garbage at us: wadded up convention programs, mustard-soaked hotdogs, half-eaten Snickers bars. My goal was to appear deceptively serene, mastering the mask of dispassion I had perfected since childhood to steel myself against any insults the outside world hurled my way. Then a glass soda bottle whizzed within inches of my skull. I heard it whack against the concrete and shatter. I didn't look back, but I glanced sideways at Louis and felt my lower lip begin to quiver. He was determined we would give our tormentors no satisfaction.

"If you start to cry," he muttered, "I'll break your leg."

It took an eternity for us to wend our way through the gauntlet, from the nosebleed rows of the arena down to the sea of well-coiffed whites on the ground floor. Security guards popped into my peripheral vision, but I knew better than to expect them to rescue us—that wasn't a realistic expectation for any African American in 1964. Louis and I pushed through the exit doors and into the darkness of the parking lot, dreading that our antagonists might trail us. When at last we made it to our car, we clambered inside, locked the doors—and exhaled.

Later I would learn that the smattering of other blacks inside the Cow Palace suffered their own indignities. San Francisco dentist Henry Lucas was ejected twice from his seat. Oakland real estate entrepreneur Charles J. Patterson, then vice president of the Alameda County Republican Central Committee, was denied his rightful place at a luncheon and discovered that none of the white Republicans there would even meet his gaze. "There was no one to complain to," he would say. "The major press seemed scared of the Goldwater people." The Tennessee delegation cited race as its reason for refusing to grant a vote to its sole black delegate. And another black delegate walked out with holes singed in his best suit after a bigot sloshed him with acid.

Jackie Robinson, who had attended as a special delegate for Rockefeller, almost came to blows with a white delegate—whose wife held him back to stop him from attacking the baseball legend. "Turn him loose, lady, turn him loose," Robinson shouted, ready for retaliation himself. The next night, Goldwater would accept the GOP nomination and proclaim his signature line: "Extremism in the defense of liberty is no vice." Although ample evidence exists to show that Goldwater personally was not racist, he had allied himself with those who were. And he would go down to defeat in a landslide, carrying only six states: aside from his home state of Arizona, all were in the Deep South. His campaign, however, set in motion an electoral realignment because a huge number of Southern whites abandoned the Democratic Party for the GOP. His campaign also laid the foundation on which actor Ronald Reagan, having charmed the 1964 convention with a passionate speech on Goldwater's behalf, constructed a conservative "Reagan Era" that would dominate the 1980s and beyond. As for Jackie Robinson, he would always recall the GOP Convention of 1964 as one of the most unforgettable and frightening experiences of his life. "A new breed of Republican had taken over the GOP," he wrote. "As I watched this steamroller operation in San Francisco, I had a better understanding of how it must have felt to be a Jew in Hitler's Germany."

That night, as Louis and I drove back to our station—our hearts still thumping and our ears ringing with echoes of the pandemonium—I was lost in thought. I contemplated the loss of President John F. Kennedy, who had been the first real hope for black people until he was cut down by an assassin's bullet. I recalled how only two weeks before, President Lyndon B. Johnson had signed the Civil Rights Act to prohibit racial discrimination. I thought about James Chaney, Michael Schwerner, and Andrew Goodman, three idealistic civil rights workers who vanished in Mississippi that summer; their murdered bodies would later be found buried in an earthen dam. And I thought about how much easier it was to change federal policy than it would be to change the hearts and minds of America.

All too many white Americans refused to believe the harsh truth about race relations in their own country. Too many turned a blind eye to the prejudices great and small that polluted the air African Americans had to breathe every day. Hatred was a powerful force. But I wondered: could it ultimately withstand the power of the press? Journalists were beginning to bring the stories of black Americans out of the shadows of the rafters and the alleys and the backwoods, out of the sharecropper plots and the inner-city ghettos, and into the light of day. They were reporting on the cross burnings and water hosings, the beatings and lynchings, in vivid details that the public could no longer ignore.

I wanted to be one of them. I wanted to broadcast the reality of my community to those who could not otherwise imagine it, to fill in that missing perspective. I wanted to do work that mattered. I wanted to tell stories that changed the world. And if it was then inconceivable for a petite, soft-spoken black woman to ever become a journalist—much less an Emmy-winning television reporter and anchor—well, chalk that up as just one more thing in the world that was about to change.

Fast forward almost a half century, to November 2008—another pivotal presidential contest. Again, the Republicans have nominated a senator from Arizona. Again, the GOP convention has featured jeering demonstrations in support of "real Americans" and against urbanites and "media elites." This time it's the Democrats who have nominated a candidate once known as *Barry*, although he now prefers his real name, *Barack*.

Don't ever let anyone tell you history doesn't have a sense of humor. Against all odds, the Democrats nominated Barack Hussein Obama, a Harvard-trained former community organizer and law professor, and the freshman U.S. senator for Illinois. His mother was white and from Kansas;

his father was black and from Kenya. Obama became the Democratic Party standard-bearer by defeating its presumptive nominee, former first lady turned New York senator Hillary Clinton. Further proof of history's twisted wit: in high school she was one of the costumed "Goldwater Girls," from the tip of her cowboy boots to the top of her straw hat, emblazoned with the chemistry pun "AuH_2O"—Au for gold, H_2O for water.

As for me, I'm in another car driving through the night, lost in thought. The world has changed in ways I never could have envisioned. I have been a reporter for almost five decades and fortunate to report on many of the major stories of my lifetime. I've talked with five presidents. I even interviewed Goldwater in his later years, when he had grown repulsed by religious fundamentalists seizing the reigns of the right away from more libertarian conservatives like him. I've been awarded eight local Emmys and a Lifetime Achievement Award from the National Academy of Television Arts and Sciences. In my seventies, I continue to host a weekly news roundtable and special reports on KQED-TV, one of the nation's leading PBS stations. My children are grown and launched into the world; and I've been happily married for more than four decades to Bill Moore, one of the country's first African American television news cameramen.

Bill and I arrive at Harris's steakhouse in San Francisco, where an election-night dinner party is underway, hosted by our close friend and California's senior U.S. senator, Dianne Feinstein. We've talked about whether the nation could possibly elect its first black president. I don't allow myself to think it will really happen.

We mingle and finally sit down to dinner and try to follow state-by-state returns, although television reception is poor. From time to time, Dianne rises, regally clinks her knife against a glass to catch our attention, and announces the latest development. Prospects appear promising for Obama, but I refuse to let myself celebrate before CNN projects him the winner.

Even when the projection is made it is unbelievable. The sound is muffled—should we check another channel?

But no one else is hesitating. Nearly a hundred guests applaud, and more than a few jump up and down and whoop for joy. As I look around, I realize that fewer than a handful of those present are black. A lump swells in my throat, and I lean toward Bill to tell him I feel an irrepressible urge to speak publicly. He looks puzzled for a moment.

"Go on then," he encourages with a nod.

So I turn to Dianne at the next table and explain. Again she clinks her glass: "Everyone please be quiet—Belva's got something to say."

The words do not flow as much as spill out, while a movie starts to unreel itself in my mind, revealing all the highlights of my life. I tell them about my father and his big dreams. I tell them how my father was denied the right to vote; my uncle was threatened with tar and feathering; and the men of my family were ridden out of Louisiana on a rail. I tell them about my mother, the silent sufferer all her life—working in laundries, cleaning Southern Pacific trains, polishing silver for tables in a dining car where she could never dine. I talk about people, such as Louis, who had borne so much with dignity.

Not that long before, I was asked to leave news conferences because no one believed I was a real reporter; and Bill was prevented from crossing police lines to get his camera shots because no one believed he was a real news photographer. We had been among the first of our race granted television jobs in the United States.

Now, as I squeeze Bill's hand tightly and wipe away tears, I speak about the promise of America that we clung to all these many years, and how on this night that promise feels fulfilled. I want these prominent people to know that we are all witnessing a miracle—not only in politics, but in the lives of people such as me.

For several seconds after I finish, no one in the room makes a sound. Then applause begins slowly and builds. Some people are wiping away tears. Others move to embrace me or Bill or anyone else nearby. Then the real party begins.

A tall, young black man has been handing Dianne notes about the vote count all evening. I don't know Christopher Thompson, who is her D.C. chief of staff, until he introduces himself to me and requests a word in private. I follow him to a quiet corner in the hallway. As soon as we face each other, he asks, "Can I give you a big hug? I just have to touch another black person tonight!" And we throw our arms around one another in a moment as tender as it is profound.

Deep down, I suspect that this glorious glow will fade into a more complex reality. Every progressive step in America seems to evoke its own backlash. In the same way that *Brown v. Board of Education* and passage of the

Civil Rights Act helped spawn the reactionary rhetoric of the Goldwaterites, so too will Obama's election trigger angry Tea Party movement protesters branding him "un-American" and clamoring to take their country "back."

Yet I choose to remain hopeful. Over the years I've followed my mantra—a note I wrote to myself years ago. Its message applies to the fate of Belvagene Melton Davis Moore from hardscrabble Louisiana, and to the Obamas and Oprahs and Christophers of the world, and to all who follow the arc of history as it bends toward justice. It begins like this: "Don't be afraid of the space between your dreams and reality . . . "

two

Up from Troubled Waters

I was conceived in Monroe, Louisiana, in the depths of the Great Depression, the reign of Jim Crow, and the "Flood of the Century" on the Ouachita River. My mother, a laundress who earned four dollars a week, was only fourteen years old.

Apparently if I was going to be lucky in life, I would have to be patient.

No doubt I would never have been born if my mother, Florene, had known how to resist the charms of John Melton. My father was a handsome, savvy but volatile man who swaggered his way through life, despite never having finished grammar school.

In 1932, Monroe was in dire straits, inundated when the Ouachita River crested fifty feet above flood level and gushed over the millions of sandbags futilely attempting to hold it back. By the beginning of February, more than a quarter of Monroe was submerged, and the Ouachita did not dip below flood level until mid-April. "The flood waters are contaminated beyond real-ization," the director of the Ouachita Parish Health Unit declared, warning that without vaccination "one is very likely to contract typhoid from merely wading and working in the flood districts." Makeshift tent cities sprang up on higher ground, as white and black families began living next to each other in a fashion that would have been unimaginable in any condition short of an emergency.

With twisted but typical Southern irony, although Monroe's blacks vastly outnumbered its white residents, whites nonetheless possessed all the political and economic power. Blacks knew all too well that their white bosses could crush them over a transgression such as knocking on the front door of a white family's house instead of the back, and that hooded Klansmen still inflicted lethal retribution against anyone they reckoned was "too uppity." It was said in Monroe that Negroes woke up every morning

11

fearing that they might be lynched, while whites woke up every morning fearing a Negro uprising. Given the discrimination and the demographics, neither fear was irrational.

The town sat at the rim of the Old South cotton belt, but by the early 1930s the cotton market had hit the skids and Ouachita Parish's agricultural income, payroll, and retail sales dropped by nearly two-thirds in five years. The Depression was challenging for Monroe's white citizenry but disastrous for blacks.

And if a flood was the last thing Monroe needed, I can only imagine that a baby was the last thing my mother needed. Nonetheless she delivered me that October inside my father's already overcrowded shotgun house—so named because you could shoot a bullet from the front door straight out the back door. The one-story clapboard was on obscure D Soloman's Alley, a dirt lane about twelve blocks north of the river.

The clerk who drafted my birth certificate misspelled both of my parents' names, and listed my father as a "com laborer" and my mother as a "domestic." I was given the name Belvagene, after my maternal grandfather Eugene Howard. But the ink on the document was barely dry before I was bundled up and hustled out of the lives of my overwhelmed, ill-equipped parents.

For my first few years of life, I had no clue that they had given me away. I was adopted by my Aunt Ophelia and her husband, who had a home, a spare bedroom, and an unfulfilled desire for a child of their own. I simply believed they were my real parents. I called Ophelia "Mamma" and can still remember how her hair was fashioned into finger waves in the front and flowed to her shoulders. She dressed me in organdy pinafores and doted on me—"primping," she called it. As I sat propped on her knee in front of her long dresser mirror, she would gently comb my hair and adorn it with fussy bows and colorful barrettes. "Belvagene, you're such a pretty baby," she would coo in my ear. "Just look at us—aren't we beautiful together?"

Life with her was sweet but short. I don't really recall her cough or the bloodstains on her handkerchief or anyone uttering the word "tuberculosis" in my presence. All I remember was that she was sick in bed, frail and quiet, and then she was dead.

My childhood died that day as well. I was three years old.

The unspeakable loneliness that seeped through me didn't abate even after I was returned to live with my mother and father and his family. They were in a different, larger house than before, but it was filled with even more people. Our home was a frenetic place, with relatives perpetually moving in or out depending on whether they had secured a job. I no longer had a room or a bed—instead I slept on a blanket pallet on the floor. Curiously, although my mother and father lived in the house, I don't remember them ever playing with me or even acknowledging my existence. Perhaps they feared that I carried Aunt Ophelia's deadly disease. More likely, they were preoccupied with their prized new baby, my brother John Jr.

All I know is that overnight I went from being blissful to miserable. I cried every day until my eyeballs were raw and my stomach ached from the sobs. People in that house pretty much stepped around me and went about their business.

My father was the head of the household, overseeing the welfare of his mother, four sisters, and younger brother—his own father had abandoned the family and taken a new wife across the state line into Arkansas. A child himself when he was forced to go to work at the local sawmill, my father used encyclopedias to teach himself to read. He was intoxicated by knowledge and could recite a trove of trivia, including the names of state capitals and lengths of North American rivers. His secret weapon was *The Old Farmer's Almanac*, which he attempted to memorize verbatim.

At the mill, he smartly made himself indispensable by tackling and mastering the most intricate and treacherous saw machinery. As a result, he earned thirty dollars a week, which was a mighty high Depression-era salary for a black man in Northern Louisiana.

His youth, quick reaction time, and keen intellect protected him: many less fortunate coworkers left severed fingers and hands on the mill floor. His intellect protected him in other ways as well. He used the weekend as a tension valve, blowing off steam in Five Points, a three-block area of "colored town" owned by the same influential white family who owned the lumber mill. The money the owners paid their workers came back to the owners via the gambling dens and saloons they operated. My father's carousing and brawling in Five Points landed him in jail on a regular basis.

He was smart enough to know he wouldn't be there long. Miraculously, an anonymous benefactor—no doubt looking out for the interests of the sawmill—always managed to secure his release every Monday morning just in the knick of time for the start of his mill shift.

My father had an explosive temper: in particularly foul moods, he was known to whip out his pistol—but everyone generally regarded "Johnnie" as a big bluffer who merely wanted to be the epicenter of attention. One way he got noticed was by joining gospel quartets. The quartets afforded him the chance to perform in sanctuaries and town halls, and to flirt with adoring young women who sat and flapped paper fans that depicted Jesus as the Good Shepherd on one side and advertised the local funeral home on the other. Gospel singing also gave him an excuse to spend part of his paycheck on snazzy suits and to slick his hair back with cans of Murray's Superior Hair Pomade. John Melton was a man who savored the ladies' attention.

My mother didn't much care for my father's extracurricular "spreading of the gospel," but she couldn't do much about it. She was a beauty herself—I used to open my candy bars to see if any of the colors of the chocolate that covered them were as pretty as the rich mocha tone of my mother's skin. She had wide-set eyes that seldom looked directly at you, but her downcast glances showed off her long, curled lashes.

Like almost all the women in my family, my mother worked for G.B. Cooley's Monroe Steam Laundry. At any given time in the 1930s, the laundry employed more than a hundred black women as laundresses. Their job was to scrub, wring dry, starch, and iron the shirts and dresses and even bedsheets of well-to-do whites. The workday was long, air-conditioning was nonexistent, the sticky heat and humidity were stifling—and for their labors, they earned less than a seventh of the pay my father received.

As for me, I tried hard to make myself useful, as though to justify my presence. Often I was sent off to deliver messages or packages to my father at the mill or to another relative's home. As simple as that sounds, I found such errands terrifying, because I was compelled to cross a lumberyard infested with huge rats. As I made my way through the maze of wood stacks, I could hear them scampering about and would catch glimpses of their beady eyes or twitching tails. At sundown, a trek across the lumberyard was a passage through my own private chamber of horrors.

I also came in handy when my maternal grandmother suffered a stroke and moved in with the Melton family. The adults would get her out of bed in the morning and position her in the rocking chair on the porch. I heard some of the grown-ups say that my grandmother adored spending time with me after my birth—I was her first grandchild. Now, my job was to sit holding her hand, help her to the bathroom, fetch her a drink of water or a sandwich, and keep her company. We were an odd, forlorn pair: she was unable to speak, rocking and humming for hours on end; and I was at her side watching her and hoping someone would pass down our street and wave at us, to bestow a grace note of excitement on the dull day.

The truth is that my family really didn't know quite what to do with me, nor did they seem to have much space in their home or hearts for a sad little girl. So I became portable—rather like an old suitcase that they would pass from place to place.

Sometimes they would send me to stay for weeks with my Grandpa Eugene in Rayville. Grandpa was what my father called a jackleg preacher— a self-ordained reverend with no education or training in the ministry. When I had outstayed my welcome at Grandpa's, I would be dispatched to Mississippi to visit my great-aunt Issaquena. Her shack wasn't accessible by any road—instead we had to drive across a meadow, undo the wires of a fence and roll it back, and then bump across the rutty terrain into the middle of nowhere.

I'm pretty sure if you had looked up the word _recluse_ in a Delta dictionary, you would have found a tintype photograph of Issaquena. Resembling an Indian, she always wore men's clothes and fastened her long hair in a single braid down her back. Her house tottered on rickety stilts near a fishing stream, and she kept a loaded shotgun by her door. I detested the snakes that slithered around her place, and I dreaded every trip to her outhouse; but otherwise I actually enjoyed my time with Issaquena. She would let me trail behind her as she gathered wood or weeded the garden, and sometimes we would sit by the stream monitoring our fishing lines, simply waiting for something to happen.

We ate nothing that she hadn't grown or killed herself. The only staples she required from the outside world were flour and lard, which my parents would deliver whenever they retrieved me.

By the time I was five, I had returned to Monroe with renewed optimism. My buoyancy had nothing to do with Monroe's having recovered from the 1932 flood or with the town then weathering the Depression better than the rest of the Delta. A huge natural gas discovery boosted its industries—carbon black plants, saw mills, and paper mills—and through the rest of the decade the town was cushioned, its white citizenry comfortable. I had no idea that that Monroe's city fathers had installed the first publicly owned streetcar line in the country, nor did I know that Delta Air Lines had been organized in the boardroom of Central Savings Bank and Trust on Desiard Street.

My newfound optimism sprang from the fact that I had a mission: to maneuver my way into someone's heart and home. And I sized up my mother's childless older sister, Aunt Pearline, as my most promising prospect.

Pearline and her feisty husband, my Uncle Ezra, had recently fulfilled their dream of opening a small grocery store. They had stocked rough plank shelves with canned goods and dried staples, and they were extending credit to people like them who strained paycheck to paycheck. In those days, a trip into a white-owned market was an exercise in humiliation: if a black customer was checking out and a white customer approached, the black shopper was obliged to reload her basket and go to the end of the line, sometimes over and over again. Our neighbors agreed it was time for a black-owned market in our midst.

Again, I strategized ways to make myself useful. I volunteered to deliver groceries to the few customers who owned telephones and thus could call in their orders; and I also picked up grocery lists and shopped for customers who were shut-ins. Eventually my aunt and uncle took me in, and I moved into the second of two rooms behind their store. The three of us felt like a real family.

I called Aunt Pearline "Tee." Like my mother and the rest of her sisters, she was frugal with conversation. The woman didn't chitchat; she sang. I could decipher her moods by the hymn of the day. "I Know the Lord Done Heard My Cry" indicated something was wrong. "Ain't That Good News" or "In the Great Gettin' Up Morning" meant it was a good day to ask her for just about anything.

Her church was the anchor of her existence. She saw to it that I attended Sunday worship, Sunday school, Wednesday night prayer meeting, and Saturday night children's programs at Zion Traveler Baptist Church. Sometimes I would sing for the children's talent show, and adults would toss pennies onto the stage to show their approval. I made a point of always donating my pennies by dropping them in the offering plate—my aunt would beam with pride. I would like to think I was a generous child, but I suspect my motivation had a lot more to do with making sure my aunt loved me better so she would keep me.

Aunt Pearline was one of Zion Traveler's "Mothers"—a group of women who aided the pastor, counseled the flock, and provided spiritual guidance to those who had lost their way. Although many of the Mothers were virtually illiterate, they could recite an impressive host of New Testament verses. Once a month, these women would march to the front of the church, in white outfits reminiscent of nurses' uniforms, to be recognized for their special role. One of their responsibilities was to prepare candidates for baptism in the Ouachita River.

As soon as I could, I declared Jesus Christ as my Lord and Savior and asked to be baptized. That testimony would become a lifelong faith, bolstering my courage and assuring me that, regardless of the circumstances of my birth, I remain a child of God, wanted and loved unconditionally. Aunt Pearline was thrilled with my decision, and she and the other Mothers went to work sewing old bedsheets into flowing white robes that we baptismal candidates would don for our journey through the river and into salvation.

Being led into the Ouachita is one of the most vivid memories of my young life. One Sunday, as soon as the church service concluded on a final round of *Amens*, we all marched blocks down to the riverbank. The Mothers walked alongside us and sang hymns; and as we neared our salvation spot, they took up the chorus, "Wa-aade in the water, wade in the water, children, wa-aade in the water. God's gonna trouble the water . . . "

My young mind suddenly focused on the lyrics, and I panicked. What did that mean, troubling the waters? Just what exactly was God going to do? But I had little time for hesitation: the pastor already was standing far from the bank when two deacons held me under my arms and solemnly carried me into the Ouachita. My body shivered from apprehension and chill as we approached the pastor. The water was at my chin, and my bare feet could no longer touch the river bottom. "Oh Lord," the pastor intoned, "cleanse this child's soul." I sucked in my breath when the deacons tilted my body backward and the current began to cover me. "I baptize you in the name of the Father . . ." Then I lost his voice as my head was dunked under water.

Just when I thought I must be on my final journey to Heaven, a cool breeze hit my face and I could inhale again, secure in the knowledge that my sinful soul was cleansed. I had been saved for eternity, and my Aunt Pearline cried with joy.

Life was pretty good. I had begun attending Miss Bessie's Brooks

Academy, a private school for Protestant Negro girls—my father boasted of what it cost him to send me to that school, which was a conspicuous symbol of affluence in our community. I was learning to read and write, speak well, and practice proper etiquette.

Unfortunately, I was about to discover how God was going to trouble the waters.

Because our grocery store was not yet sufficiently profitable, my Uncle Ezra had retained his grueling job at the Armour Meat Packing Company. One day he was hit hard by a swinging side of beef, injuring his back so severely that he could no longer work. Without Ezra's weekly paycheck, my aunt and uncle were forced to shutter the market they had worked so hard to establish; and they moved us all back into the already jam-packed Melton house.

So my uncle did something unheard of in Monroe, Louisiana: he sued the company. My relatives warned him that he was crazy—no colored person had ever sued a white company in Monroe. Amazingly, he found a young white lawyer to take his case; and even more incredible, a Louisiana judge found in his favor and ordered Armour to pay him two thousand dollars in damages. We were overjoyed—but it was like licking syrup from a serrated knife. Ezra's lawyer came to alert him that, according to the talk of the town, Monroe's white businessmen had no intention of letting him collect a dime. Instead they were plotting to make an example of him with tar and feathering.

Fear ricocheted through our entire extended family, and with justification. Twenty-one blacks already had died at the end of ropes in Monroe; and while the last lynching had been in 1919, it was seared into adult memories as though it were only yesterday. My father took charge. All the men in the family were determined to be in imminent danger by association and would have to leave immediately. They scattered into the night in various vehicles. Ezra hopped a freight train to keep him off the roads.

I don't know why the men chose to rendezvous in California, except that it was far, far from Louisiana.

As for me, eventually I was packed up and farmed out yet again— this time in the company of my little brother—to our paternal grandfather Horace Melton and his wife, in El Dorado, Arkansas. I'm certain our step-grandmother had a name, but we knew her only as "The Lady with the

Switch" because of her penchant for whipping us for the petty crimes of childhood. She had no children of her own, and thus she could never fathom why two youngsters couldn't keep the red clay of Arkansas off their shoes and out of her immaculate house. We would watch in utter trepidation as she broke a branch off the peach tree in her backyard, rubbed her hand up to strip off the leaves, and then called us to bend over and brace ourselves. She played no favorites in her house. The welts on our young skin never healed before another offense would inspire a fresh whipping.

I hoped desperately for a rescue. I wasn't sure anybody cared enough to reclaim me, but I secretly counted on the strength of my father's love for my brother motivating him to come get us both. Within half a year he did.

The segregated train bound for California had no seat for me, so I sat on the floor on top of my suitcase and silently prayed about my new life. I knew that God loved me and Jesus loved me. But I also wanted somebody down here to love me—and it didn't seem like too much to ask.

three

• • •

Truth Isn't What You Want to See

I shared my journey with row upon row of uniformed soldiers. They filled each segregated car as the Southern Pacific train chugged across one state line after another. We all were bound for a common destination—a place on the eastern shore of San Francisco Bay whose oak-studded hills had prompted settlers to christen it Oakland. By the 1940s, Oakland was a thriving metropolis and a western terminus of the transcontinental railroad. As we arrived, stretched our stiff limbs, and climbed onto stationary soil, I felt a curious combination of bone-weary exhaustion and antsy anticipation.

"End of the line!" announced the Southern Pacific Railroad conductor. *Nope*, I thought to myself, *the beginning*.

As I clutched my small, battered suitcase and struggled to follow my father bobbing through the crowd, I couldn't help but be struck by the sheer number of white faces. In Monroe, whites were outnumbered about ten to one by blacks, and they never ventured into colored neighborhoods. But Oakland was overwhelmingly dominated by Portuguese, German, Irish, Italian, and Greek immigrants and their children. Blacks were barely more than 2 percent of the city population.

My family had fled from a tattered and fraying Deep South culture, the racist remnants of plantation slavery—but strands of bigotry also were woven into the fabric of Oakland. Only fifteen years before my arrival, the stately Oakland Auditorium had hosted a conclave of nearly ten thousand Ku Klux Klansmen and their women from across the country, cheering the induction of five hundred new members into the national order. A year later, the local citizenry had elected Klansmen to powerful posts, including county sheriff—in fact, a burgeoning Klan patronage apparatus was dismantled only after it had become the focus of a graft and corruption inquiry. The zealous Alameda County district attorney who prosecuted that case would years later deliver the U.S. Supreme Court decision outlawing racial segregation: His name was Earl Warren.

Blacks began to trickle into Oakland via the railroads, which offered them a variety of jobs. The relatively fortunate were the Pullman porters who served as butlers to the most luxurious travelers. George Pullman hired only black porters, not only because they worked cheaper than whites, but also because he considered them better at "keeping a social distance between passengers and servants"—and it was common practice for passengers to address every Pullman porter as "George" without any thought to the man's real name.

Soon a colony of Pullman porters settled into West Oakland. And as more blacks worked the railroads, they recruited relatives up and down the line, promising them that California afforded more opportunities than Jim Crow ever would.

Some of the men of my family, fleeing the threat of a Monroe tar and feathering, had landed jobs working for Southern Pacific in Oakland in 1941.

East Bay locals had been growing nervous about an influx of job seekers. That year the *Richmond Independent* issued an editorial warning: "The man who thinks he will get a job building ships because he built a woodshed somewhere is doomed to disappointment." Then the Japanese bombed Pearl Harbor, the headlines screamed *WAR!* and a torrent of migrant workers began to flood into California to work the shipyards and railways to aid the war effort. My father, a carpentry wizard, was one of the first people hired to work at the Oakland Naval Supply Depot—his job was building pallets and other containers for holding cargo—and eventually he saved enough money to retrieve his children from Arkansas.

And so I became a tiny part of the so-called Second Great Migration west during World War II. Nearly one-third of those who moved to Oakland in the early 1940s, and two-thirds of those who were black, came from only four Southern states: Texas, Arkansas, Oklahoma, and Louisiana. By the time the war ended a few years later, Oakland's population had increased by a third and its black population more than tripled, so that one in five Oaklanders was black. Locals occasionally railed against how the "Okies and Darkies" would undermine their job base and quality of life.

I, of course, knew none of this. I scarcely noticed the disapproving glances aimed at a little black girl in pigtails trekking across West Oakland to her new refuge.

The topography of Oakland has always been a vivid illustration of its stratification. The wealthy claimed the desirable hills with the scenic vistas of San Francisco Bay. The middle class populated the foothills. To the working class were left the flatlands that stretch to the railroad tracks, the industrial port, and the bay. West Oakland was flatland, and when I arrived it was a multiethnic neighborhood where blacks congregated. Black-owned businesses flourished along the Seventh Street corridor, which was an amalgam of respectable businesses and "black and tan" jazz and blues clubs where people of all races were welcomed.

My father, brother, and I journeyed one block off to Eighth Street, following it into a mixed residential neighborhood. Our house itself was stunning to my eyes—a rambling Victorian on Eighth Street near Peralta, surrounded by other colorfully past-their-prime "Painted Ladies." The few that recently had been painted were coated in navy surplus paint, rendering them battleship gray. Still, all were far roomier and more inviting than the tiny shotgun house on D Soloman's Alley. My dream seemed to have come true. I admit that I privately had dared to fantasize about an idyllic family home, where my mother and father would welcome my brother and me. I would have an actual bed—perhaps even a room—all my own.

I should have known better.

My new home proved to be the Victorian's unfinished basement. Its walls were dirt, giving rise to a musty, earthy odor that permeated the entire place, which consisted of two rooms plus a bathroom. When my eyes adjusted from the bright outdoors to the shadowy dimness of the basement, I could make out a makeshift kitchen that had been thrown up in one corner. Old but freshly scrubbed sheets and cheap chenille bedspreads dangled from wooden clothespins spaced across the clotheslines that criss-crossed the ceiling—a desperate attempt to create zones of privacy for the eleven relatives who would share this space.

Yet again, I would have to "make do" with a cold, hard floor as my bed. The adults had to sleep in shifts.

We had no yard in which to play in the front or back. The adults advised my brother and me to avoid sitting on the front steps in search of a shard of sunshine, because after all, our family didn't own the steps or the house. The owners, our landlords, were a Portuguese family—nice enough people, but they preferred not to mix with us.

I remember feeling excitement and trepidation the day my mother walked me over to nearby Prescott Elementary to register for school. My writing was rudimentary but still better than my mother's, so I carefully penciled both of our names on the enrollment forms. My third grade teacher was unimpressed. "Your mother's name was obviously meant to be Florence, not Florene," she intoned. "There's no such name as Florene." She shot my mother a look of slightly veiled exasperation. And in that fateful instant, my poor shy mother—unable to cite a reason to justify her own name to this stranger—became Florence for the rest of her life.

I wasn't so easily coerced. "Obviously your parents didn't know how to spell your name," my new teacher continued. "If your name is Belvagene, then the proper spelling is Belva Jean—*j-e-a-n*," she said impatiently, punctuating her sigh with a roll of her eyes. "*Gene* is the masculine form. *Jean* is the feminine." But no matter what she said, I refused to change my name. I knew I was named after my grandfather Eugene, and I continued to proudly write "Belvagene Melton" at the top of all my schoolwork.

Like many of my fellow pupils, I confronted a double-barreled prejudice as a black and a Southerner. Teachers continually corrected our Southern speech and admonished us to shed our accents quickly if we wanted to advance. They were annoyed even by our Southern custom of referring to them as *ma'am*. "I'm not your ma'am," they would snap, "I'm Miss Jones!" Or, "I'm Mrs. Smith!" Some days, the retribution for our polite Southern habit was our being ordered to clean the chalkboards during recess.

I was an atrocious speller but sharp at math, and I relished history. At Prescott Elementary I established a pattern that held at every other school I attended: I remained a diligent, good student. Diligence is the solace you have when you don't know what else to do.

My Uncle Ezra and Aunt Pearline lifted the spirits of everyone in the basement when they announced that they had secured housing in Alameda. A small island town across the estuary from Oakland, Alameda featured green parks, a nice beach, an architectural treasure trove of well-tended

Victorians, and inhabitants who were—almost without exception—white. The town was about to get its first black residents, and they would be living in the projects.

Government housing projects were a novel concept—no one in my family had ever lived in one—but we regarded them as a classy step up from the cramped conditions we were accustomed to. Uncle Ezra was walking with a cane, could sit in a chair only with back pillows, and had yet to collect his two-thousand-dollar judgment against the Monroe meatpacking plant. Because of his disability, he and Aunt Pearline were among the first to be granted subsidized housing. What most interested me was the news that they would have two bedrooms—that meant a spare. I hinted, then lobbied, and finally wheedled an invitation to move in with them. My parents had no reservations about losing me once more, and I had no hesitation about leaving them. So, the next semester I transferred to Lincoln Elementary in Alameda.

The white students at Lincoln had little use for black kids from the projects. At best, they treated us with cool indifference. At worst, they were on the lookout for any opportunity to harass us into retreating. How I dreaded my walk home from school, when gangs of little white boys hung out on the street corners taunting me, chasing me, yanking the long braided rope of my hair, or simply hollering that I didn't belong in Alameda. But they couldn't possibly understand my resolve. I had a bed. I had my own room. I was learning to read, and the library offered a seemingly limitless supply of books. This was the closest I had been to nirvana. I had no intention whatsoever of leaving.

Unfortunately, the choice wasn't mine to make. Uncle Ezra's older brother Alex sent word that he had left Louisiana headed for California and would need a place to stay. When he arrived with his wife and six children—including a daughter who was about to have a baby—it was clear that I had to go.

Once again I felt like a plant ripped out by my tender roots and stuck in yet another parched patch of ground. In this case I was sent back to Oakland, to a second-story, two-bedroom apartment in a barracks-style housing project on Twenty-Fourth and Poplar. Both my parents now were living there, along with an assortment of other relatives. The only vacant spot for me was on the kitchen floor.

I wasn't particularly happy to be reunited with my parents, who had never come the few miles to visit me in Alameda. I suppose it's an understatement to say we didn't have a normal parent-child relationship—I'm quite sure I didn't even know what that was. Life just seemed to keep them in a state of constant turmoil. New Louisiana relatives and friends seemed to be forever crawling out of the woodwork. They would write my dad to seek his help, and he would send some money to get them to California and squeeze them into our place for a while; despite his bluster, he was known as a soft touch whose greatest attribute was his willingness to share what he had with his family. Sometimes they would get homesick for the Delta and ask him for the money to go back. He would swear and kick the walls and, often as not, give them the money for their return fare.

Perhaps our way of life wasn't that unusual for people from the South. Your luck was in, then out; and you would keep on keeping on and trying to help the rest of your relatives when you could. When I think of how we had to live—practically on top of one another like crabs in a barrel—it amazes me that any of us made it to the top.

To make matters worse, Oakland's housing supply fell far short of demand during and after the war. Residential vacancies were an already low 2 percent in the spring of 1941. By the fall of 1942, vacancies had plummeted to a preposterous 0.06 percent. Still, people kept coming. From 1940 to 1945, the population density of West Oakland had increased fourfold. Within a few years, all West Oakland was designated a "blighted" district. When organized labor and the NAACP persuaded the city council to authorize construction of three thousand units of federally subsidized housing, property owners and the Oakland Real Estate Board blasted it as "socialistic," beat it back, and pushed every councilman who supported it out of office.

The day I enrolled at Oakland's Hoover Junior High School was the day I met the girl who would become my dearest lifelong friend. Rose Mary Prince and I spotted each other across the chaos and felt an instantaneous connection. We both were black girls with our hair styled into three tight braids; but what really distinguished us was that we both wore thick glasses. Rose Mary's mother, whom I would forever call Miss Anna, eyed me, smiled, and gave her daughter a nudge.

"Look here, Rose Mary, there's another little girl with glasses. See, it's not so bad."

We were assigned to the same homeroom and soon became more inseparable than sisters.

Rose Mary and I shared a love of books. Usually we perused the school library and checked out proper literature. I was captivated by a book titled *Ramona* by Helen Hunt Jackson, a melancholy drama about a mixed-race orphan girl raised by a relative who loves her son but not Ramona. I would tuck it under my covers and read by the diffused yellow glow of my flashlight, submerging myself in her world and her struggles. I must confess that on occasion Rose Mary and I would wander over to a downtown department store that rented romances for a nickel. These paperbacks were slightly racy—meaning they might feature a torrid kiss or two—and we thrilled to the illicit savoring of the romances and then stashed the books under our bedcovers.

We also loved picture shows. I would save up milk-bottle tops, which on summertime Wednesdays could gain me free admission to the small, rundown Rex Theater on Broadway that usually showed Westerns. My favorites were swashbuckler movies, elaborate musicals, and anything starring Alan Ladd or Margaret O'Brien.

As I grew older, my favorite place to be was at Rose Mary's house, which she shared with her mother. She was an only child, having lost her father when she was but a baby. I surreptitiously studied the interplay between Rose Mary and Miss Anna and marveled—theirs was the first intimate mother-daughter relationship I had witnessed. I couldn't be jealous, because I was grateful to be able to soak up the extra love in the house. Miss Anna was the only adult who had ever sat down and really conversed with me. She sought my opinion, and in her diplomatically oblique fashion, tried to give me the motherly guidance I needed. "You know, honey," she would say, "I don't know if I'd do that if I were you."

My home was overstuffed with people but lacking in affection. And it was about to get worse.

I returned home from school one day to find that my mother had simply vanished. Her belongings also were gone. My father was livid, suspecting, correctly as it turned out, that she had taken a boyfriend. That was rather out of character for her—usually my father was the one who did the philandering. She'd left no note, no explanation—only an anxious pall that descended upon our apartment.

I was utterly devastated, and I felt alone.

If ever I doubted our family hierarchy, it was etched in my mind the afternoon that my father arrived home with John Jr., who then strutted around the apartment in a suit my father had paid a tailor to make for him. The rich fabric was soft yellow with black stripes on a cream-colored base, and it cost a ridiculously extravagant sixty-four dollars. I had to content myself with frugal basics. I had long recognized that my brother was whip smart and cute as could be, but now I had irrefutable evidence that my father loved him far more than me. I was so jealous, but all I could do was sit on the stairs, hug my book tightly to my chest, and blink back the burning tears.

I don't think it ever occurred to my mother that she was leaving her young daughter to be the sole female in an apartment full of men. The reality of my situation crept upon me one awful night like a fog hugging the bay . . . silently. The first finger was almost imperceptible, its caress hardly noticed. Then fear—but along with fear, something new. I could only wait to see if it would hurt; and by the time I sensed danger in the mist, it was too late: I was engulfed in its seduction and its unbearable guilt.

That was the beginning of my journey down the road of exploitation and into a private hell, as though I had been captured by a devil who moved only in the shadows. As a child, I didn't know this devil's name; but the silent hands that invaded my body at night knew everything. My lips were sealed in guilty confusion as I lay on my pallet on the kitchen floor of the projects, afraid to sleep and afraid to remain awake. Night after night, throughout each molestation, I kept my eyes tightly shut. I didn't want to know which man in the house was taking pleasure with me. It might be someone I loved and trusted in the light of day, and then what?

I told no one, not even Rose Mary. As close as we were—all those afternoons when I would walk her home and then she would walk me home and we would keep going back and forth until it became suppertime or dark—I could never speak of the hell being visited upon me at night. In truth, I barely talked to her about how much I missed my mother. Withholding the details of my life was my survival technique. I told myself that nobody likes a victim: *They may feel sorry for you, Belvagene, but they won't respect you.* Nor would I risk disclosing anything that might jeopardize my lifeline to Rose Mary, or to Miss Anna.

But I prayed to God for deliverance, and finally my prayer was answered. A new batch of relatives moved in, with two newcomers assigned to floor space next to the kitchen. My unknown molester was not bold enough to tempt discovery. At long last, the physical torture ceased.

The mental torture, however, continued unabated. Deep inside I felt damaged, destroyed, deserving of death.

But I had no idea how to actually kill myself. I searched the library for methods that might be relatively painless. Ultimately I found nothing that I had the courage to carry out. I contemplated throwing myself in front of the A Train that ran in front of our apartment, but the train moved too slowly to do fatal damage.

All my father's coiled frustration and my bottled-up emotion were about to burst into one histrionic crescendo. The impetus was hardly more than the common cold. I contracted a bad one, and my father decided what I needed was a dose of castor oil. I had been made to take castor oil once before and nearly gagged: to those who have never swallowed the stuff, I can only describe it as akin to rancid melted Crisco.

I said "No."

He said "Yes."

"No!"

"Yes!"

My father unstrapped his belt and lunged in my direction. I bolted into the bathroom of our barracks-like apartment in the projects and locked the door. His fists pounded on the door as my heart pounded in my chest. I scurried up onto the toilet seat and tugged at the window screen.

"Belvagene," he thundered, "open this goddamn door!"

"No," I yelled back. "I'm not gonna take it, do you hear me? I'm not going to take it!"

I had no courage at that moment—just the opposite. All those years of being bullied and ignored smacked against my psyche. I no longer had any way to deny the truth: surely the people who were supposed to really care about me didn't care enough. I had raised myself, tried to protect myself from harm, and I had failed miserably at it. I had spent my life desperately trying to please anyone who paid me any attention, and I was exhausted by the futility of it all. I just wanted to be dead.

I felt the force as he threw his body against the door: "Open. This. Door. Now!"

I looked out the window at the concrete sidewalk below and envisioned myself jumping and surviving, spending the rest of my life maimed and miserable. My one thought was *Please God please, don't let me jump and* not *die.*

four

...

Strained Mercies

What I had yet to learn is that the consequences of suicide are simply too risky—you never know what's in your future that you might miss.

But Divine Providence must have intervened that day as I stood tottering on the toilet by the window, grieving the loss of my mother, my dignity, my will to live. All that was left in me was a determination not to swallow my father's castor oil. Through the bolted bathroom door I could hear a neighbor, no doubt alerted by my screams, talking my father down from his rage. By the sound of the muffled tenor, I suspected it was kindly Mr. Toney, also a refugee from Monroe: his son Robert would, decades later, become a rear admiral in the navy and president of the Oakland Chamber of Commerce.

I waited to emerge until I was sure my father's maelstrom had subsided. Sullenly he put away his belt and the castor oil and reverted to ignoring me. After that clash, we ceased all conversation and he rarely came home at night. I could not possibly understand the impotence he must have felt as a black man in the 1940s, just as he could not fathom the deep recesses of my adolescent anguish.

But the encounter steeled my resolve to find an escape hatch—a way out of this apartment bursting with the menace of men. My hopes soared when my Aunt Pearline and Uncle Ezra, who had finally received that elusive two-thousand-dollar settlement check from his lawsuit, asked whether I could take a streetcar ride with them to Berkeley to look at a house for sale. We disembarked from the Grove Street line and strolled a few blocks down Ashby Avenue, bracketed with cheery single-story wood-framed homes surrounded by small green lawns and brightly colored roses.

"Look how many are vacant," my aunt murmured, looking up and down the street.

"It's a shame what's happened to those people," my uncle replied, putting his hand on her back to hurry her along. They knew that the vacancies were the result of the U.S. government forcing Japanese families to relocate to internment camps for the duration of World War II. Soon the former homes of families with names such as Ito and Kobayashi were up for grabs, and cheap. Who could blame my aunt and uncle for lunging at the chance to own their own home for the first time in their lives? And who could fault me for presuming that they had brought me along because they intended for me to join them in this bargain paradise—a two-bedroom home with a living room, dining room, and cozy back yard?

But my aspirations came crashing back to earth when I overheard my uncle explain to the real estate agent that this house would be perfect because they were adopting a teenage relative's baby. The significance of my presence was suddenly crystal clear: I wasn't to live in this house with them, I was present merely to help them read and decipher the real estate documents.

I tried not to dampen my aunt and uncle's celebration when they signed the papers; but that night, as I climbed the steps back to our apartment in the projects on Poplar Street, I felt as though the air were hissing out of my spirits, leaving nothing behind but deflated emptiness.

Not long after my thirteenth birthday, I received word through an intermediary that my mother was safe and wanted to rendezvous with me in downtown Oakland. This time I stamped out any embers of hope that she would reclaim me. When I went to meet my mother, I told myself to expect nothing so I couldn't be disappointed.

She was subdued, although she did say she was sorry for leaving without telling me good-bye. "I just wanted to be sure you're getting along all right," she said.

She explained that she was sharing her own place with a man named Nathaniel, who also worked for the Southern Pacific and was a dining car waiter on trains that ran from Oakland to Chicago. Rather obviously she had no intention of taking me with her—after all, the apartment they had taken near Oakland's deFremery Park was a tiny studio. But when she didn't offer, I asked. Not that I disclosed the details of what I had suffered in her absence, but perhaps she sensed that I had to get out. In any event, I was a complication she would have to deal with.

During the time I was staying in that Sixteenth Street studio with my mother and Nathaniel, I experienced my first real brush with death—and ironically, it was unintentional. We used the small gas kitchen stove to heat the apartment. One afternoon when I was home alone and the air was chilly, I knelt down, struck a match, and opened the oven door. It blew off its hinges as a blast of heat knocked me back against the cabinet, the door still in my hand. My face was scorching while I frantically slapped at the sparks coming from my blouse. I don't remember crying out, and I barely remember a neighbor bursting into the apartment and wrapping my head in a towel to cover my singed and smoldering hair.

The skin on my face peeled off in sheets for days, but miraculously, the accident would leave no permanent damage. My wounds, however, took weeks to heal. And they led me to an oasis shimmering in the midst of my desolation: while recuperating, alone and bored out of my mind, I wandered over to the deFremery Park Recreation Center.

Chances are no one who grew up in my corner of West Oakland in the 1940s and '50s could ever forget the deFremery Center. An enormous Victorian mansion with its own swimming pool and basketball courts, it had been a banker's estate and USO headquarters before it reverted to the city in 1946. For the first time ever, city officials hired a black woman to run its youth programs.

Dorothy Seels had earned a master's degree in French from Howard University, and she was thrilled by the prospect of instilling culture and a love of learning in the neighborhood's boys and girls. Shortly after she was hired, she scoped out her charges by slipping into a local concert featuring the popular Johnny Moore and the Three Blazers. Miss Seels didn't like what she observed: the room was too dark; the dancing was far too intimate; the girls displayed atrocious posture; and the boys would leave them stranded on the dance floor as soon as the music stopped—not to mention their improper penchant for slipping their hands under their dates' coats. deFremery's new recreation director was mortified, and she left the concert determined to teach social graces.

She tried to gauge the neighborhood's interest in a charm-school class—and got an emphatic "no!" So she repositioned the idea as a class in modeling. "The word," she would later recall, "was like magic. Now, they really wanted a modeling class."

But that was merely the beginning. The rec center began hosting dances (with appropriate lighting and "proper" dance steps), talent shows, synchronized swimming exhibitions, museum field trips, moonlight picnics, hayrides, service clubs, job fairs, piano lessons, and dozens of other activities designed to educate and enrich the youth of West Oakland. It must have worked—from 1947 to 1955, the juvenile delinquency rate in West Oakland plummeted. Many of my neighbors who later became luminaries would credit the deFremery influence: Ron Dellums, who later became Berkeley city councilman, congressman, and Oakland mayor; Ruth and Anita Pointer, whose Pointer Sisters act would throw more than a dozen songs up to the Top 20 on the *Billboard* chart; and Bill Russell, from my hometown of Monroe, who ultimately became a five-time winner of the NBA's Most Valuable Player Award as center for the Boston Celtics. Russell later extolled deFremery's staff for teaching him life's most valuable lessons. "For example," he said, "they were the first ones to inform me that 'mother' was a word by itself."

As another beneficiary-to-be of the deFremery magic, I arrived wearing sunglasses and a scarf designed to conceal my healing burn scars. I was so self-conscious as I made my way across the deFemery Park lawn and up the steps of the mansion that I almost turned back. Every room in the rambling structure buzzed with energy. But when I crossed the creaky threshold, I knew I had found a home away from home. Immediately to the right of the front entrance was a cozy reading room filled with books. Upstairs, young people were engrossed in a dominoes tournament. Downstairs, they were playing ping-pong and pool.

Soon Rose Mary and I joined the deFremery SUBDEBS—a club for girls too young to be debutantes. We would promenade around the neighborhood in SUBDEB club jackets, which looked like letterman jackets with hearts on them.

Spending as much time as possible at the rec center, I volunteered to help Miss Seels prepare for craft classes. By now I had my formula down to a science: *Make yourself useful, Belva,* I would tell myself. *That way some adult might actually want you around. Who knows, maybe they'll even learn to love you.*

I deployed the same strategy trying to endear myself to my mother. I wrote checks for her, paid her bills, and ran her errands, particularly if it enabled her to avoid encounters with intimidating sales clerks. One day she dispatched me to Woolworth's.

"I'd like to buy some blues records . . . ," I began to explain to the snooty white salesgirl.

"I don't understand you," she said, giving me a blank stare.

"I'm looking for blues . . . ," I began again.

"Do you mean blue dye?" she interrupted, addressing me as though I were six years old. "Blue clothes? Blue what?"

Given that we were conversing over the record counter, my purpose was hardly a mystery. I walked out—and by the time I walked home, I was fuming. My mother just chuckled: "Well, lucky I've got you to do the talking to those clerks for me."

Meanwhile my father had gotten wind of the fact that Nathaniel was living with my mother and me, and the family warned us that trouble was brewing. For reasons that still elude me, the three of us descended upon my Aunt Pearline and Uncle Ezra and their new daughter.

So I wound up living in the Ashby Avenue house in Berkeley after all, sleeping on the dining room floor.

Months passed. And then one Sunday morning, my father showed up on the front porch—with a fully loaded gun—threatening to kill my mother and Nathaniel. Perhaps he knew what I didn't know: my mother was pregnant with Nathaniel's child. As fate would have it, Nathaniel wasn't even there.

Uncle Ezra tried to calm my father down and disarm him, which seemed only to make him more livid. My Aunt Pearline pleaded with him to put away the gun.

My mother hid in a closet.

And as none of the adults seemed to be producing a solution, I took matters into my own hands and called the police.

When the squad car rolled up, my father looked frantically for a place to hide the gun, ended up stashing it in his pocket, and then cranked his charm up to its full wattage. The gravity of the situation was starting to sink in, both to my father and to me.

"We received a report of a man with a gun. Who made the call?" the officer asked. We all froze in silence. "Who made that call?" he repeated in a louder voice.

I stepped from behind the screen door. "I called," I said. "I was scared someone was going to get hurt so I made the call."

The policeman zeroed his interrogation in on me. "So who has the gun?" he demanded.

I couldn't look up. With my eyes focused on the planks of the porch floor, I raised my arm and pointed in the direction of my father.

"Officer, this was nothing—just a little family quarrel, but it's all fine now."

The police weren't having it. They searched him, found the gun, secured him with handcuffs, and transported him to jail.

I went to the backyard and sat on the steps the rest of the day. No one came to scold me, or comfort me. I had no idea when I would see my father again, but I had no doubt there would be hell to pay for what I had done.

Across the country, seventeen states maintained segregated public schools in 1948. California was not one of those, so I enrolled at Berkeley High as one of about three hundred blacks among its three thousand students. Because the town had a single public high school, teenagers from posh hills and the hardscrabble flatlands shared the same classes. But it was academically rigorous and progressive, sitting only a few blocks from the edge of the famed University of California campus. The teachers were nurturing and caring; and I tried to soak up everything I could. Of course I missed Rose Mary, who remained in our old neighborhood and attended Oakland Tech High School. I made new friends at Berkeley High, but I refused to hang out at the Smoke Shack with the fast black girls who streaked their hair and gathered at lunchtime to kiss the air with smoke rings. Most of the girls who were regulars had deep ties to South Berkeley—their families owned their own homes, and their parents held good, middle-class jobs. My mother and I enjoyed neither.

As a newcomer to Berkeley High, I had a hard time finding my place. I soon was adopted by a group of white girls, opening a window for me to glimpse what it was really like to be middle class in white America. The world these girls lived in included theater, opera, museums, private dance lessons after school, tennis with their dads on the weekends. I had known about these things only from movies—now I was befriended by people who actually lived that way.

Never had I been treated so equal to white students. Some of my class-mates invited me to their houses to study for algebra and calculus exams, and the color-blind casting of the theater department permitted me to appear in several roles on stage. My star turn as Portia in *The Merchant of Venice* was a de facto illustration that our drama teacher did not strain the quality of mercy: suffice it to say my thespian skills left a lot to be desired. But I studied Shakespeare along with business communication, because I felt the need to improve my English skills and had a lot of catching up to do.

Even Berkeley was no utopia of racial harmony, however. I occasionally walked with my white friends to their social dancing classes and clubs, but then we parted ways. We all tacitly understood that our friendship did not extend to my dancing with white boys or breaking the color restrictions at their whites-only private clubs.

For a brief interlude, I tried playing basketball. I hadn't considered that a girl who wore eyeglasses and stood barely five feet tall might not be a natural at the game. But then I joined the bowling team; and although I had never bowled before, I set out to conquer the art of bowling strikes. Scraping together enough money for the bowling shoes and lane rental required for team practices was hard, but my job dusting and stocking shelves at the South Berkeley Five and Dime paid off. One Saturday I decided to splurge on a private session so I could improve my approach to the starting line and practice a smooth release of the ball.

The bowling alley was quiet that afternoon as I excitedly approached the check-in desk for a lane assignment. No one else was at the counter while I waited, money in hand, for someone to help me. I tried to catch the attention of the alley employees, but they ignored me. Minutes ticked by. Finally a man strode over.

"You have to go," he declared. "We don't let Negroes bowl here."

What he said made no sense. I told him I had the money. He merely stared at me.

"I bowl here every week with the Berkeley High Bowling Club," I explained.

"I don't care," the man retorted. "You can't bowl here now, so just move along."

Words failed me. I didn't know what to say or how to fight back. I looked around to see if anyone else heard him. After all, this was Berkeley, not

Monroe, Louisiana. But there were no apparent witnesses, or at least no one willing to back me up. Crushed and confused, I turned around and walked out the door.

As always, I told no one. I didn't know whom to tell anyway. Instead I focused on my original intent, which was to better my game. If I couldn't bowl in an alley, our driveway would have to do. I chalked an outline of a bowling lane on our concrete driveway, lined up cans of Del Monte green beans and creamed corn as substitute pins, and began to practice every day after school. One afternoon when I was deep in perfecting my back swing, I heard a voice ask, "What are you doing?"

It was our bowling club sponsor, Miss Entz. She had been driving by in the stop-and-go Ashby Avenue traffic and saw me at work.

Startled, I stammered out that I was practicing.

"I'm just curious as to why you are bowling on concrete."

I took a deep breath, and then all the pent-up hurt over my ejection from the bowling alley poured out of me.

She was quiet for a moment, pursing her lips. "Well," she said, "we shall see about that."

At our regular bowling alley team practice a few days afterward, Miss Entz pulled me aside. "You can practice here anytime you want. And let me know if you are ever turned away at a public place in town, ever. From now on, your bowling is on me, because you are so good at the game."

Unbeknownst to me, she had talked to the school principal and they had agreed that all Berkeley High activities would be pulled from the bowling alley unless the management agreed to welcome all students at all times. Faced with a potential boycott, the management backed down.

I was speechless. Nobody had ever stuck up for me before. I was struck by the power of one woman to confront bigotry head-on and defeat it. She had just given me one of the most critical lessons of my life.

Typically, mothers worry about their teenage daughters accidentally getting pregnant. My own family legacy was sufficient to keep me away from any boy who wanted to "go too far." Instead, I worried about my mother's pregnancies. By the time I entered twelfth grade, she had given birth to two babies by Nathaniel, only eleven months apart. Then he up and left.

I admired how she carried on. Without complaint she took care of her children during the day and worked the graveyard shift cleaning dining cars at the Southern Pacific rail yard. I was responsible for the babies after she left for work at eleven at night. Aunt Pearline supervised the children from the time I left for school every morning until my mother returned home. I honestly have no idea when my mother slept.

In the spring of 1951, I became the first person in my immediate family to graduate from high school. My aunt came to my graduation. I wasn't surprised that my mother was too busy or exhausted to attend—I understood her burdens.

At Berkeley High, I completed what was called a double major; mine was both a business track and a college prep track. All my friends were planning to go off to college, and I was overjoyed when I received my admissions letter to San Francisco State University. I wanted to become a junior high school teacher, not only to kindle a love of knowledge in students, but also to give them the extra emotional support that I had sorely lacked. I was pursuing college on my own, however, without the involvement of family or counselors. My naïveté was about to cost me dearly. I had missed the deadlines for scholarship applications, and I suddenly was confronted with an urgent need for three hundred dollars to pay for registration fees and books. In our cramped household on Ashby Avenue, requesting that money would have been like asking for a million bucks.

I was earning money myself—both at the Five and Dime and by assisting Mrs. Davis, our next-door neighbor, who ran the hatcheck operation at Sweets Ballroom and also waited on guests at elaborate soirees in the hills. She was a nice woman, but she regarded my family as vaguely disreputable and didn't quite approve of me or the amount of time I had begun to spend with her oldest son, Frank. But she needed a hard worker, and I knew how to make myself useful. My job was to retrieve dirty plates and empty the ashtrays.

But some of the money I made was channeled into helping pay for utilities and food on Ashby Avenue. None of us were maintaining a savings account. So, before long I had extinguished every other possible option for college financing. And then, with the greatest reluctance, I called my father.

We had barely spoken since my earlier phone call had sent him to jail. He was locked away for a few months, was released, and eventually ended up working as a carpenter. He was making a comfortable living for himself and for the woman who would become his new wife—he could take one look at a space and build a cabinet that would fit it perfectly.

I told him I had gotten myself into college and explained that unless he would lend me a few hundred dollars, I could not go. There was an awkward pause.

"I don't have it," he said. "If I were you, I'd get a real job. Plan ahead. You've got the brains."

And in an instant, my dream of college evaporated.

That summer, as Rose Mary and my Berkeley High friends prepared for college, I passed the civil service exam and was assigned to a GS-2 typist position at the Naval Supply Center. My mother and Aunt Pearline were flabbergasted that I wasn't as overjoyed as they were by my good fortune.

So when Mrs. Davis's son Frank dropped out of college, joined the air force, and asked me to marry him, I agreed. While my friends were pledging sororities and studying for midterms, I clocked in and out at my typist station, and I spent my weekends shopping for wedding and bridesmaids' dresses.

We set the date for New Year's Day 1952.

I was eighteen years old; and except for my future husband, I had kissed only one boy. Rose Mary and my other friends threw a bachelorette party on the eve of the wedding, and they were utterly mystified that I sobbed all night long. All I remember saying is, "I don't want to get married, I don't want to get married, I don't want to get married . . . "

five

In the Driver's Seat

As dawn broke on my wedding day, I sat up in bed and tried to convince myself I was experiencing normal bridal jitters. In only a few hours, the fairy tale I had planned would unfold. McGee Avenue Baptist Church would be scented with bouquets of carnations; my four bridesmaids would be in place; and admirers in the pews would be glancing over their shoulders as I floated down the aisle to become Mrs. Frank Davis Jr.—for better or for worse, til death do us part.

If I were to back out now, what else could I do with my life?

So I got married.

Afterward we held the reception at Frank's house, given that it was fancier than ours. His house was filled with our friends—all teenagers barely out of high school. We girls stood around in our gowns as we nibbled hors d'oeuvres; we were striving to appear as sophisticated as those in the wedding parties depicted in bridal magazines. Frank and his groomsmen clustered around the black-and-white television, watching Illinois cream Stanford in the first nationally televised Rose Bowl game.

The next day, the air force dispatched Frank to Texas for training, and I took another apartment in Berkeley with my mother and her children. But it wasn't for long. Later that year Frank was reassigned to Andrews Air Force Base outside Washington, D.C., and sent for me to join him. My mother put her Southern Pacific connections to good use, alerting all the porters on the California Zephyr to keep an eye on me, feed me well, and make sure I changed trains correctly in Chicago, as I made the three-day trek across country. She also schooled me on survival in segregated territory, warning me to use only the colored bathroom, to drink out of only the colored water fountain, and to make sure I didn't wander by mistake into a whites-only waiting room. When I got off the train in Washington and plunged into the frenzy of Union Station, I couldn't find the "coloreds" bathroom or Frank. By the time I spotted my new husband's face in the crowd, I was a nervous wreck.

Washington, D.C., was in transition in 1952, as it began to look in the mirror and confront its racism. Just a few years earlier, the Truman Committee on Civil Rights had released the first comprehensive survey of its kind, which was damning. The committee singled out the capital as "a graphic illustration of a failure of democracy.

"For Negro Americans, Washington is not just the nation's capital. It is the point at which all public transportation into the South becomes 'Jim Crow.' If he stops in Washington, a Negro may dine like other men in Union Station, but as soon as he steps out into the capital, he leaves such democratic practices behind. With very few exceptions, he is refused service at downtown restaurants, he may not attend a downtown movie or play, and he has to go into the poorer section of the city to find a night's lodging. . . . In addition, he must endure the countless daily humiliations that the system of segregation imposes upon the one-third of Washington that is Negro." The inconsistencies were ludicrous: Constitution Hall seated whites and blacks with no distinction but refused to allow black performers on stage. Other theaters cast black actors but refused to allow blacks in the audience. And foreign officials with dark skin were typically mistaken for "American Negroes" and refused service until they established they were not Americans.

The exception to all this senseless segregation was the federal government. As an experienced GS-2 clerk typist, I landed a job with the Wage and Salary Stabilization Board. Every day in Washington was an education for me. It was the first time I had worked with so many black professionals: lawyers, economists, and managers. Our office set wages for most major industries. One day the thunderous and fiery labor leader John L. Lewis of the United Mine Workers Union—the man who infuriated the nation when he took his miners out on strike in 1943 during World War II—stormed into our office during the Korean War, threatening to do the same thing again unless the agency would approve wage increases for his miners. He was a man to be feared; and there I was, a recent high school graduate at the front desk, asking if he had an appointment.

My coworkers and I even made a trip up to Capitol Hill as spectators for one of Joseph McCarthy's anti-Communist witch-hunting hearings.

Within a year, I gave birth to my son, whom I named Steven Eugene. Yes, I kept *Eugene* in the family tradition.

But no sooner did Steven arrive than he was whisked away from me. I was diagnosed with hypertension, and the hospital ordered us separated so I could rest and receive treatment. For the crucial first week of Steven's life, I couldn't hold him or care for him the way other mothers did.

When we returned home, Frank and I continually clashed over how to raise our son. We were merely kids ourselves, neither of us knowing the first thing about caring for infants. Given my upbringing, the maternal instinct was a mystery I had to discover on my own. Nonetheless, I believed you could never hold a baby too much; he disagreed. One evening when Steven was about a month old, fussy and inconsolable, Frank put him on the bed and locked me out of the room, determined to let little Steven cry himself dry. As his wailing grew more shrill and frantic by the minute, I pleaded with Frank, pulling at his arm and begging him to unlock the door and let me get to my baby. He refused.

I would never truly forgive him.

Washington, D.C., desegregated city parks and facilities in 1954, and that same year the Supreme Court jettisoned the "separate but equal" doctrine for public education. I watched the burgeoning civil rights movement from afar—by that time, I had joined Frank at his new posting in Hawaii, near Pearl Harbor. News from the mainland reached us a day late, after newspapers and filmed TV news segments had been flown over the Pacific.

By the time we returned to Oakland in 1956 for Frank's discharge, Rosa Parks had been arrested in Montgomery, Alabama, for refusing to surrender her seat to a white passenger; and the resulting bus boycott, led by Dr. Martin Luther King, was shaking the foundation of segregation throughout the South and beyond.

Frank began work as an electronic technician at the Hunters Point shipyard in San Francisco. I secured an after-school babysitter for Steven, and I landed a post handling top secret weapons manuals for the navy, working out of a huge warehouse on Treasure Island in the middle of the bay. Soon our small unit was melded into a much larger one at the Naval Supply Center. Then it became a tedious eight-to-four job—and when the clock approached 3:59 p.m., most of my coworkers had their handbags at their sides while they waited to punch out and head home. In that environment I was a veritable workaholic, even winning a few employee awards for my dedication. Before long I could recite the naval names and numbers of larger vessels, the newest types of missiles and rockets, and assorted minutia about a host of weapons of war in the Pacific Fleet.

Needless to say, this expertise limited my conversation within my circle of friends. I certainly couldn't chat about my work.

To keep some spark in my life, I joined several black women's organizations. Soon I was volunteering to write about their activities for local small black weekly publications, most of which would print anything that was fairly well written and that landed in their lap free of charge. Admittedly, I was an amateur—one of the first outlets to publish my reports was the *San Francisco Shopping News*. Eventually I teamed up with popular photographer Chuck Willis; I wrote small stories that accompanied his pictures of community and social events.

I never expected Chuck to pay me a dime—I considered it sufficient reward that I was meeting interesting people, and he had valuable contacts. Among his clients was *Jet*, a magazine that was becoming indispensable to tens of thousands of black readers across the nation.

The creative force behind *Jet* was John H. Johnson, a young Chicago entrepreneur who sensed that a magazine aimed at the emerging Negro middle class would be, in his words, "a black gold mine." He used his mother's furniture as collateral for a five-hundred-dollar loan and catapulted into the magazine business, first with a *Reader's Digest* style *Negro Digest* and the romance confessional *Tan*. In 1951 he introduced *Jet*, and a few years later, he debuted the glossier *Ebony*.

Jet was a mix of human-interest features, celebrity profiles, and political news, as well as practical guides, such as how to apply for scholarships and register to vote.

Its formula for success: covering the stories that white publications downplayed or completely ignored—stories of crucial interest to African American readers. As Johnson later observed, "If you had relied on the white press of that day, you would have assumed that blacks were not born."

So when fourteen-year-old Chicagoan Emmett Till was lynched, beaten, shot, and his body dumped in Tallahatchie River for the "crime" of whistling at a white woman in Mississippi, *Jet* ran the story on its cover. Emmett's mother, after threatening to bust his sealed casket open with a hammer to see her son, was sickened to see that the boy's tongue was choked out; his right eye hung from its socket; his nose had been broken in several places as though someone had taken a meat cleaver to it; and his body had been held underwater for three days by a seventy-pound cotton-gin fan tied to his neck with barbed wire. The Chicago funeral director asked if she wanted him to "touch the body up."

"No," she replied with vehemence. "Let the people see what I have seen. I think everybody needs to know what happened to Emmett Till."

The only national publication to feature the photo of Emmett's corpse was *Jet*, but the photo made it impossible for decent people to ignore the results of racist hate. And when an all-white-male jury in Mississippi took less than an hour to find the accused white men "not guilty"—and boasted that the verdict would have been even speedier if they hadn't taken a soda break—the case of Emmett Till became a major turning point for civil rights.

I was an avid reader of *Jet* and was pleased when Chuck asked me to write captions and fact sheets for the freelance photos he was sending off to the company's headquarters in Chicago. One day *Jet* editor Bob Johnson phoned with a question:

"How would you like to be a stringer for the magazine? We can't pay you much—five dollars an item if we use it." I would not get a byline: Anything useful I submitted would probably end up in Gerri Majors's popular "Society World" column.

I couldn't have cared less about the low pay or the lack of credit. In fact, I was elated.

I began submitting community news items, blurbs about the most fascinating black people in the Bay Area, rundowns of charity events. As it turned out, Johnson (no relation to the publisher) was a talented and patient editor, from a distinguished family—his grandfather had been the first African American to serve as a U.S senator. Each week after the magazine was "put to bed," he would call me and go over my copy, ripping it apart. "How do I know it was a great party—what did you tell me about it, except for that flat line?" he would ask. "Girl, you have got to take me there!" From him I learned to meticulously record the details that bring a story to life.

I was interning with a mentor two thousand miles away, working for the most popular black magazine in the world.

At the same time, I was more or less trying to be the submissive, traditional wife that Frank clearly desired. I cooked, I cleaned, I attended church, I played hostess, I cared for our son. But I also was moody, distant in the bedroom, and not inclined to invite him into the world of my imagination.

He was jealous, kept close tabs on my whereabouts, didn't want me to drive, objected to my dancing with other men, detested it if I wore short skirts and low necklines, and saw "this writing stuff" as a complete waste of time.

I defied him and continued reporting for any publication that would take my copy. For *Ebony*, I prepared short profiles about Bay Area notables for consideration in its "Bachelors of the Year" and "Bachelorettes of the Year" features; and I relished the opportunity to spend time in the company of fascinating people. One of my successful bachelor submissions was George Wiley, a brilliant UC Berkeley professor who would later be regarded as the father of the welfare rights movement.

Eventually I received my own bylined column, "Society Swirl," in the *Bay Area Independent*, a small weekly, based in San Francisco. I wrote about the progress black people were making—local civil rights leaders; budding politicians; and everyday people, such as the first local black man hired as an automobile showroom salesman and the first black woman to work at a cosmetics counter.

I was juggling a lot: working a full-time job with the navy, freelancing for *Jet* and *Ebony*, writing my column, and of course, my family. And on that front, things were continuing to crumble.

Steven was not a happy child. My husband's rules were strict, and the repercussions for violating them were harsh—he expected young Steven to "be a man." He showed no sympathy for the fact that Steven was frightened of the big dog in the backyard and terrified to walk the nine blocks down MacArthur Boulevard to kindergarten all by himself. My son had few friends, and a mother who was changing every day. I think his childhood must have been as lonely as mine. He began stuttering. We both were out of step with the head of the household.

And then I found out I was pregnant again.

The arguments between Frank and me only escalated—about Steven, my work, and particularly my perpetual deadlines. In my final trimester, I began to rely on a new friend, the warm, easygoing photographer who worked in Chuck's darkroom. Bill Moore was a godsend. Many times when I was banging into a deadline, he bailed me out by driving to my home to retrieve my newspaper copy and delivering it where it needed to be.

The final showdown with my husband came three nights before Christmas 1959. I had been rushing to finish my column, decorate our Christmas tree, wrap presents, and keep my life from unraveling. I can't even recall what ignited this particular explosion, but soon Frank and I were toe-to-toe screaming at one another in the bathroom; and I was doing my fair share of the screaming. I told him I wanted a divorce.

"Get over it—divorce is not acceptable in this family," he hissed. And then another, more chilling declaration: "I'd rather see you dead than go through a divorce."

What happened next would forever remain a matter of dispute—with me believing Frank struck me, and him contending it was only a shove—but the impact sent me toppling backward into the bathtub. My water broke, and my daughter, Darolyn, began her journey into this world.

Now I had a son and a daughter. The world around us was awakening, stirring, changing. In the face of snubs, jeers, fire hoses, attack dogs, and bigots backed by the power of the state, black men and women in the South and throughout the country were risking everything for equality, freedom, and the dream of limitless possibilities—the enticing "what if?" In that milieu, I allowed myself to dream along with them. And I feared that if I waited much longer to leave my marriage, I'd get too worn down to take a risk, and my dreams would wither and die.

I had to get out of there.

For three months, I schemed with the precision of plotting in a detective novel. First I informed the navy that I would not be returning from maternity leave and requested my full retirement disbursement: three thousand dollars. I paid cash for a used car—a huge blue and white Plymouth sedan—that I bought only on the condition that I could store it on the sales lot until I needed it. I spent hours hovering over the counter at the AAA office, perusing cheap motel listings and maps as I plotted our route along desolate country roads that meandered south toward Los Angeles. And I hired a moving van, which was to appear at our house at 9:30 a.m., about an hour and a half after Frank left for work; to load up the furniture, toys, and clothing the children and I would later need and deposit them in a rented storage space. To avoid confrontation, the timing had to be perfect.

I left Frank some food, our bed, and a letter informing him that he could keep the house we had jointly purchased on Seneca Street. I hoped that might create at least a sliver of good will.

As the moving van arrived, neighbors were peeking out from their curtains along Seneca, one of two streets in the East Oakland hills that accommodated black homeowners. Owning our first home there had been a symbol of progress and pride, but I knew I could never live there again.

As I loaded the children into a waiting taxi, Rose Evans made a beeline across the street. She was the sort of woman who tracked the comings and goings of the neighborhood, and she'd clearly concluded that she needed to launch her own inquiry.

"What's up with the moving van? I just saw Frank, and he didn't say anything about you guys moving," she said, scanning my face for clues.

"Good," I replied. "And the less you know about this the better. Wish me luck!"

With that, I bade good-bye to my old life and moved into the great unknown. I had confided only in my mother, who thought this impulse was terrible and feared we would surely be caught or hurt or both. But in the words of the old Negro spiritual, we had "crossed over" now, and there would be no turning back.

An opaque fog enveloped us as we sped through the night, our own headlights reflecting back to cast a luminous halo around our lumbering Plymouth. Tule fog is notorious in California's Central Valley—it causes more weather-related deaths than any other force of nature in the state. Every few years, the highway linking Northern California to the Los Angeles Basin experiences a massive pileup in which up to a hundred cars and tractor-trailers plow into one another in fog-induced oblivion. For the most part I avoided venturing onto any easily traceable highways. Our greatest danger was that if we would need help, no other living soul was around for miles.

For the sake of my children, I feigned calmness. But I was inexperienced behind the wheel—an awful driver who kept hitting the brakes at the slightest cause. The bassinet on the backseat, with baby Darolyn tucked inside, would tumble forward; and six-year-old Steven would grab it and slide it back into place. He asked where we were going. I told him only that we couldn't live with his father anymore and needed to find someplace else to be for a while. Mostly he was quiet.

We changed motels every night, and at each we propped a chair against the door. None of us slept soundly.

In Los Angeles, I checked us into a flashy Hollywood motel with a shimmering blue swimming pool on Sunset Strip. We stayed three nights, giving Steven a chance to swim, relax, and pretend to be on vacation.

A phone conversation with my mother shattered our fantasy refuge: Frank's mother had put a private eye on our trail. Mrs. Davis was a strong-willed woman who was devoted to her grandchildren, and I knew she would never give up. For a few frantic hours, I considered driving us into Mexico. Then the rational part of my brain kicked in, and I realized I couldn't speak a phrase of Spanish and we would have no one to help us. Besides, I was running out of money.

I could only hope that Frank's temper was similar to my father's, and that with the passage of time, he had simmered down. For all my master-minding of this elaborate escape, I really had no plan for what would come next.

six

. . .

Vapors and Black Ink

I drove the Grapevine highway straight back toward the Bay Area, making as few pit stops as humanly possible traveling in the company of a six-year-old boy and a baby girl.

We hoped to lie low while I obtained an apartment and a job. My mother agreed to let Darolyn and me squeeze into her place, which already was housing enough relatives to remind me of D Soloman's Alley. My old best friend, Rose Mary, offered to take Steven in for a while—an act of bravery considering she had no experience whatsoever with small children. Nor did Steven make it easy for her, considering that he somehow managed to crawl out of a tiny upstairs window and onto her roof, necessitating a Fire Department rescue.

Returning to my mother's home one night, I observed a car parked across the street and the glow of a cigarette from the driver's side. Mother, watching anxiously out the window, saw me rushing up the steps; and she quickly opened the door and closed it behind me. She continued to watch from the corner of the window in the darkened room. I sat on the sofa in silence, trying not to panic. Finally, she saw the glow of the cigarette extinguished, the headlights switch on, and the car pull slowly away. Now Frank knew where I was. I had to move, and move quickly.

The next day I accepted an apartment in South Berkeley near where my mother and mother-in-law lived. Race and money dictated that I stay near those who knew me; intuition told me that sooner or later, Frank would find me.

I was right. Shortly after our furniture arrived from storage, the children and I returned to our apartment past dusk. Shifting Darolyn on my hip, I entered the bedroom, and my heart stopped: a dark figure was rising from beneath the bed. Time froze. I couldn't scream. Did the shadow have a knife? A gun?

And then I heard that sarcastic voice say, "Belvagene. So, you thought you could get away."

In the split second between caution and terror, I flipped on the light.

The baby squirmed, and I instantly decided that an offense was my best defense.

"What are you doing in my house?" I shouted. Darolyn began to cry. Steven burst over the threshold and ran to his father. I snapped out questions with the rapid fury of a Gatling gun: "Why were you under my bed? How did you get in here? What gives you the right? Get out of my house!"

Taken aback, Frank actually began to apologize for frightening us so. He told Steven he had missed him and would see him again soon, and then he agreed to leave. But I knew we would never have another peaceful night in that apartment, so we moved again—this time to a second-floor three-bedroom apartment with only one door—and I took another African American woman who held a civil service job as a roommate.

But the smartest thing I did was hire UC Berkeley nursing student Karen Lind as a part-time live-in babysitter. Karen was so tenderhearted that she had adopted a Korean orphan from one of those television appeals. She fell in love with my children, and on weekends often would take Darolyn to her home in Redwood City, south of San Francisco. Unbeknownst to me, she was taunted by strangers who mistakenly presumed the black baby was hers.

Meanwhile, Frank wasn't finished with me yet. I was served with legal papers accusing me of child neglect and of being an unfit mother. Frank and his mother were seeking custody of both of my children. Somehow I didn't blame my mother-in-law; they were her only grandchildren. But he knew better.

Granted, I had vulnerabilities he could exploit: the manner in which I left him could be portrayed as unfair and erratic, and I was subsisting on a string of jobs through a temp agency plus my stint as "Society Swirl" columnist for the *Bay Area Independent*. But after I enlisted the services of Carl Metoyer, a black lawyer who was the epitome of respectability, the case was dropped before it even went to trial. Only many years later would I discover a possible explanation for Frank's surrender: in the final months of our marriage, he had been carrying on a surreptitious affair, fathering a child born about the same time as Darolyn.

Declaring myself an independent woman was a costly endeavor, but at last I had my freedom. I just had to figure out how to earn enough money to keep the children and me afloat, given that I had forfeited to Frank my share of our house on Seneca and had not fought for or received any child support. Occasionally he sent them a twenty-five-dollar savings bond, but that was it.

So I became a wizard at living on *vapor*—a word I preferred over *handout*. I never asked anyone for help, especially my parents; but somehow help materialized at pivotal moments. One example was my friend Lillian Fortier, who was raising five children and pursuing her dream of a career in public relations. She rented a house near our apartment, and she had a small garden in back that produced an overabundance of tomatoes that she shared with me—a valuable *vapor*. One particularly memorable week, we had tomatoes every day: fried tomatoes, corn bread, and Kool-Aid one night; "hot water corn bread" with tomato sauce another; crispy fried patties made from corn meal, flour, tomatoes, and pinches of sugar and salt yet another. I imagined these were old slave recipes and that by fixing them I was establishing a communal connection to ancestors. My children, just plain hungry, were under no such delusion. Our week culminated in a meal of spaghetti and tomato sauce. Steven let me know he was well aware that the hamburger meat that belonged in the sauce was inexplicably missing.

Our household celebrated on the day Don Welcher, the publisher of the *Bay Area Independent*, offered me a full-time job. I had no set hours, only a requirement to work as much as necessary to get the paper out. My salary was forty dollars a week—scarcely sufficient to cover rent and childcare—but I was delirious with joy.

My mind flashed back to my high school years in Berkeley, when every Saturday morning I would journey down to Rumford's drugstore in search of news from the nation's leading African American broadsheets. Proprietor and pharmacist William Byron Rumford became Northern California's first black legislator, eventually winning passage of landmark laws outlawing discrimination in employment and housing throughout California. At Rumford's I would buy Uncle Ezra the newest editions of the *Chicago Defender*, the *Amsterdam News*, and the *Pittsburgh Courier*; and I'd help him read them. Now I was going to be a real reporter, too.

The *Independent* was one of two black weeklies then operating out of San Francisco's Fillmore District, a black cultural mecca with a thriving commercial core studded with cafés, hair salons, jazz clubs, shops, and churches. Southern blacks had moved into the area during the war; they often occupied the homes of Japanese residents ordered into internment camps, and the blacks had found steady work in the shipyards and other military facilities. Now the jobs were gone and the people poor, but the vibrancy lingered; the cool syncopation of jazz and blues still punctuated the night air; and the savory tastes of home cooking—gumbo, fried chicken, candied yams, greens, and corn bread—continued to lure people to the pulsing Fillmore.

As the *Independent*'s publisher, Welcher was a capitalist through and through, a black Republican who strove for objectivity and wanted his newspaper to play it straight while turning a profit. He had little interest in writing editorials, preferring to spend his time persuading local merchants that they should invest their ad dollars with us. The *Independent* was by far the smaller of the two publications.

The other, the *Sun-Reporter*, was its opposite—a fiery crusader owned by the legendary Dr. Carlton Goodlett, a black physician with socialist sympathies who claimed, "A people who fails to control or have access to the media . . . is a psychologically enslaved and deprived people. As crucial to democracy as the concept of 'one man, one vote' is the concept of 'one man, one voice.' "

Both papers filled the void that existed in local coverage of so-called Negro news. Despite the fact that the Bay Area's black population had soared in the post-war era, major white papers largely ignored the community as transient and unworthy of attention. Tom Fleming, the *Sun-Reporter*'s editor, recalled that after a press conference in the late 1940s, then San Francisco mayor Roger Lapham cornered him and asked, "Mr. Fleming, how long do you think these colored people are going to be here?" Fleming looked him in the eye and replied, "Mr. Mayor, do you know how permanent the Golden Gate is? Well, the black population is just as permanent. They're here to stay, and the city fathers may as well make up their minds to find housing and employment for them, because they're not going back down South." According to Fleming, Lapham turned red in the face and never spoke to him again.

By 1961, the *Sun-Reporter* had a zealous following. Its motto was "That no good cause shall lack a champion, and that evil shall not thrive unopposed." To those ends, the paper vigorously advocated desegregation, fair employment, housing laws, and new requirements that San Francisco's Muni hire blacks. Goodlett liked to say he wrote editorials to "spank the butts" of the powers that be. None of us imagined then that four decades in the future, the street address of San Francisco City Hall would be renamed Dr. Carlton B. Goodlett Place.

At the *Independent*, we could only hope for a fraction of the *Sun-Reporter*'s influence, not to mention its advertising base or news staff. In fact, we had the distinct disadvantage of having a newsroom staff of merely two: my editor and me. And to complicate the issue even further, he was white, with a Southern drawl to boot.

His name was Darryl Lewis. He had spent years as an Asian bureau chief for the Associated Press, but he hit the liquor bottle one too many times and blew one too many deadlines to keep his job or find another in the mainstream press.

"I'll be honest with you—you're going to have to give Darryl a lot of help, and you're going to have to defend him, too," Welcher said the day he offered me the job. "He's experienced and he knows journalism. But he doesn't know the Negro community, he doesn't know the Bay Area, he doesn't even know America that well—the man's been out of the country for years. Our people aren't gonna want to talk to him. But Belva, they'll talk to you."

That was the literal truth, more than Welcher could have imagined. One day Darryl and I were both working in the back room of the *Independent*'s rickety building on Turk Street when we heard the bell jingle on the door to let us know someone was entering the office. Darryl strolled up front to handle the situation, and before long he called out for me.

"Belva, could you come up front?"

"Just a minute," I called back, intending to finish up what I was doing.

"No, right away, please," he insisted.

Grumbling silently about the interruption, I approached the front and saw three clean-shaven men, standing ramrod straight, all dressed in somber suits, crisp white shirts, and bow ties. One of them was a dead ringer for Malcolm X.

"Good afternoon, sister," said one of his lieutenants.

Uncertain about Black Muslim protocol, I simply said, "Good afternoon."

There was an awkward silence. Darryl glanced at me and ventured an explanation: "These gentlemen want to place something in the paper."

I stared back at him blankly. *Fine,* I thought, *so why do you need me?*

One of the lieutenants provided the missing information: "Brother Malcolm don't talk to white folks."

Without thinking, I blurted out, "But don't you guys have your own newspaper?"

Of course they did. Black Muslims in the early 1960s could often be found on urban street corners, hawking copies of their new publication, *Muhammad Speaks.* It debuted in 1961 with a cover title "Some of this Earth to Call Our Own or Else." The Nation of Islam—founded in Detroit in the 1930s and led in the early 1960s by Elijah Muhammad—preached pure living, black brotherhood, and racial separatism. At the time, Malcolm X was one of Elijah Muhammad's key disciples and was functioning as the public face of the faith. Although he would later break with the Nation of Islam and espouse a more unifying message, at the time he had unnerved whites by labeling them "devils" and troubled many blacks by labeling civil rights leaders, including Dr. King, as "stooges" and "chumps."

And there he stood, only a few feet away from me, with a gaze so intense I felt as though his eyes were lasers piercing right through me.

"Sister, we have some information here that we want to give to our black brothers who might miss our paper." He went on to add that he would like his text to be printed unedited, at its full length, and at no charge.

I pivoted to face Darryl, addressing him as though he didn't understand English: "Brother Malcolm would like his text to be printed unedited, at its full length, and at no charge."

Darryl responded that we could run the copy and do so for free—let's face it, neither of us wanted to cross the Black Muslims—but the next edition simply had no room left to fit it in without trimming his text.

Again, I turned to Malcolm X and relayed Darryl's comments as though they had been nothing but incoherent gibberish to his ears.

Darryl: "Perhaps I could split it and run it in two editions?"

Me: "Perhaps he could split it and run it in two editions?"

Malcolm X: "No, I want it all to run at one time."

Me: "No, he wants it all to run at one time."

This farce continued back and forth while Darryl and Malcolm X negotiated a solution to the snag, with me "translating" every verbal volley in their exchange. At last they agreed that Malcolm X himself would do the cutting, and everyone waited as he took out a pen and excised the few paragraphs he deemed most expendable. Then he handed the copy over to me, and the trio strode briskly out.

For the rest of my life, I would always wonder whether this demand for a "translator" was ordinary behavior for Malcolm X, or if he was having a bit of fun at Darryl's expense.

At the *Independent* I learned to write compelling leads, craft snappy headlines, pick up the Safeway supermarket ads that kept the paper going, deliver copy to the printer, file tear sheets, retrieve the first run of the paper for distribution, and sober up Darryl on his bad days. In short, I got a real education in publishing a small paper.

Darryl, a small man with brown wavy hair and blue eyes who walked with a slight limp, brought a global perspective to his coverage of racial affairs in the early 1960s. He believed that people of color all over the world bore similar burdens and shared a very rich history, and he encouraged me to follow world events so we could discuss their implications. During his sober spells, I couldn't have had a better teacher. He put me at ease about my lack of a college education—telling me to just write accurately about what happened and capture the emotions of the people I interviewed as well as I could. These people were the story; I was merely their messenger. He imparted a wonderful way to learn.

Best of all, he corrected my spelling, grammar, and punctuation errors. Suffice it to say that my spelling and syntax skills would someday make me a natural at broadcasting.

Never did we lack news to cover. San Francisco's Geary Street Expressway was ripping the neighborhood apart: Its dividing line between north and south, rich and poor still stands. James Baldwin swept into town to promote his literary manifesto, *The Fire Next Time,* and I interviewed him over at Mary Ann Pollard's intellectual private club, the Rainbow Sign, in Berkeley. But the greatest thrill was the day Cassius Clay came to town.

Clay was on a winning streak in the ring, but he was not quite yet the world heavyweight boxing champ he would become in 1964, much less the "Sportsman of the Century" that *Sports Illustrated* would crown him in 1999, after he had assumed the name Muhammad Ali. He had won the light heavyweight gold medal at the 1960 Summer Olympics and left Europe a hero, although he claimed that after returning home he was refused service at a "whites-only" restaurant and was harassed by a white gang—experiences that prompted him to disgustedly toss his medal into the Ohio River.

In any event, he came to the Fillmore one sunny afternoon to soak up the adoration that surely awaited him. I was on hand with photographer Chuck Willis to cover his visit for the *Independent* as well as *Jet*; although my babysitter arrangements had fallen through, so I had both Steven and Darolyn in tow. The boxer with the strikingly handsome face entertained his way down the thoroughfare, loving the backslaps, the blown kisses, and the jive talk as he led a pied piper's parade through the establishments along the Fillmore.

It took us hours to travel a few blocks. Beauty shop patrons with their hair in various stages of washing, pressing, and curling squealed and ducked under their salon capes. The men tried to play it cool—the shy ones flashing him smiles accentuated by gold-capped teeth, the braver ones slapping his hand in congratulations. I was urging Steven along, carrying Darolyn, and frantically scribbling notes on my pad when Clay asked me why I wasn't home taking care of my children. Then with a crinkly smile he said, "Gimme that child," and scooped Darolyn up and onto his shoulders. She was delighted and was content to remain up there in the limelight for the rest of the afternoon. The most disappointed person of the day was Steven. He, too, wanted to be carried by this icon, but he begged to no avail. Clay said, "You're a big boy. Come on. Stop crying. Act like a man." Although Steven had heard these words from his father, it pained him more to hear them from the one and only Cassius Clay.

Chuck supplied pictures to *Jet* and the *Independent*, and we published a major spread that was one of our most popular editions, selling out at newsstands throughout the city.

Still the *Independent* struggled financially and grew increasingly out of step with the rising liberalism of the Bay Area. One day Darryl didn't show up for work and never came back. I got the chance to move to the more influential *Sun-Reporter* and never looked back.

My column at *Sun-Reporter* became more political. One story I relayed was about black businessmen who had attempted to dine at Trader Vic's shortly after the eatery was required to remove its No Niggers Served sign, only to have the waiter smash the men's glasses on the floor. I covered controversial W. E. B. Du Bois—who, as the first African American to graduate from Harvard, fought for civil rights and, at the age of 93, joined the Communist Party USA—when he spoke at San Francisco's Third Baptist Church.

But in addition to my column, I also was the *Sun-Reporter*'s women's editor. Dr. Goodlett decided that my duties included going to tony clothing stores, such as Macy's and City of Paris, and persuading them to use black women as models in their ads. I saw this as a crusade for the dignity and pride of dark-skinned women, although in retrospect I'm sure he was mindful of the advertising potential, too. I recall telling him that I had secured a commitment from Macy's to use black models and run ads in our paper if we followed Macy's suggestion that the *Sun-Reporter* hire a fashion editor. He readily agreed; then he added, "So, I guess you'll just have to share your salary."

I knew then that my time at the *Sun-Reporter* would come to an end—no way could I live off a reduced paycheck—but I had made a crucial connection with the paper's political editor, Edith Austin. Heavy, dark, her hair in a "natural" that looked as wild as a revolutionary's, Edith blew into rooms like a hurricane—a concentration of force and mass to be reckoned with. She wrapped herself in long ethnic garbs, refused to take any lip off anyone; and she could take the top Democratic politicos of the day, wrap them around her pinkie, and kick 'em on the way out the door. She knew a lot of things that a lot of people didn't want known, and she knew how to leverage that power for maximum effect. I knew I never, ever wanted to make her mad.

Most Sunday mornings, Edith hosted her salons, where up-and-coming black politicians such as future Berkeley congressman Ron Dellums would gather for grits, eggs, biscuits, and strategizing. The attendees would crowd into her Telegraph Avenue apartment in Berkeley, filling the available sitting space on the furniture and floor. She called them her "main horses," and all were men except Edith and me. I was the only woman invited, and I understood from the outset that I wasn't there to speak but to listen—listen and learn.

Just as I was beginning to understand the newspaper business, a new opportunity materialized. Herb Campbell, the lone newsman at white-owned, black-programmed San Francisco radio station KSAN, phoned me to ask whether I'd like to read my social column on the air. The only other black woman I had ever heard do such a thing was Tarea Hall Pittman, the West Coast regional director for the National Association for the Advancement of Colored People, who in her staccato voice recorded a weekly *Negroes in the News* report for Oakland station KWBR. I was intrigued and immediately said yes.

I was going to be on the radio.

seven

· · ·

Lucky 13

I always suspected that the white family who owned KSAN never actually listened to it. But seemingly resigned to the need to give their San Francisco station its initial "black" voices, they made two cynical moves:

The first was to put their own black handyman on the air, introducing him as "Rockin' Lucky." The poor man had no experience or training in radio, and he spoke in a broken English that left black professionals cringing. But "Rockin'" became locally famous for his live remote broadcasts—usually done sitting in the window of a small business in a black neighborhood—in which he invited passersby to stop and chat between records.

The second move was to place in the prime afternoon-drive slot "Ole Jumpin' George Oxford," a polished DJ who spun rhythm-and-blues platters and percolated through his show with a patter of soulful slang. Acclaimed the most popular DJ in local Negro broadcasting for more than a decade, he would sign off with, "I love everybody—'specially you, baby!" Many listeners automatically assumed he was black, but he wasn't, although he was always completely at ease at black events. In person, Oxford bore a resemblance to Walt Disney. He was KSAN's hottest star until January of 1960, when rival Oakland station KDIA shrewdly hired him away. The desperate KSAN sued to preempt him from using either the name "Ole Jumpin' George" or his signature sign-off on KDIA, insisting those were KSAN trademarks. Ultimately KSAN agreed that he could occasionally use "ole" on the air as a word, given that the guy did have a natural Southern accent and thus couldn't stop himself.

I became a new black voice on KSAN, and its only female. And I was, of course, a complete novice. But mellow DJ John Hardy took me aside and gave me a million dollars' worth of advice in only a minute: "Take your copy and a tape recorder, go stand in front of a mirror, and practice reading," he said, making it all sound so simple. "But when you look in the mirror, watch the way your lips and tongue interact with your words. Make sure you enunciate properly, so you can distinctly hear each syllable.

"And when you're done—and this is very important—listen to the tape to hear your phrasing and your breathing pattern," he continued, placing his hand atop his stomach. "Most of all, you should talk from the diaphragm, not the throat."

I practiced and practiced until my reflection in the bathroom mirror seemed to be saying, "Ah, you again?" But my delivery grew clearer and stronger. I heard that management liked the sound of my voice, and occasionally I would receive a pittance to cover my gas bill or bridge toll. Otherwise, my compensation was in experience rather than dollars.

For years I had gotten along by gluing together the chips and pieces of part-time and freelance paychecks into a mosaic that did not quite yet depict a career. Then one day my friend Odessa Broussard phoned with a job offer. Odessa was the traffic manager at powerful KDIA, with its mixed-race listening audience and celebrity DJs, including Oxford and basketball star Don Barksdale. Resting at 1310 on the AM dial, KDIA billed itself "Lucky 13" and was a grab bag of offerings—from the nightly saying of the Rosary to the calling of the horserace results. The station played soul, jazz, rhythm and blues, church services; and news director Louis Freeman even pulled double duty as a gospel DJ. The station's goal: to offer something for everyone, every day.

Odessa was expecting a baby, and she wondered whether I'd consider taking her place. "You should do this," she said. "First off, I'm not sure I'm coming back from maternity leave. Second, you just might be able to talk your way into an on-air spot. You know, women are our biggest block of listeners in the mornings, and we've got nothing special for them right now. Think about it."

I didn't need to think about it, I said yes. But I had one question for Odessa: "What is a traffic manager?"

She laughed. "First, it has nothing to do with the traffic on the streets. It would be your job to control the traffic of commercials that air on the station. You'd schedule them in the time period the salesman promised the clients.

You'd make sure competing products aren't advertising next to each other. And that's how you might get your own show.

"Those salesmen are gonna need you to get their commercials aired in the best time slots, especially during drive time," she continued. "I'm sure one of the new guys would be very receptive if you approached him about finding a lead sponsor for a new women's program. As I said, they *need* you."

"Odessa," I whispered, "that sort of sounds like blackmail."

"Well . . . ," she said with a conspiratorial chuckle that propelled both of us into giggles.

Odessa did not return to KDIA, although radio had been good for her. She had once fielded an inquiry from a prominent attorney seeking free airtime for some worthy cause; and while nobody remembers whether he got the airtime, he certainly got Odessa. Allen Broussard was yet another Louisiana transplant who had graduated from UC Berkeley's law school; he opened a private practice with my divorce attorney, Carl Metoyer, and Lionel Wilson, who would someday become Oakland's first black mayor. As for Al, he was destined to be the first African American president of the California Judges Association and an associate justice of the California Supreme Court. And he was ultimately eulogized for his commitment to civil rights, his intricate legal mind, and his smoking hot gumbo. But back then, he preferred that his wife stay home with their baby, so that's what she did.

Just as Odessa predicted, it was our newest salesman, Bill Morrison, who enlisted the first sponsor of *The Belva Davis Show*—Beauty Pleat Drapes, located on Thirtieth and Broadway. My show aired for two hours on Saturday mornings and for one hour on weekdays. As for the format of this unprecedented "women's show," the men at the station shrugged and left it totally up to me.

So I incorporated every stereotypical concept of women's programming available in the early 1960s: recipes, childcare tips, interior decorating advice. Although my manic work schedule guaranteed long days into night, I insisted on having dinner with the children every evening. Their weekends took them wherever our schedules demanded—sometimes to places they should have been, sometimes not. I was almost never home and scarcely had time to take care of myself, but my listeners would never have guessed reality from the opening of my first show:

"Hi—welcome to the premiere of *The Belva Davis Show*, a program designed for the woman with an interest in making herself and her home more beautiful," I cooed, my voice clear and confident while the violins of my theme music faded away.

Only a few minutes into that inaugural show, my audience heard from Beauty Pleat, which I characterized as "designer of the world's finest draperies" with its "sixty thousand yards of quality fabrics" and a patented system eliminating the need for drapery pins and traditional rods. Another commercial featured a dialogue between a fictional married couple—"John and Mabel"—about why Mabel had hung Beauty Pleat drapes not only on the inside of her windows, but on the outside as well. Her reason, of course, was that she wanted even the neighbors she didn't know to see how beautiful her drapes were!

My first guest was none other than Ella Fitzgerald, who made a brief appearance to promote her show in the Venetian Room of the Fairmont Hotel that week. It gave me an excuse to play some of her jazz classics. I also spun "Release Me," a cover by Little Esther Phillips that had just topped the R&B charts; "Work Song," by Oscar Brown; and "Trouble in Mind," by a hardly known vocalist who would in the future be crowned the "Queen of Soul" and the first female inducted into the Rock and Roll Hall of Fame: Aretha Franklin.

I plugged an *Ebony*-sponsored fashion show to benefit the Booker T. Washington Community Center. I profiled some of my nominees for *Ebony's* "Most Eligible Bachelors" feature. And I shared my recipe for holiday "spirit balls": crushed vanilla wafers, nuts, and liqueur, all rolled in powdered sugar. "Serve them," I urged, "and watch the spirits rise."

As I settled in behind the studio microphone, I realized that I wasn't a bit nervous. This felt *natural*. Actually, this felt *fun*.

A parade of budding singers and comedians made live appearances on *The Belva Davis Show*, typically on Saturday mornings after opening a run of local performances the night before in San Francisco or Oakland venues. Our Saturday show was broadcast in front of a live audience in the largest KDIA studio, which featured seating for one hundred and a grand piano. My studio guests included jazz crooners Nancy Wilson, Mel Tormé, and Diahann Carroll, and comedians Dick Gregory and Bill Cosby. Cosby was frequently booked at clubs like the hungry i, and came around so much that he recorded a promo with my daughter. "Hi, this is Bill Cosby. Listen to *The Belva Davis* Show," he intoned. And then Darolyn's toddler voice chirped, "'cause that's my mommy!"

I attempted to coax performers into appearing in person by promising them more airtime, unedited. Some, of course, were nocturnal folks—as far as they were concerned, the crack of dawn didn't arrive 'til afternoon—and they couldn't be cajoled into a morning appearance for any reason whatsoever. In those cases, I hauled my clunky tape recorder to their clubs and halls, where I recorded interviews either before they opened or between sets. Not that I was always successful.

When trumpeter extraordinaire Miles Davis opened at the Jazz Workshop, I resolved to persuade him to talk to me despite his reputation for hostile press relations. I showed up, spotted him at the bar, and casually sidled up to the empty stool beside him. He failed to acknowledge my presence.

"Good evening, Mr. Davis," I ventured.

Silence.

I swallowed. "You know, here's a coincidence—my last name is Davis, too."

A grunt.

Choosing to interpret any audible response as progress, I sucked in a deep breath and soldiered on. "Mr. Davis, I have a radio show on KDIA, Lucky 13 on the dial. And I know you don't do many interviews, but I would so appreciate it if you would give me a break just for tonight and let me ask you just a few questions."

He smacked his glass down on the bar and cocked his head my direction with a look that could freeze vodka. "Girl, what the hell's the matter with you?" he rasped in a voice full of porcupine quills. "Don't you know I don't do no damn interviews?"

I felt the sting of such rejection more than once, but I refused to let it deter me. When Frank Sinatra played the Cow Palace, I hoisted my gear over my shoulder and joined the throng of white newsmen clustered outside his trailer door. As he returned from a preshow rehearsal, press photographers began snapping away, their flashbulbs popping in his face. He threw up a hand to shield himself and cursed the lot of us. Then he eyed me, raised his eyebrows, and crooked his finger as though to reel me in.

"Girlie," he said, "you can come on."

Trying not to look dumbstruck or starstruck, I followed him up the stairs and into his trailer. He took a seat, lit a cigarette, crossed his legs, and leaned back, scrutinizing me as I frantically fumbled to untangle my microphone cord.

"So how come you're shaking like a leaf?" he asked me.

"I'm sorry, Mr. Sinatra, I'm so sorry," I said, feeling tears starting to brim at the rims of my eyelids. "It's just that I'm terribly nervous. I know I shouldn't be nervous, it's just that . . . "

He raised a hand. "Stop. Let me tell you something." He leaned forward and stared intently at me. "The day I walk out on stage and I'm not nervous is the day I quit. So you don't ever have to apologize to me about nerves."

I nodded and gave him a grateful smile, and he proceeded to give me one of my best radio interviews.

One of my worst was with provocateur comedian Lenny Bruce, who relished being as noxious as human ammonia.

He opened his show at Basin Street West by carpet-bombing the place with a slew of racial and ethnic pejoratives sufficient to insult virtually everyone in the crowd. I stiffened as he began a staccato repetition of the word *nigger*.

"Well, I was just trying to make a point," he said, "and that is that it's the suppression of the word that gives it the power, the violence, the viciousness. If President Kennedy would just go on television, and say, 'I would like to introduce you to all the niggers in my cabinet,' and if he'd just say 'nigger nigger nigger nigger nigger' to every nigger he saw, 'boogie boogie boogie boogie boogie' and 'nigger, nigger, nigger, nigger, nigger, nigger' 'til nigger didn't mean anything anymore, then you could never make some six-year-old black kid cry because somebody called him a nigger at school."

I was shocked speechless, which I suppose is what Bruce intended, but I wasn't buying his rationalization either. I only lasted through part of his monologue before walking out. Still wanting the interview—if for no other reason than to demand a better explanation—I returned during the break. We spoke briefly on tape, sparks of antagonism flying like electricity between us. I asked him how he could possibly justify using such a hurtful word; and he pretty much said that he didn't care whether he hurt anybody because that was his act, baby—take it or leave it.

Although Bruce was white, black artists have been deploying the word for decades since then in a misguided attempt to lance its hate. In 1964, Dick Gregory authored the book *Nigger: An Autobiography*, and he wrote in a foreword, "Dear Momma—Wherever you are, if you ever hear the word 'nigger' again, remember they are advertising my book." Later, comedians from Richard Pryor to Chris Rock would build performances around what more polite society has come to refer to as *the n-word*, and rap artists would make it their mantra. Nonetheless, I would argue that a half-century after Lenny Bruce thought he was disarming the word, it has lost none of its lacerating power to wound.

The Belva Davis Show was becoming a hit, and I was beginning to lead a life I could not have imagined merely a couple of years before. The show drew bigger sponsors, which inspired me to prepare and serve a free lunch to my Saturday studio audience.

Staying up until the wee hours the night before, I would fix batches of fried chicken courtesy of Foster Farms; potato salad with Best Foods spread; finger sandwiches made from Wonder bread; and for dessert, cobbler baked with Del Monte Cling Peaches.

My silent partner was my old friend Bill Moore, the good-hearted guy who had worked in Chuck Willis's darkroom and delivered my copy when I was running late. In the intervening months, our friendship had only grown deeper. When I was struggling to learn radio, Bill was my listener. When my babysitter would cancel, Bill was my substitute childcare. And when I was utterly exhausted and the moon was full, Bill would pick me up in his Volkswagen Beetle convertible and drive us to the Valley of the Moon in Sonoma County, the wine-growing region of California made famous by author Jack London. Sometimes Darolyn would accompany us and sleep in the back while Bill and I listened to John Coltrane on the radio and drove with no destination whatsoever. It was magic, as though the silvery glow of the moon was washing away all my worries. Often I would fall asleep—the most luxurious sleep I had ever experienced.

Still I was astonished when sultry singer Nancy Wilson pulled me aside at KDIA and said, "That Bill's a nice guy. In fact, he's the best thing that's come around in a long time. You should marry him and stop running around with these musicians."

Nancy, then at the crest of stardom as a jazz singer, had become a regular visitor to KDIA; and we had struck up a warm friendship that would last the next fifty years. Yet, I was taken aback. First off, I had casually dated a few musicians but certainly did not consider myself "running around." More to the point, I had never thought of Bill as anything other than my dearest comrade.

The more I thought about it, however, the more I realized that we had begun to function like a single organism—leading and following, challenging and supporting, understanding each other's whims and idiosyncrasies. I was needy; he nourished. He needed someone to protect him from his own generosity of spirit; I protected. I had never before experienced true joy; Bill had a need to bring joy to everyone around him. He was everything that no man in my life had ever been.

Our relationship was like melting chocolate, changing so gradually that we didn't even notice we had fallen in love.

It took a child to see it. Steven, loving the new father figure in his life, tugged on Bill's sleeve one day and asked, "When are you gonna marry my mom?" He continued this somewhat embarrassing campaign until Bill and I applied for a marriage license.

Bill's family had the stability my own family sorely lacked. His mother, Isabelle, could trace her ancestors to Ellis Island. His father, Edward "Poppie" Moore, had hopped a ship from the Caribbean island of Barbados to Panama, and then another on to California, where he settled but chose to remain a British subject for the rest of his long life. Our families' sagas intersected at the Southern Pacific Railroad yard in West Oakland, where my mother worked so many years and where Poppie, like my mother's boyfriend Nathaniel, "ran on the road" as a waiter. The Moores shared a successful marriage and four well-adjusted children.

Photography was Bill's passion, having studied it at Laney College and apprenticed in Chuck's darkroom. Photo supplies were pricey, so occasionally Chuck would collect the deposit for a client's portrait sitting and slip the money to Bill, who would sneak out the back door to go purchase the film and flashbulbs required for the job. Unbeknownst to the client, Chuck would simply fake it, clicking away at his empty camera until Bill strolled back in and nonchalantly tossed him some "extra" film.

Each of us dreamed of bigger and better careers, and we determined to pursue them as a team.

Our first official step was tentative. We drove out of our home county of Alameda and over to Martinez, the seat of adjacent Contra Costa County, to apply for a marriage license. That would keep our names out of the Oakland press in case we decided to back out. Weeks passed. We were busy.

To say that our wedding was spontaneous would be an understatement. Looking at my radio log calendar one Thursday morning, I realized that our license was set to expire the next day. I called him with the update.

"Well," he said, "do you want to get married today or tomorrow?"

I thought I remembered that Odessa had gotten married in Carmel, the romantic seaside resort set on a spectacular strip of Pacific coastline south of the Bay Area. I phoned the Highlands Inn there and confirmed that yes, they had availability that night and could book a minister on our behalf— apparently not a lot of people scheduled their nuptials for late on a Thursday night.

Next I once again summoned Rose Mary.

"It's Belva. Two questions: One, are you free tonight? And two, do you have something I can borrow to wear? Bill and I are getting married, and I'd like you to be my maid of honor."

Rose Mary confirmed that she wouldn't miss this for the world, and also that she could lend me a cream-colored brocade suit with a matching pillbox hat and small veil. What's more, she could arrange for her boyfriend, Ralph, a wry-humored mathematician, to stand in as Bill's best man. We were relieved, chiefly because Bill and I didn't trust our cars to make the trip, whereas Ralph had a shiny new VW bug coupe certain to get us the eighty-three miles to Carmel and back.

The four of us piled in and headed across the Bay Bridge into San Francisco, at which point Bill suddenly realized that he needed a proper bachelor party. So we pulled off the highway and into a South of Market neighborhood in search of a bar. Ralph parked, and the two guys headed inside, leaving Rose Mary and me joking about how much time would pass before we might see them again. To our amazement, they returned in no time flat. As we headed south, they kept looking at each other and cracking up, all the while refusing to share their inside joke with Rose Mary and me. Finally, after at least a half hour, we teased out the truth about the winks, smiles, and flirtations they attracted from other patrons in the bar—and our men's dawning realization that there was not one woman in sight: Bill had just held his impromptu bachelor party in a gay bar.

The sun was setting over the Pacific when we arrived at the inn and I realized I had no bridal bouquet. The desk manager gave me permission to snip a few hydrangeas from the hotel grounds. A pallid Presbyterian minister arrived, and soon the chapel was filled with the off-kilter sound of an old 45 rpm record galumphing around the turntable as it blared Mendelssohn's "Wedding March." The ceremony was brief. Bill set up his camera on a tripod with an extended cable so he could snap a few of his own wedding pictures.

By this time we were famished, but the hotel's restaurant had already closed. We had no prospect of a honeymoon: I had a babysitter waiting; we both had work the next morning; and we didn't have the money to pay for a room at the posh Highlands anyway. So we loaded up the VW and headed back to the Bay Area. Ralph dropped Bill off at his family's home in Oakland and then took me to my house in Berkeley. The next evening, we announced to the children that Bill was moving in. They were overjoyed.

Everything was going so well that at last I was willing to believe Lucky 13 had brought me good luck as well—that is, until the night I realized I might have just pulled the plug on my broadcasting career.

Late that night I had finished the weekend radio traffic logs while chatting with ad salesman Bill Morrison a couple of cubicles away. I was repeating some juicy gossip I'd just heard about temperamental soul star James Brown's latest tantrum with his traveling band: Word was he had ordered some of them off his bus and left them on a desert road. "What a guy," I said sarcastically. And then, recalling that Brown was scheduled to make a late night show appearance on KDIA, I called out "I got to hurry up and get out of here before that little old ugly James Brown shows up."

At that moment I heard a man clear his throat behind me, and I whirled around to see none other than James Brown himself standing in the doorway. In an instant I could see myself joining his evicted band on that deserted road to nowhere. Brown's music was incredibly popular with our audience. The station treasured his drop-in chats with our DJs and even sponsored his concerts. No doubt I would be fired for insulting one of our biggest stars.

"Oh, Mr. Brown," the words rushed out of me, "I'm so sorry, I shouldn't have said that."

As I stumbled through a profuse apology, a broad grin swept his face. For whatever reason, he had decided to be merciful.

"Aw, that's all right darlin'—I know you didn't mean no harm." Then he added, with gold teeth shining, "You really don't think I'm good looking?"

eight

Lend Me a Tiara

In the 1960s, valiant Americans put their bones and bodies, their livelihoods and lives on the line to halt the ravages of racism. At the decade's opening, black people in many places could not safely vote, attend integrated schools and universities, marry a white person, purchase a home in a nice neighborhood, or sit at a Woolworth's lunch counter. We had never had a post-Reconstruction U.S. senator, major airline pilot, Supreme Court justice, network TV drama star, mayor of a large city, NBA coach, congresswoman, member of the New York Stock Exchange, or *Vogue* magazine cover girl.

By the end of the decade, African Americans—determined that the blood of civil rights martyrs not be spilled in vain—were rewriting history with a vengeance. Ed Brooks was sworn in as U.S. senator from Massachusetts. Marlon Green was hired as a passenger-airline pilot. Thurgood Marshall became associate justice of the U.S. Supreme Court. Bill Cosby was a co-star of NBC's *I Spy*. Carl B. Stokes was elected mayor of Cleveland, Bill Russell coached basketball's Boston Celtics, Shirley Chisholm was seated in the U.S. House of Representatives, Joseph Searles III joined the New York Stock Exchange, and model Donyale Luna graced the cover of British *Vogue*.

As an aspiring journalist and mother of two small children, I did not march or sit in; nor did I face down lacerating fire hoses, snarling police dogs, or swinging clubs. Like most African Americans, I watched the explosive confrontations on TV news and felt profound respect for our freedom fighters on the front lines. But also like many African Americans, I became more attuned to everyday injustices—and I began to look for everyday ways to advance the causes of equality and black pride.

One such opportunity presented itself in September 1960, when I was among the 85 million television viewers who tuned in to watch the Miss America pageant broadcast from Atlantic City.

Nobody had to tell me that a dark-skinned girl was ineligible to be Miss America: everybody knew the crown was reserved for white girls only. The rare occasions when the pageant included African Americans had been demeaning, such as the 1923 competition in which blacks played the roles of slaves during a *Court of Neptune* musical extravaganza. By the 1930s, the exclusion was made explicit with Pageant Rule #7, which required that Miss America contestants "be of good health and of the white race."

By the 1940s, contestants were required to complete a biological data sheet tracing their ancestry as far back as possible—preferably to the Mayflower. And in 1945, when pageant grand maestro Lenora Slaughter watched concert pianist Bess Myerson compete in a pageant preliminary, she proposed that Myerson change her name to something that sounded less ethnic. "I was a Jew and proud of it, and I was going to stay a Jew," Myerson would later explain. "I was already losing my sense of who I was; already I was in a masquerade, marching across stage in bathing suits. I kept telling myself it was OK, that if that's what I had to do to win, then I could do it. But whatever was left of myself I had to keep." She kept her name and won, becoming the first Miss America who was Jewish.

But not until 1970 would a state be so rebellious as to send a black contestant to the Miss America Pageant; and ironically the color barrier would be broken by one of the whitest states in the nation: Iowa. It would be 1984 before we would see one of our own crowned Miss America. Vanessa Williams of New York would set two precedents, winning the title and then resigning several months later after the appearance of old photos of her posing nude. Her first runner-up and her ultimate replacement, Miss New Jersey Suzette Charles, also was African American; and in recent years, several black women have won the pageant.

That future was unimaginable in the early 1960s—a time when black females never saw themselves celebrated as beauties in the movies, on television, or in best-selling fashion magazines; and when TWA had recently defended its decision not to hire its first black stewardess on the grounds that the applicant wasn't "attractive enough." Popular media gave us limited bandwidth: we were portrayed either as maids, Aunt Jemimas, or prostitutes.

The prototype of a "beautiful woman" in the mainstream culture of the day had a slim build, blonde hair, and blue eyes. Social science research would later establish that mulattos and lighter-toned African Americans had better employment prospects than their darker counterparts.

Internalizing this racism, many black females put themselves through a tortuous process trying to appear "less black"—straightening the kinks out of their hair, bleaching their skin, minimizing their curvaceous bodies, and even occasionally clamping their wider noses with clothespins in a preposterous attempt to narrow them. I inwardly winced every time we at KDIA aired a spot from one of our national sponsors, ARTRA skin lightening cream. On the other hand, I joined millions of other black women in treating my hair to make it smoother and straighter.

But I also had no doubt that attractive girls and women came in all colors, from pale porcelain to glorious ebony. And if the Miss America Pageant was too stubbornly prejudiced to see that, I decided, we should simply initiate a contest all our own.

Negro beauty pageants had been around for a while, although all too often they rewarded contestants with the most "passable" Caucasian complexion. This inflicted "pigmentocracy," however, was destined to fall out of favor. At Harlem's Miss Fine Brown Frame Contest in 1947, when the judges passed over dark-skinned, curvaceous audience favorite Evelyn Sanders and selected instead a light-skinned competitor, turmoil ensued. As *Ebony* magazine reported, the crowd—which included World War II veterans impatient with their own country's prejudices—let the judges "know that, for once, white standards of beauty would not be forced upon them." Organizers sought to mollify the audience by offering to bestow the title upon the lighter contestant and award Sanders the three-hundred-dollar cash prize: a Solomonic solution that left the outraged audience shaking their fists. Before the night was over, Sanders had the title and the cash.

By the 1960s, a patchwork of Negro beauty pageants was thriving coast to coast, but they tended to be haphazard, bargain-basement imitations of Atlantic City's main event. An exception was a pageant launched in Southern California by glamour photographer Howard Morehead, whom I knew because of his work for *Jet* magazine. Freelancing had allowed him daily contact with a bevy of black beauties around Hollywood who were ambitious, talented, and frustrated. His awareness of this untapped potential led him to create a beauty contest that offered not only prizes and scholarships, but also screen tests with major film studios for the winners and top talent contestants. His Miss Bronze California Pageant had been going strong for a few years before I decided, in 1961, to produce a Miss Bronze Pageant for Northern California.

"Let's face it—Negro girls never get selected in beauty pageants," I told the *San Francisco Examiner.* "That's what inspired the Miss Bronze contest, and we hope in time to make it so popular the other beauty events will also want our girls."

The pageant was open to unmarried African American women ages seventeen to twenty-five, from the Oregon border all the way south to Fresno. I recruited contestants in the Bay Area via my newspaper column, my radio show, and even church appearances. Eventually Sacramento, Merced, and Fresno staged their own local pageants, with their winners advancing to the Miss Bronze Northern California finals. The winner and first runner-up, as well as the talent-competition victor, were awarded free trips to Los Angeles to compete in the Miss Bronze California Pageant finals.

I did everything I could to make the competition affordable to all young women. Entrance was free, as were the required charm school classes. We secured donated swimsuits for the contestants—always modest one-pieces, to keep the churches happy—and provided stipends for their evening gowns. Local merchants donated other supplies; Gallenkamps, for example, gave contestants free shoes and charged only the cost of dyeing them to match the gowns.

At the outset, the price tag for an authentic tiara exceeded our budget, so we arranged to borrow the one Howard used for the Southern California Pageant, which he in turn had borrowed from Miss Universe Pageant officials. While I wouldn't stake my life on it, the pearl-encrusted tiara was said to be valued at a million dollars.

"Productions like the Miss Bronze California will do more for integration than all of the money spent down South," the crown's creator, James Boutross, brazenly claimed, "because you show the Negro in a dignified light."

Also in the interest of affordability, out-of-town qualifiers for Miss Bronze Northern California stayed at my Berkeley house for a week or more before the pageant. They slept on couches or our living room floor, which made for one gigantic, giggly pajama party—with Bill, Steven, Darolyn, and me accommodating these effervescent young women.

As the unofficial mother hen, I laid down firm rules: No smoking. No drinking. No inappropriate language. Curfew at a respectable hour. And absolutely no dating any men connected with the pageant.

More than once I had to cross my arms and place myself between a naive contestant and a male sponsor who mistakenly presumed that his contribution entitled him to special access. The girls nicknamed me "The Steel Fist inside the Velvet Glove."

Each young woman was put through her paces at Charm Unlimited, a Berkeley poise and grooming school founded by my ex-husband's second cousin, Shelby Davis, and his wife, Tonita. Shelby—an elegant looker whose favorite word was *glitter*—eventually served as a pageant co-producer. Tonita, the school's directress, cut a striking figure in stockings and high heels, long nails perfectly polished, hair impeccably coiffed, carriage erect. Behind the carefully constructed image, both had checkered pasts, including financial finagling that had once landed him behind bars. But they were determined to forge reputable new careers—Tonita, for example, enrolled in every conceivable modeling class. Their charm school became popular with Southerners transplanted into the foreign culture of California, because it promised to "open so many doors for ambitious and forward-looking Negro women." The advertisements that Tonita wrote for Charm Unlimited appealed to the insecurities of these black women, who craved greater opportunities but were unschooled in the intricacies of bourgeois life:

> There are times, I am sure, when you have just hated yourself because you were overdressed at an important social function, or you stammered your way through an interview or a simple introduction, or you weren't quite sure how you would come off when your big moment arrived, or what to discuss in casual conversation with new acquaintances, or even what to do with your hands or feet in a conspicuous gathering when all eyes would eventually be focused on you. Bring your courage to Charm Unlimited and we will guide you along the way to grace, glamour and good looks.

Tonita instructed our contestants on how to glide in heels, to sit with their legs discreetly crossed at the ankles, and to delicately pat the corners of their lips with table napkins. "And ladies," she would whisper in a confidently conspiratorial tone, "always carry a little room deodorizer to spray after you use the restroom. Remember, a lady *never* leaves an unpleasant odor behind her!"

To underscore that beauty is more than skin deep, we required contestants to fulfill hours of community service through organizations such as the Red Cross. And they were to perform a talent of their choice, be it a poetry recitation, an Afro-Cuban dance, or a vocal solo.

The finalists then fielded questions posed by judges before an audience. "Could you tell us what kind of social change you would like to see in your lifetime?" the judges asked contestant Stephani Jo Swanigan, an Oakland City College criminology student who would go on to become Miss Bronze California 1963. "As grateful as I am for the Miss Bronze Pageant," she replied, "I look forward to the day when there will be no need for a separate contest for Negro girls."

The Miss Bronze Northern California Pageant debuted at the Surf Club at San Francisco's Playland at the Beach, and it played to a full house of about five hundred spectators. I was adamant that it be a regal affair, and I supervised the design of an elaborate set.

Over the next few years, the pageant moved to the Jack Tar Hotel, which had opened in 1960 to protests for having hired only a few African Americans—and only as doormen and maids. Pressure from groups such as the NAACP soon forced the Jack Tar to hire at least one black person to fill each of these staff positions—clerk, room-service attendant, accountant, and bartender; and the community was encouraged to reward this compromise by patronizing the hotel. In later years we moved the pageant to the San Francisco Hilton near Union Square and, finally, to the crown jewel of San Francisco hotels, the Grand Ballroom of the Fairmont atop tony Nob Hill.

Our first winner, Cynthia Badie, was a stunning beauty with a dark complexion, all the more accented by her sleeveless ivory gown and long gloves. She had grown up with relatives teasingly calling her "Blackie"; but they had also complimented her for being adorable, and she later said she never had any trepidation about competing against young women of a lighter hue.

"We try to avoid those who are too Caucasian in their features," I told reporters in the early years. "And skin color varies, but I might tell you this—the fairer she is, the less chance she seems to have of winning. The girl should look like a Negro."

But having made my point early on, I ultimately had to confront the reality that we risked perpetuating our own form of discrimination by penalizing lighter contestants. In the six years I produced Miss Bronze Northern California, we crowned African American girls with a variety of complexions.

I always secured an integrated panel of judges. That meant enlisting black friends including Nancy Wilson and Don Barksdale as well as *Ebony* magazine West Coast editor Louis Robinson and *Mission Impossible* TV star Greg Morris. Approximately half of our judges were white, and they included KDIA station manager Walter Conway, *San Francisco Chronicle* "Advice to the Lovelorn" columnist Monique Benoit, Columbia Records rep Del Costello, and Miss San Francisco 1962, Sally Ann Hamberlin.

We also one-upped the Miss America Pageant in the crooning serenader department. *Let Atlantic City have its Bert Parks,* I thought. *We snared young newcomer Lou Rawls.*

Still, we struggled to garner coverage outside the black community press. For our first news conference, we assembled all the girls in bathing suits around the outdoor pool at the new Jack Tar Hotel. Only one photographer showed up, and he was lackadaisical about the assignment, admitting that it was unlikely that his paper, the *San Francisco Examiner,* would deem the pageant worth a photo.

"Look," he cracked, "the only way you're likely to get any attention is if you toss one of those girls into the pool."

We huddled with the girls; we evaluated our options and calculated whose hair could emerge from a dip in chlorinated water and still look good; and then, settling on a plucky willing contestant, we obligingly tossed her in the pool.

The photographer was right: the *Examiner* ran the picture alongside an advance story on the Miss Bronze Northern California Pageant.

Our sponsors likewise extracted a toll for their support. They created ads featuring our contestants, clad in swimsuits, posing while pumping gas at Art Dickens Chevron Service Station, alongside a car from the Merit Lincoln-Mercury dealership, and in front of cases of soda from the Pepsi Bottling Company. But the young women had no objection, given that many of them aspired to be models and therefore valued the exposure.

We promoted the pageant with motorcades and receptions, and even had the contestants introduced at a Giants game, where they were thrilled to meet legendary slugger Willie Mays. By 1966, California governor Pat Brown sent a congratulatory letter, which we of course incorporated into the program.

Miss Bronze Northern California received an array of thirty prizes, including expenses to the state pageant, a diamond wristwatch, a day at Disneyland, a case of Coca-Cola, a portable TV, one hundred gallons of Gulf Oil gasoline, and a "100 percent human hair wig" from the Purple Poodle Wig Shoppe.

The talent competition was judged separately, with "Miss Grand Talent" garnering an all-expense-paid trip to the state pageant and prizes—including a silver fox stole, two hair permanents, a charm school scholarship, a gift package of Frito-Lay products, and a photographic portrait shot by my husband.

As the 1966 program said, Miss Bronze contestants "entertain, innovate and they integrate. For as they project poise, personality, talent and ability, many doubts are dispelled; there is no barrier that can withstand their charming challenge."

I remain proud of our success stories. Some contestants would go on to careers in the entertainment industry and credit Miss Bronze for making it possible. Marilyn McCoo and Florence LaRue won the state pageant talent competition in 1962 and 1963 respectively, and a man named Lamonte McLemore was one of the pageant's photographers. The three went on to become three-fifths of The 5th Dimension, a 1960s pop musical sensation that recorded classics such as "Up, Up and Away" and "Aquarius/Let the Sunshine In." McCoo later recorded with her husband, Billy Davis Jr., and collected a lifetime total of eight Grammys.

I took a direct role in managing the early career of vocalist Carolyn Blakey, a Sacramento standout with her 1963 pageant rendition of "When Sonny Gets Blue." I helped book her initial gigs in Barksdale's club and other local venues. Because she was merely nineteen years old, I shielded her from predatory advances by requiring her to sit at the side of the bar under the watchful bartender's eye, or wait in the club manager's office between sets. A concert promoter in the pageant night audience offered her an international booking, and soon she had circled the globe—singing in Australia, Iran, Pakistan, Lebanon, Greece, and in Italy with doomed rocker

Jimi Hendrix. Eventually she was cast on Broadway in *Hair* and posed for a *Playboy* magazine spread on the "American Tribal Lock-Rock Musical," although she was adamant that she would only be photographed wearing her tie-dyed costume.

Another Miss Bronze Pageant winner, Beverly Johnson, would go on to become the first black woman to grace the cover of American *Vogue* magazine in 1974. And contestant Margaret Avery would later be nominated for a Best Supporting Actress Oscar for her role as the blues singer Shug Avery in the film *The Color Purple*.

Throughout their Miss Bronze experience, the contestants felt pampered and validated—and also exhilarated to jettison the racist stereotype that Negro girls could not be honored as beautiful. Our pageant came of age along with the "Black is Beautiful" movement, and our goal was to take us as black women out of the realm of "the other."

Sociology professor Maxine Leeds Craig would later produce a thoughtful analysis of the historic role of Negro beauty pageants in her book, *Ain't I a Beauty Queen? Black Women, Beauty and the Politics of Race.* As she astutely noted, those of us who organized the Miss Bronze Northern California competition "attempted to uncouple race from beauty, and color from class."

If anyone had feminist objections to Miss Bronze, nobody complained to me, even though each program not only featured pictures of the women in swimsuits, but also listed their precise bust, waist, and hip measurements. By the time my career demanded that I give up producing, after the 1966 pageant, no one else was willing to pick up the pieces, and Miss Bronze Northern California ceased to be.

Two years later, a small cadre of women converged on the Atlantic City boardwalk to protest the Miss America Pageant for denigrating and objectifying women. After symbolically crowning a sheep, the women tossed girdles and bras into a trash can—and although the can was never set afire, the event spawned the urban legend that early feminists were "bra burners." It's worth noting that they borrowed the tune of the civil rights anthem "We Shall Overcome," substituting the words "We Will Not Be Used."

Only a few doors down from the main pageant and protesters, the first Miss Black America Pageant was holding its inaugural competition under the direction of J. Morris Anderson of Philadelphia, who had spent time observing our pageant. The next year, the Jackson 5 would make their first television appearance—on the pageant. And in 1971, the competitors would include Miss Tennessee, Oprah Winfrey. The pageant, she would say, "put a flower in my mind."

I first approached Oakland television station KTVU with the idea of airing a promotional preview of the Miss Bronze Pageant, featuring highlights from the talent competition. It wasn't an easy sell, but I was persistent. At last, KTVU community affairs director Ian Zellick said, "Well, you know, I can give you the time, but I don't have any staff to produce this show. So if you can get a producer and a director, we'll give you the slot and you can do it."

"Why, of course," I said with a smile, "I'd be happy to handle that."

Then I sashayed out of the station and made a beeline for the Oakland Public Library, where my old school chum Rose Mary then was a librarian.

"Rose Mary, help," I pleaded, "I think I just agreed to direct and produce a Miss Bronze show for television . . . and I have no idea what a director or producer is supposed to do."

She calmly led me to the reference area and helped me locate instructional books on TV production, which I checked out and studied, trying to fathom the expectations of my newest unpaid job. I learned how to "backtime" a program, subtracting the required commercials and station announcements to figure out precisely how much air I had to fill. KTVU provided a studio camera crew, I served as the program's host, and our production went off without a hitch. *The Miss Bronze Showcase* drew one hundred thousand viewers.

And I had just gotten my first taste of television.

nine

· · ·

Dreams Deferred

I can truthfully say that my first television appearances drew nothing but positive reviews; but in the interest of full disclosure, I'll also say that the shows drew only one review. A *Richmond Independent* newspaper columnist, who watched me host a production of *The Miss Bronze Showcase* on KTVU, wrote that somebody should find someplace for me on television. In a burst of naive optimism, I bought up copies of that column and mailed it off to every TV station in the San Francisco Bay Area, daring to dream that someone would take the hint and hire me. I don't know what I was thinking—to my knowledge there was not a solitary black woman in TV news.

But in the early 1960s, the aspirations of African Americans were taking flight like never before. We were inspired by a Baptist minister from Georgia with a firm faith in nonviolence and a devotion to equality. He had held aloft his own dream that someday all God's children "will be able to join hands and sing in the words of the old Negro spiritual, 'Free at last, free at last, thank God Almighty, I'm free at last.'"

I still remember the night I was working late to finish KDIA's traffic logs when I looked up to see two men in dark suits walking slowly across the darkened office outside my door. One of them, whom I recognized by his gait, was Frank Clarke, handler of the station's lucrative national ad accounts. The man silhouetted next to him was shorter, broad chested, his face indiscernible under his fedora—and yet there was something oddly familiar about him.

"Good evening, Belva," said Clarke, who always managed to sound as though he were speaking into a microphone. Then they came into focus beneath a flickering fluorescent light and I caught my breath. "I trust you know Martin?"

I nodded, recognizing the preposterousness of the notion that Belvagene

Melton Davis was on a first-name basis with Dr. Martin Luther King Jr. I had heard office gossip that Clarke was a close chum of King, that the two had met in Boston, and that Frank had been a participant in King's wedding to Coretta Scott—but I had my doubts. Now the evidence was irrefutable.

"It's an honor to meet you," I said, stretching out my hand.

He took it, replying that he was pleased to meet me as well. We exchanged a few pleasantries that I was too nervous to commit to memory: something about his appearance at the Oakland Auditorium to raise money for the struggles down South. His appearances always drew a packed house, from a young lawyer named Willie Brown to an impatient activist named Bobby Seale. Local black leaders would pass the hats and exhort all of us to dig deep, and we did. Bill and I believed the cause was righteous. And donating helped assuage the subconscious guilt many of us felt for failing to join the front lines in Birmingham. But Dr. King never tried to make anyone feel guilty. He'd say you can help pay for the buses, you can help pay for the food, and you can pray for us.

Whatever Dr. King specifically said to me that night, what I would always recall was impressionistic: his sonorous, soothing voice and his extraordinary politeness.

"If you'll excuse us," Frank interjected, "we're on our way to my office to smoke a couple of good cigars and unwind."

"Of course," I said, waiting until the door to Frank's office clicked shut before I reached for the telephone.

"Bill," I whispered into the receiver, "you are never gonna believe who's here . . ."

In 1963, Dr. King traveled more than 275,000 miles coast-to-coast and, in defiance of crackpot death threats, delivered more than 350 speeches—many of them to raise funds for a planned convergence on the nation's capital. In his California appearances, he mingled erudite observations with soul-stirring simplicity: "I say good night to you by quoting the words of an old Negro slave. 'We ain't what we ought to be and we ain't what we want to be and we ain't what we're going to be. But thank God we ain't what we was.'"

At an Emancipation Centennial rally in the Oakland Auditorium, Dr.

King exhorted audiences to boycott businesses that were refusing to train or hire black workers. He often made such suggestions with a twist of wry, suggesting, for example, that people quit buying Wonder bread until "we make Wonder bread wonder where the money went."

On August 28, 1963, the March on Washington drew an estimated quarter of a million people. Millions more who heard Dr. King articulate his dream began investing in dreams of their own. I was one of those dreamers.

While the national focus was on Jim Crow practices in the Deep South, blacks suffered their insidious effects in California too. Remember, San Francisco Giants star Willie Mays was barred from purchasing a home on Miraloma Drive in the city's tony, lily-white Sherwood Forest neighborhood after neighbors objected that his family's presence would drive down property values. One of those neighbors told the *Chronicle*, "I certainly wouldn't like to have a colored family near me!"

The slugger's wife, Marghuerite, summed up the situation this way: "Down in Alabama where we come from, you know your place, and that's something, at least. But up here it's all a lot of camouflage. They grin in your face, and then deceive you."

Only after then mayor George Christopher, a Greek immigrant, invited the Mayses to be his houseguests did the seller relent. But the Mayses didn't last two years in the house; during that time they endured humiliations including a bottle that sailed through their front window with a racist note attached.

With wartime jobs gone and blacks staying put, the lit fuse of frustration was burning toward a tinderbox. *San Francisco Chronicle* reporter Art Hoppe described the incendiary landscape:

Racial discrimination, as practiced in San Francisco, is a subtle thing. True, unlike the South, there were no signs saying "COLORED ONLY." The signs said something far more ambiguous: "We Reserve the Right to Refuse Service to Anyone." The Negro newcomer who walked into a lunch counter in the Richmond, the Sunset or the Mission was never sure whether he would get a sandwich or a scene. . . . The shipyards closed down and there weren't enough cranes and welder's tools and shipfitter's jobs to go around. It was the old adage of the Negro being the last hired and first fired. Many drifted back to the South. For those who remained, with their skills no one wanted and their memories of high wages, the defeat was thorough."

By 1964, the local NAACP was plotting lawsuits to force recalcitrant Bay Area businesses to halt discriminatory hiring.

But then a new tactic, swifter and more effective, began to catch on: the demonstration. The first big one was against Mel's Drive-In, a burger joint that served blacks but refused to hire them. Targeting the San Francisco diner—which was co-owned by San Francisco supervisor and mayoral candidate Harold Dobbs—more than one hundred people occupied *all* the seats, and they refused to order until Mel's hired blacks. Pickets went up at the diner and at Dobbs's home. After losing the election, he signed an agreement to integrate hiring for up-front jobs.

At Lucky's grocery stores, protesters would fill their shopping carts to the brim, unload their contents at the counter, wait until cashiers had rung up every item by hand, and then declare, "I'll pay for these items when you start hiring Negros!" As checkout registers clogged, shopping ground to a standstill.

At San Francisco's swank Sheraton Palace Hotel, which employed 19 blacks in only menial cleaning jobs out of a staff of 550, about five hundred demonstrators clasped hands and encircled the hotel inside and out; then they staged a "sleep in" that transformed the lobby floor into a wall-to-wall carpet of protesters.

And because the car dealerships that lined "Auto Row" along Van Ness Avenue also hired blacks only as janitors, hundreds of white and black protesters staged demonstrations at both the Cadillac dealership and the Lincoln-Mercury dealership to force a hiring accord.

As challenging as the situation was for blacks, women faced multiple obstacles, especially in media. Although a few females had been working as reporters, columnists, and editors for newspapers, and a handful more as DJs or radio hosts, we mostly were consigned to covering life's curlicues: fashion, entertainment, society happenings. Whether white or black, females did fluff.

But I knew I wanted more. I felt as though someone had hit the fast-forward button and the world around me was advancing in a blur. I was captivated by the big stories, and I wanted to be a part of them.

One of my entrées was through KDIA news director Louis Freeman, who was stretched too thin doing every newscast and all the station's field reporting, not to mention its gospel music show. I volunteered to be his "pick-up person," gathering notes and quotes at Berkeley City Council meetings, community organizing sessions, and the like.

We were in the incubator of a new political consciousness. Tens of thousands of black families such as mine—having deserted Louisiana, Texas, Mississippi, and Tennessee and having resettled in California—were discovering the potency of politics. It was heady stuff. Back home, our parents had been unable to even register to vote. Here, not only could blacks cast ballots, but they even could elect a few of their own. California, which had dispatched its first black legislator, Frederick Roberts, to Sacramento in 1917, sent its first black congressman, Gus Hawkins, to Washington in 1963. He would go on to author Title VII of the 1964 Civil Rights Act to establish the Equal Employment Opportunity Commission.

I was acquainted with many of the East Bay's rising political wizards. Brilliant bon vivant Willie Brown, who would someday dominate state politics as speaker of the assembly and then serve as mayor of San Francisco, was dating a high school friend of mine while both were students at San Francisco State. Future congressman and mayor Ron Dellums was a member of Edith's "Kitchen Cabinet" and one of her "main horses." And of course William Byron Rumford, proprietor of my old local drugstore in Berkeley, became a state assemblyman and hometown hero in 1963 after he won enactment of the Fair Housing Bill outlawing discrimination in private housing. The real estate industry and angry white property owners persuaded state voters a year later to amend the state constitution to nullify the act, although ultimately the California and U.S. Supreme Courts would uphold Rumford's law.

The white backlash was indicative of the growing notion among California whites that we were pushing too far, too fast. As San Francisco human relations coordinator James Mitchell, a former Eisenhower labor secretary, told *Time* magazine, "What Negroes have to remember is something they tend to forget: that they are a minority, and that they can only achieve what they want with the support of the majority." White resistance was unmistakable as it whipped through the Cow Palace during the 1964 GOP convention—the experience that solidified my determination to become a real reporter.

I had little hope of achieving that dream at KDIA, which was moving away from individualized radio and fast embracing corporate-directed, rigidly formatted playlists. The impetus may have been the payola scandal, which revealed that record company reps were bribing DJs to guarantee more play for songs on the reps' labels. I was flabbergasted by the revelations—nobody had ever offered me a dime, perhaps because they figured that housewives listening to *The Belva Davis Show* composed an inconsequential sliver of the record-buying public.

But radio was becoming more robotic, and I didn't want to be a robot. So I decided to quit KDIA even though I had no other job lined up. Within days, we learned that Bill was about to lose his job at the Berkeley Camera Shop. The logical course of action might have been to reconsider my ill-timed resignation, but suffice it to say we defied logic. Instead, Bill and I doubled-down to buy our first house together before the bank would discover we were losing our sources of income.

We swiftly settled on a tidy eighteen-thousand-dollar ranch house in El Cerrito, a suburb north of Berkeley, where real estate was comparatively cheap. In fact, our mortgage payment of $143 a month was less than the rent on our more fashionable place in Berkeley. The El Cerrito house was nondescript, save for a large portrait of Jesus Christ painted directly on the dining room wall. The house had only two bedrooms, but we subdivided the attached garage, making half of it a bedroom for Steven and the other half a darkroom for Bill's new freelance photography.

For a while, the sacrifice of our garage appeared prescient: we fell behind on our Mustang's payments, prompting the bank to repossess it. But a former KDIA DJ—who had gone to work for the bank—intervened and helped us retrieve our car.

Although we didn't encounter discrimination when purchasing our house, El Cerrito's predominant whiteness would carom through our lives at random. My heart broke the day young Darolyn came home and crumpled into a chair with a forlorn sigh. "Dee Dee, what's wrong?" I asked. She explained the inexplicable as best she could: The Brownie troop leader at her elementary school had told her she would not be allowed to join the all-white troop. "I don't understand why I can't be a Brownie—I'm brown!" my daughter exclaimed. I complained to the school, but I was told the matter was out of their hands because, although the troop met on school property, Girl Scouts is a private organization.

Soon I lined up another radio job, this time as a clerk and occasional DJ for KJAZ—a station that, as its call letters suggested, played jazz to the exclusion of everything else. Profitability was elusive, and the owner often collected trade-out merchandise instead of cash from small advertisers who couldn't pay. Then, in turn, the owner tried to cajole us employees into accepting the trade-outs in lieu of salary. Example: a tire shop might advertise on the station and offer a free set of tires to the DJ. On our old Mustang, that free set of tires came in handy. Usually, though, I held out for the cash.

After a few months, I landed a job as the unlikely new voice of the station that in 1966 became KNEW. I say *unlikely*, because KNEW was a pop station of monochromatically white on-air personalities and the station reveled in playing the bland tunes: Petula Clark singing "Downtown"; Wayne Newton crooning "Red Roses for a Blue Lady"; and the Beach Boys and Annette Funicello extolling the "fun, fun, fun" of surfing. I doubt any black listeners tuned in. But with President Lyndon B. Johnson signing Executive Order 11246, which required federal contractors to use affirmative action to help alleviate racial inequities, and with the United Church of Christ and NAACP challenging the FCC licenses of stations that turned a blind eye to the black community, a growing number of broadcast stations felt compelled to make at least a token minority hire.

I would come in to KNEW a couple of days a week to voice its public service announcements and promotional spots. In addition, the station used me as DJ of its late weekend music shows, from nine at night to one in the morning Saturday and Sunday. I was instructed to strictly adhere to the station's approved playlist. Sometimes around midnight, my inner rebel got the better of me, and I would sneak in a cut by Miles Davis or Duke Ellington. On a couple of occasions, the edgier track hadn't finished before station manager Varner Paulsen was phoning me on the studio's inside line, demanding to know why my show was broadcasting unapproved music. I would fib and tell him I thought the track had been approved, and he would grumble and hang up.

But I was most mystified the night Paulsen called in for what he said was simply a private chat.

"So how are you feeling about how things are going at the station?" he ventured.

"Fine—I'm having a great time," I lied, desperate to retain a steady paycheck even if it meant that my brain replayed bad surfer tunes in my dreams.

"Well, good, that's good . . . ," he said. After an interminable pause, he followed with, "You know, Belva, I don't know quite how to say this . . . but I was just wondering about your sound."

More awkward silence.

"My sound?" I asked. "Is there a problem with the way I sound? Do you need me to lower my pitch?"

"No, no, nothing like that. It's just that we'd like our listeners to know who you are."

"I don't understand."

"I mean, who you *really* are."

"Mr. Paulsen, I am who I am, and this is what I sound like."

"Well, maybe if you could sound a little more, you know . . . "

"A little more what?"

Then it hit me. The station had gone to all the effort of hiring a black woman, and they wanted to be sure they got full credit for their gesture. The unspoken word, the word Varner Paulsen was too squeamish to utter, was *Negro*.

Radio was paying my mortgage, but my dreams still were invested in television. I zeroed in on KGO-TV in San Francisco as the station most likely to take a chance on me. It had a reputation for unconventional programming, with a lineup including local fitness guru Jack LaLanne and ex-striptease artist Gypsy Rose Lee, whom the station had made a talk show host. Of course I didn't know a soul with hiring authority at KGO; but I worked every possible peripheral connection. And when I discovered that the station had an opening for an anchor to launch a new early morning news show, I managed to snare an interview with the station's general manager, David Sacks. But he kept me waiting outside his office for two hours—perhaps hoping I would either give up or go away—at which point a receptionist told me he had to cancel. Undaunted, I rescheduled for another day. On my way out, I ran into a friend, fashion designer LaVetta Forbes, who designed gowns for Nancy Wilson and the Supremes and was at the station arranging a fashion exhibit for Gypsy Rose Lee's show. LaVetta in turn introduced me to actress Ingrid Bergman's daughter Pia Lindström, a guest on Gypsy's show because she had completed an American Express–sponsored cross-country trip using only her credit card. Pia asked what brought me to KGO, and I gave her all the details about the new anchor post I was hoping to win, surprised by her keen interest in what I had to say.

But my rescheduled interview with the station manager a few days later was a disaster. Sacks beckoned me into his office and listened to me discuss why I thought I could do a good job. Then he smiled sympathetically, as though someone in my family had just died. I can only imagine that, in his own inept way, he was trying to be pleasantly complimentary. "I'm sorry, but we're just not hiring any Negresses," he said with mild chagrin, rising to his feet to usher me out. "Besides, we've already filled the morning anchor job. But I want you to rest assured that if we ever *do* decide to hire a Negress, you'll definitely be on our list."

Speechless by his casual likening of me to a caged tiger, I felt sick to my stomach and barely made it to the parking lot before bursting into tears.

KGO debuted its early morning news show soon after. Its newly hired anchor was Pia Lindström.

ten

· · ·

New Station in Life

Debating whether television was "to be or not to be" a national pastime, a *New York Times* reporter in 1939 dismissed it as having an inherently fatal flaw:

> The problem with television is that people must sit and keep their eyes glued on a screen; the average American hasn't time for it. Therefore the showmen are convinced that for this reason, if for no other, television will never be a serious competitor of broadcasting. Radio can flow on like a brook while people listen and go about their household duties and routine. Television, on the other hand, is no brook; it is more of a Niagara.

Well, by the 1960s, the Niagara that was television gushed on with more thunderous force than ever. In the Bay Area, as elsewhere, radio was stricken with an identity crisis—and newspapers were closing and consolidating or going out of business. I perceived that radio and newspapers were not journalism's future. No, the future of journalism was in television: immediate, vivid, powerful.

What television was not, in those days, was in any way representative of the population. But TV stations began hiring women and minorities for three reasons: A few realized that broadening their viewer demographics was smart journalism and smart business. Others began hiring blacks because they realized that when stories such as a small riot in Hunters Point or a big riot in Watts would erupt, the station would be uncomfortable sending reporters with white faces into the melees. And a few did it because critics were filing federal complaints seeking to have the broadcast licenses of recalcitrant stations revoked. The NAACP and local black leaders such as San Francisco supervisor Terry Francois and newspaper editor Dr. Carlton

Goodlett were pressuring stations to break their color barriers and were threatening boycotts and license challenges. Stations feared being forced into compliance.

When KGO-TV hired a woman reporter, statuesque Swedish blonde Christine Lund, a station executive explained that he would gladly have hired a puppy if that were what it took to keep the station's license.

After my KGO rejection, I picked my ego up, dusted it off, and kept trying. In the fall of 1966, I noticed a newspaper column in which Nancy Reynolds, then a co-anchor at KPIX-TV, San Francisco's CBS station, was quoted saying that she was a big fan of Ronald and Nancy Reagan and would love to work for them if Reagan were to be elected governor. The day after Reagan won, I fired off a letter to KPIX program director George Moynihan saying that I understood Nancy Reynolds would be leaving and I'd like to apply for her job.

My phone rang.

"Mrs. Davis, this is George Moynihan. I received your letter, and I just have one question. What makes you think Nancy Reynolds is quitting?"

"Well, I read it in the newspaper."

"You did? Where?"

Moral of story: never announce someone else's resignation before she's had the opportunity to do so herself. Reynolds was furious that I had let the cat out of the bag. I apologized profusely—but I was proved right. She did accept a post as a press aide for then governor-elect Reagan. Moynihan called again and asked me to come in immediately to test for the opening.

I knew the station had recently hired its first black reporter, Ben Williams of the *San Francisco Examiner*, although I wasn't sure whether his successful presence on staff improved or worsened my chances. I arrived and was introduced to KPIX's savvy assignment editor, Fred Zehnder, who explained that I should rip some news wire off the Teletype and draft some copy to film a test stand-up. The photographer assigned to capture my endeavor was a heel-clicking Hungarian immigrant named Steve Paszty. After typing up several sentences of wire copy, I headed out with Steve at my side, toting his sound-camera equipment.

"Well, I hope you know what you're doing, because I sure don't," I confessed. "I don't even know what the heck a stand-up is."

He looked at me with an impish grin. "Don't worry, *babee*," he said. "I'll take good care of you, *babee*. Just leave everything to me."

In a Hungarian accent thick as goulash, Steve explained that a stand-up is when a reporter appears on camera and, using a portion of the story script, addresses viewers directly: "You write something, you memorize it, I take your picture—that's it. Just look into the camera, babee, and tell it to me. See? Easy."

I was nervous and my voice quavered as I stumbled through the first take. "That's good for starters," he encouraged. "Let's do it again." The second time I was a bit more relaxed; and by the fourth or fifth time, my confidence was peaking. Once Steve was satisfied that we had a usable take, he arranged for the film to be placed in the capable hands of the station's most charitable editor. But because it had to be processed, I couldn't see how my audition came out. I was officially done for the day. On the way out, I learned that the station was considering sixty-seven applicants for the job. Well, I told Bill when I got home, no sense getting my hopes up.

But KPIX called me a week or so later and asked me to return to the station for filming behind the anchor desk. In those days, a newscast script consisted of seven color-coded copies, one of which went into a teleprompter that was turned by hand. They also had a mock "guest" come on the set for me to banter with. I felt more comfortable now—this was akin to my work in radio. Again, I was thanked and sent home.

Around Christmastime, Moynihan called again. "We think we'd like to hire you," he said, "but there's a problem."

Oh, God, here it comes, I thought. Mentally, I braced myself for all the expected impediments: I was black; I was female; I had no college degree; I had no TV experience. But I wasn't prepared for this: "We think you're about ten pounds overweight. Can you lose ten pounds in a month?"

"Yes!" I said in a heartbeat. "Yes, absolutely."

Although I was a size 6, television is notorious for adding weight to your face—and apparently I appeared too puffy on screen. The solution to my problem: the grapefruit-and-steak diet. I had to consume a grapefruit at breakfast, a grapefruit at lunch, and another grapefruit at dinner, plus drink grapefruit juice before every meal. Only then was I allowed to eat lean steak and steamed vegetables seasoned with salt and pepper. If I craved a between-meals snack, it had to be—you guessed it—another grapefruit. But

I made sure the diet worked. I would have eaten nothing but grapefruit if I thought it would land me a TV reporting job.

In those early weeks of 1967, I felt as though I were walking on Jell-O. Actually, I was so fretful that the rug might be pulled out from under me that I didn't quit my radio job until the day I went on the air at KPIX.

And I had even forgotten to ask Moynihan what my salary would be.

It was two hundred dollars a week. That was more money than Bill and I had ever seen—the year I left KDIA, the two of us combined had earned less than eighty dollars a week. Overjoyed, we celebrated my TV offer with a fancy dinner, which by our standards then meant anyplace that wasn't a pancake house.

My previous newsgathering experience was exclusively in the black press, where reporters tended to take more of an advocacy role. KPIX station manager Lou Simon, a fatherly gent who knew his days at the station were numbered, sat me down to offer some guidance: "You have to remember that you're not just reporting for black people anymore. You have to be a reporter for everybody. That means you've got to keep your reporting balanced if you want to succeed here."

I knew he was right, and I was grateful for previous mentors who had stressed the importance of striving for objectivity, accuracy, and fairness. As a reporter, I wanted those to be my goals.

The station held a press conference and luncheon to announce that it had hired the first black woman TV reporter west of the Mississippi. Every stylist at my regular beauty shop offered an opinion about which new hairstyle trend would best flatter me on the air. LaVetta provided me with a beautiful outfit—a long-sleeved, white silk, shift dress with a black half-belt slung just below the waist. Little did we know that the dress color was all wrong: The creamy white of the fabric posed such a contrast juxtaposed against my dark skin that the cameraman had to dial the exposure down, rendering my face so black its features were indistinguishable except for the whites of my eyes.

Also, on the morning of my debut news conference, I scooped up my only pair of black pumps and discovered a hole in the sole of one shoe. With no time or money, the ever-resourceful Bill cut out some cardboard, stuck it into the shoe, and painted over the patched sole with black shoe polish.

The press described me as "the bright-eyed young Negro woman who wouldn't take 'no' for an answer to her TV aspirations." *San Francisco Examiner* reporter Mildred Hamilton wrote that I had a "practical, determined and hard-to-resist enthusiasm that melts most obstacles." Effective February 5, I was hired as an "eyewitness reporter."

That night Nancy Wilson invited us to stop by her room at the Fairmont to celebrate, and she ordered an expensive bottle of champagne. I had to giggle realizing that had I encountered Nancy's generosity earlier, perhaps I could have skipped the champagne and used that money to buy a new pair of shoes.

In TV news, your photographer is either your savior or your nemesis. A good camera operator helps you look smart; gets great visuals so your story will snap, crackle, and pop; and generally has your back. At KPIX, Steve Paszty was one of the saviors. But a number of the cameramen made it quite clear that they didn't want to work with a Negro reporter, they didn't want to work with a female reporter, and they positively did not want to be teamed with someone who was both.

One photographer was too embarrassed to even be seen on the street with me. When we left the newsroom together on an assignment, he invariably came up with some reason to return for something he had "forgotten." "You go on ahead to the car—I'll meet you there," he would say. When we arrived on scene, he would pull the same stunt, sending me on my own while he would find some reason to linger at least twenty paces behind. Some of the photographers joked about how I would react upon seeing my first stiff. In truth, the memory of seeing my first dead body on a story is indelibly etched in my memory—a young woman was sitting on a bench in Alamo Park, her eyes open, her body already starched by the onset of rigor mortis. I was shaken to my core, but I never let on to anyone in the newsroom.

My baptism by fire came the day we picked up chatter on the police scanner that the cops were in hot pursuit of a car of armed robbers. I was thrust into the assignment alongside cameraman Lou Calderon, a good-old-boy newshound who could sniff out a story like nobody's business and pursue it relentlessly. He was tight as a tick with the cops. In fact, upon his death decades later, Alameda County's Sheriff Charles Plummer would acknowledge, "We all felt like he was one of us. . . . He was like a combat photographer. He had ice water in his veins. He had no fear."

On February 7, 1967, I saw firsthand exactly what he meant. Lou and I scrambled into one of the station's raggedy Peugeots, roaring out of the parking garage toward the chase. We made it to Oak Street and saw the careening getaway car, followed by a police cruiser with sirens wailing and lights flashing. One of the suspects stuck a pistol out the passenger window and opened fire on the cops in pursuit. Lou accelerated, weaving around San Francisco traffic to catch up to the action. He simultaneously continued yakking on the two-way radio, telling the assignment desk what a hot story we'd gotten. Then, to my stupefaction, he floored it and swerved around and in front of the cop car, sandwiching us between the shooter and his targets.

"Here, take the wheel!" he shouted, digging for his Bell and Howell camera. He let go of the steering column and climbed out the car window, aiming first in the direction of the live ammunition whizzing past us from the getaway-car shooter, and then backward at the livid cops now on our tail. I ducked my head as low as I could while keeping my eyes on the road. My knuckles gripping the steering wheel, I tried to maneuver around the honking traffic. Fortunately, the shooter was a bad shot.

I said a prayer aloud when the police pulled in front of us and Lou put the camera on his lap and retook the wheel. The chase got away from us, but Lou had his film.

Throughout the entire ride back to KPIX, neither of us uttered a word. My role would be invisible—the story would be handled in a voice-over by the six o'clock anchor. Back at the station, Lou could be heard hee-hawing about how he had "scared the holy hell out of her today."

I later learned that he had placed a wager with fellow cameramen: The little black lady reporter would be gone in two weeks.

Lou Calderon lost that bet. I stayed at KPIX, and I thrived. A few photographers took a long time adjusting to my presence in the newsroom, and they had a tendency to shoot me from a deliberately distorting low angle so that my breasts and the flare of my nostrils dominated the picture. I knew that the last thing a woman breaking into the business needed was to be labeled a whiner, so I never complained. Eventually the editors and producers put a stop to the practice. Meanwhile, Fred proved to be an extraordinary assignment editor, giving me a fair mix of hard news and soft feature stories, as well as the time I needed to learn the ropes. The station had only four reporters—Pat O'Brien, Rollin Post, Ben, and me—to cover the entire Bay Area during one of the most tumultuous, glorious news periods in our history. We had plenty of great stories to go around.

Still, KPIX had no black news photographers—in fact, not a single one worked at any commercial station in Northern California. I could personally vouch for a guy who I knew had the potential to be a great one: Bill. He had been doing only freelance work while serving as the primary caregiver for Steven and Darolyn, because we had agreed that I would need his support at home to master the demands of my new career. But I knew he had big dreams as well. The roadblock was the union, which required that applicants for membership be vouched for by three other union members. Soon I was badgering every camera guy I worked with: "When are you going to sign for my husband?"

At last two of them did, along with cameraman Will Sobey, an old school friend of Bill's who was working at KTVU-TV in Oakland. Bill got his union membership, and Will helped him land his first job as a news photographer for KTVU. Now we both were pioneers.

But we knew it wasn't going to be easy. You can't tear down walls without suffering a few scrapes and bruises in the process.

More than once when I attended San Francisco's renowned Commonwealth Club gatherings to cover a noteworthy speaker, staffers tried to shoo me away. They'd say, "I'm sorry, you have to leave now. This table is reserved for reporters." A San Francisco judge, unaware of his Jewish club's rules prohibiting women, invited me to the Concordia Club for lunch. Club officials balked at seating me in the dining room, and they engaged in a loud debate before arriving at a Solomonic solution: I was seated at the head of a long table that stretched from the dining room into the hallway, enabling me to be seated at the same table albeit not in the same room as my host and his other guests.

But the occasion I remember most clearly was when KPIX sent me to cover a fashion show extravaganza in the Grand Ballroom of the Fairmont. Weaving through the frenzy of models and technicians setting up for the event, Steve Paszty and I approached the show's coordinator, a grand dame well known in the society pages. She looked right past him and focused urgently on me. "Where have you been? You're late, and there is so much pressing to do," she snapped in exasperation.

It didn't strike me that a fashion show was that pressing a story, and besides, we had arrived well in advance—so I was momentarily speechless.

"You are the woman here to do the ironing, aren't you?"

I found my voice then. "I don't think you need a film cameraman and lights to do that, do you?"

I turned on my heels and walked out, with Steve right behind lugging his gear. I phoned back to the station, explained what had just happened, and told Fred that if he still wanted this story, he'd have to find somebody else to report it. He said come on back.

But that was the only time I ever recall kicking an assignment at KPIX. I worked hard and was as agreeable as humanly possible. So I was elated when, after a few months on the job, I was summoned to Moynihan's office and he announced he was going to almost double my salary.

Only later did I learn that the station had long been paying my colleagues more than twice as much as it had paid me.

eleven

...

His-and-Hers Gas Masks

✳ I went to war in 1967, 1968, and 1969. I didn't go overseas, and I didn't engage in combat. Instead I went to Oakland and Berkeley, reporting on the bitter, often brutal clashes between authorities who held power and the counter-culture that challenged them—whether over the Vietnam War, the draft, ethnic studies, or a 270-by-450-foot plot of University of California land dubbed "People's Park."

Often my days would begin at 4:00 a.m., my alarm clock blaring like a trumpet hailing Judgment Day. I would dress quickly, slipping into comfortable shoes, because I was certain to be on my feet all day, come rain or shine. Bill—working first as a freelance photographer for news outlets including the Associated Press and then as a cameraman for KTVU—would drive. Together we would make our way from the flatlands of El Cerrito to the scheduled scene of the day's showdown. Anything could happen, and often did. Whatever fear we felt was alloyed with thrill: The Bay Area seemed like ground zero in a generational battle for the soul of the country.

My first day on the battlefield—October 16, 1967—I didn't know what to expect. My job was to cover several hundred protesters who planned to picket and block the doors to the Northern California Draft Induction Center in Oakland, which was processing about three hundred draftees a day. It was the kickoff of a weeklong "Stop the Draft" action. Folksinger Joan Baez smiled serenely as she sang a few protest songs and then joined the group of young bodies stretched out across the concrete to block all three entrances. When the first buses of draftees arrived at nine in the morning, the inductees had to climb over and across the jigsaw puzzle of prone protesters. As soon as police managed to clear the doorways by arresting those protesters, another group simply would take their place.

101

Although police arrested 125 people—including Baez and her mother and sister, all of whom were sentenced to ten days at the Santa Rita prison farm—it was peaceful.

But the next day had a far different vibe.

The October 17 crowd of some three thousand was rowdier and angrier—the air had the feel of an electric storm. Many of the students had been up all night after a banned teach-in turned into a vociferous antiwar rally, held on the UC Berkeley campus in defiance of a court order. Anticipating more trouble, KPIX again assigned two reporters, half of its eyewitness news team, to the scene that day. Ben Williams was the reporter on the ground; I was stationed atop a municipal garage that police had transformed into a riot control center. Several times after dawn, a sharp-voiced officer on loudspeaker warned that the demonstrators constituted an illegal assembly and must disperse or face arrest. They retorted with catcalls.

At nine o'clock in the morning, the cops answered back in full force. About two hundred helmeted officers from the Oakland Police Department and the California Highway Patrol marched in unison from the garage into the throng—the officers swinging clubs and spraying Mace in the faces of anyone who failed to clear out. In the confused frenzy, reporters and cameramen on the ground felt the brunt of the cops' wrath. I knew Bill was shooting freelance stills somewhere in the crowd below and, although he carried a press card, only a few photographers knew him as a professional.

As the arrest rate climbed, both sides amped up the aggression. The more the cops swung their clubs, the more agitated the crowds became—using taunts and verve as their weapons. I studied the scene below me, wondering what possessed the draft objectors to be so zealous that they voluntarily threw themselves in harm's way. Even from above, I could spot the body language of those eager to get into the fray. The protesters had the nervous energy of sprinters poised before a race. Most came out of heartfelt opposition to the war; a few were out to wreak havoc. The cops were tightly coiled, a few hitting their batons against the palm of their hands as though warming up for a bravado performance. I marveled at the human determination required to stand up to authority, the courage to face down a man in full armor with a weapon in his hand. I had seen similar scenes from the

South in the fight to overthrow segregation, but those were on television. Now the violence was occurring right before me. Whenever I saw a baton coming down on someone's head, my eyes would close no matter how hard I willed myself to keep looking.

I had pushed for this assignment, and I felt that complaining would only make me sound like a "girl" to the rest of the newsroom—I was the station's sole female reporter. But I confess that I breathed a sigh of relief that Thursday morning when Fred Zehnder, without comment, diverted me to cover a routine rally elsewhere. By Friday, more than seven thousand demonstrators—some slashing tires, dragging debris, and pulling trash cans and benches into the streets—temporarily obstructed eight Oakland intersections that led to the induction center.

Nor was the issue about to go away. In a UC Berkeley referendum on Vietnam policy held in November 1967, only 13 percent of the students supported escalation of the war or the status quo—the overwhelming majority wanted negotiations and an end to the bombing, or total withdrawal. In fact, antiwar sentiment ran stronger at Berkeley than at any other major university in the country.

The number of troops deployed had sharply escalated that year—485,600 U.S. soldiers were then in Vietnam—which prompted a new wave of antiwar protest and more arrests. Joan Baez and fifty others were arrested again for blocking access to the induction center, and this time the legal consequences were more severe. She was sent back to Santa Rita on a three-month sentence. Not long after, I received a tip that Martin Luther King was planning an unannounced visit to the jailed Baez, who had worked alongside him in the South. In April he had denounced the war, losing him the support of some in the civil rights movement as well as access to President Johnson. So on January 14, 1968, a misty Sunday morning, KPIX photographer Dick Reizner and I drove south of Oakland to the prison farm. We eyed two black cars parked on the side of the road just outside Santa Rita. The guards at the gate told us they would not permit us to enter and that they knew nothing about a King visit.

"What do you think we should do?" the photographer asked.

"Wait," I said.

Undaunted, we parked behind the other two idled cars. I could see black faces in at least one of the vehicles. I called on the two-way radio to let the station know that King was there but had been denied access to the prison. No one had been allowed beyond the main gate, where the guards said permission to pass could only come from Sheriff Frank Madigan himself. I asked the assignment desk to try and reach him.

Then, in the cold drizzle, I walked back to the nearest car, which I recognized as belonging to Fouche's, a black funeral home that usually loaned King its finest sedan when he was in town. King's aide Andrew Young was in the front passenger seat and recognized me, so I asked what was going on. Some sort of mix-up, he explained: the group had obtained permission for the visit, but their clearance hadn't been relayed to the guards on site. I looked in the back seat and saw Reverend King sitting quietly, impeccably dressed in a dark suit, white shirt, and tie—after all, it was Sunday. But he stared blankly ahead as though lost in thought. I said hello, wondering whether he would remember our occasional encounters at the Oakland radio station, but he didn't acknowledge my greeting.

Other reporters began trickling to the scene; by midday a full contingent of reporters and Baez supporters had arrived. The King people kept checking with the guards' gate, and I kept checking with them. The KPIX assignment desk was worrying as hours ticked by. I assured them we would have a story, sometime. And I hoped I was right.

Impatient reporters gathered around the window of King's car trying to coax out a comment, but he insisted he would have nothing to say until he had seen Baez. Finally, the guards received the OK for King's party to enter, sans press.

While we continued waiting, the drizzle turned into light rain, and I felt my hair begin to revert to its natural curl and rise. I had neglected to bring an umbrella or even a large scarf, and yet I knew that eventually I would have to face the camera. We began shooting backup stand-ups, and suddenly my photographer squinted his disapproval and ventured, "Um, Belva, what's wrong with your hair?"

"What do you mean?" I asked.

He looked embarrassed and dropped the subject.

I retrieved a small handkerchief and tried to stretch it over my bushy natural. Here I was—a serious reporter standing at the precipice of this historic moment—and my hair was expanding like a giant puff ball.

At last, King emerged and conferred with his entourage. We were feeling somewhat frantic, because we were losing the daylight that we needed to get good pictures. Finally he addressed the press, noting that Baez and her mother were in good spirits because "when you go to jail for a righteous cause, you can accept the inconvenience of jail with an inner sense of calm and an inner peace."

Knowing how some critics were complaining that he was straying from his civil rights mission by denouncing the Vietnam War, King stressed that he could not, and would not, segregate his moral concerns.

"Amen, amen," said supporters gathered around the press. "Peace, brother," said one. "Tell it like it is," urged another.

"There can be no justice without peace," King said, "and there can be no peace without justice."

Then, borrowing the language of those more radical, he called for a "revolution of values . . . even if that means breaking unjust laws" and quoted the spiritual "Down by the Riverside," with its lyric "I ain't a gonna study war no more." The crowd erupted in song, finally leaving King with us reporters.

I jumped right in with a question that I had carefully crafted in my head to tease some new insight out of the oft-quoted reverend: "Can you explain what you're quoted as saying, that you're for escalated nonviolence?" I asked. "What did you mean by that?"

"Well," he replied, "I made it very clear that the anger of our ghettos is very extensive and the bitterness is very deep, and in order to give that understandable anger a kind of creative and constructive expression, we've got to escalate nonviolence to the point that we make it much more militant, much more demanding, much more insistent, even if it takes on the dimensions of civil disobedience." Nonviolence, he added, "must now be strong enough to be an alternative" both to those who wanted to block change altogether and those so desperate for change that they could be lured into violent revolt.

Not only did that sound bite lead our evening news, but it was picked up by the national media as well. Within four months, King would be struck by an assassin's bullet in Memphis. But his words, including those he spoke that day outside Santa Rita, would resonate for years to come, and the quote

I elicited would be included in later documentaries to help explain his political evolution.

I started to realize that I could really do this job.

Of course at times doing the job was extremely difficult. Berkeley was in an
almost perpetual state of restless agitation.

I can still feel the sting of a particular day in February 1969 when I was
covering demonstrations on one side of UC Berkeley's Sather Gate staged by
the Third World Liberation Front, whose nonnegotiable demands included
the establishment of an ethnic studies department. On the other side of the
gate, faculty members represented by the American Federation of Teachers
were picketing the arrest of protesting teaching assistants. Law enforcement units from the campus, together with Berkeley police, the California
Highway Patrol, and the Alameda County Sheriff's Department, formed
a line that stretched from one side of Sather Gate to the other, creating an
impenetrable barricade.

Following my photographer and other reporters, I attempted to pass
through the line, which the press card I held high entitled me to do. At that
moment, the deputies—whom the students nicknamed "the Blue Meanies"
after the fun-sucking characters in the Beatles' film *Yellow Submarine*—
apparently decided it was time to give me my comeuppance. One reached
out, grabbed my shoulders, and began spinning me like a top down his
entire row of buddies. Each took their turn twirling me. The buildings, the
laughing students, the smirking cops—everything and everyone whizzed
into and out of my line of sight in a blur. My stomach lurched. By the time the
last officer released my shoulders, it took all I could muster to stand still, eyes
squeezed shut, waiting for the world to stop hurling around my humiliation.

I said none of what I wanted to say to them: they were armed with guns,
Mace, and clubs, and had shown little hesitancy to use them when chal-
lenged. But when KPIX filed a formal complaint, Alameda County sheriff
Frank Madigan wrote me a letter of apology.

I fared far better that day than did Clifford Vaughs, a black former
photographer for the Student Nonviolent Coordinating Committee, who
documented civil rights struggles in the South before being hired on as a
reporter for KRLA radio in Los Angeles. He, too, was at Berkeley covering
the riot that day and incurred the wrath of the cops. When I came out of

my daze, I could see that he was being badly beaten. I wanted to yell, "Stop, stop!" But then I saw my cameraman and remembered that I was a reporter not a bystander, and I hoped he had shot pictures. The student newspaper, the *Daily Californian*, carried a front-page story with a picture of Vaughs surrounded by deputies, batons drawn, as he cowered—head down, microphone raised high—in the grips of other deputies. The photo was captioned, *KRLA reporter Clifford Vaughs being held and beaten by officers of the Alameda County Sheriffs Department*. Moments later he was dragged down a flight of concrete stairs, feet held in the air, to the campus police office in the basement of Sproul Hall. Even in moments of tension and confusion some things resonate and are hard to forget: The thump of his head bouncing off those concrete steps still echoes in my ears.

Vaughs was charged with assaulting a police officer, resisting arrest, and obstructing a public pathway. His injuries were serious and required hospitalization, which led him to eventually file a federal suit against various law enforcement agencies.

The cops didn't much care for the press—particularly reporters who were black or female, or in my case, both. The officers regarded us as closet left-wingers who no doubt sympathized with the radical protesters. Conversely, many student protesters didn't like us either, denouncing us as capitalist tools of the establishment. Offenders on both sides were irritated by the presence of cameras capturing and recording acts for which they would have preferred not to be accountable.

My reputation with both sides was good, but that credibility didn't count for much on the battlefield. The very day I was harassed by the police, my photographer Tony Frazita and I also wound up dodging stones and bricks flung by students; perhaps they were aiming at police, but they didn't seem to care that we were caught in the cross fire. On the other side, cops were tossing tear gas canisters. We made a mad dash for shrubs along Strawberry Creek, which runs through campus, with Tony balancing his heavy camera and me lugging his heavy tripod—and we managed to avoid getting hit by either side. Tony, a born-again Christian, known to often pray fervently for a parking space, found himself praying much harder for our safety.

All the animosity coursing through Berkeley reached its zenith in May 1969, over a small plot of land that students and social dropouts referred to as the "beautiful little slice of reclaimed nature" and "Power to the People Park" but that then mayor Wallace Johnson labeled "a diabolically clever idea by that motley bunch of Bohemians and hippies." To then governor Ronald Reagan, it was nothing more than "an excuse for riots."

At issue was a patch of university-owned land a few blocks south of campus that the University of California intended to develop; to conservatives clinging to their historic control of Berkeley, the move was long overdue. Berkeley's state assemblyman, Don Mulford—a Republican who already had suggested the death penalty for marijuana dealers—had been urging the university to demolish area buildings on its property to "get rid of the rat's nest that is acting as a magnet for the hippie set and the criminal element." But some of the free-spirited locals planted sod and trees; others installed sandboxes, slides, and swings; and many simply camped out in the park, often under a light haze of marijuana smoke. So before dawn on May 15, a couple hundred cops rousted about six dozen street people huddled around a bonfire; and within a few hours, crews had erected a steel mesh, eight-foot-high fence.

No more than an hour later, thousands of students came together in a noontime rally on the campus's Sproul Plaza. When news of what had happened at the park spread through the gathering, students' outrage swelled. Law student and student body president-elect Dan Siegel spoke, and after he said the words "take the park," the students never heard the rest of his sentence. Instead, the cry "Take the Park" echoed back from the crowd, which immediately surged toward narrow Telegraph Avenue toward the park beyond.

They ran smack into cops who, unbeknownst to them, had been authorized not only to unleash canisters of tear gas but also to open fire—using bird shot and even buckshot—on protesters. Reagan, the Hollywood actor who won the governorship on a vow to crack down on unruly demonstrators, had taken control out of the hands of university authorities and placed his top aide, conservative former Alameda County district attorney Ed Meese, in charge. The directive: get the situation under control by any means necessary.

Keeping pace with the throng from campus, I saw demonstrators running up the street. Someone opened a fire hydrant, which sent water spewing in all directions. I heard storefront windows shattering. Tear gas permeated the air, seeming to singe my lungs and eyes. Today, of all days, I had forgotten to bring along my station-issued gas mask, but I was instantly grateful for the bit of protection afforded me by heavy studio makeup and contact lenses.

The *Berkeley Daily Gazette* would later accurately describe two Telegraph intersections as "open-door gas chambers."

Our station car was parked on Bancroft Avenue, which parallels the south side of campus and serves as a de facto border between the university and funky Telegraph Avenue. The street now was jammed with students, bohemians, street people—people angry about the park, the war, the draft, racism, and the news media. We swiftly loaded our equipment and tried to extract the car from the turmoil. But protesters swarmed our car, beating on the windows and refusing to let us budge. We had heard rumors that a news car had been set afire.

I looked at my cameraman, soaked with sweat and fear. Gerd Rausch would have preferred to never have to partner with me, but particularly not on this assignment. In my cameraman's eyes I was too small, too short, and a girl, to boot—useless, he figured, if things were to get out of control.

Well things were pretty out of control, and Gerd didn't seem to be of much use, himself. Without thinking, I told him to stay behind the wheel and keep edging the car slowly forward. Then I climbed out, put my hands on my hips, and invoked my strongest "black mother" voice to address the angry students towering over me. "Do you know what you're doing?" I demanded. "If you don't let us report what's happening here today, no one will know what really went on."

"The press lies!" "You all work for the establishment!" "You only report what your right-wing bosses tell you to report!"

"Tell me one story where I didn't tell the truth," I shot back. "Give me one example when I didn't report something accurately. Just one instance when I wasn't fair."

Nobody offered one, so I kept talking. "Look, a lot of you know me, you see me here all the time. I'm saying what I've always said—it's not my job to protest the war or the park or anything else. My job is to report your protest. And I'm trying to do my job."

With the students' attention focused on me, Gerd managed to guide the car through the sea of bodies. Soon I lost sight of him. Then a horrific roar rose from Telegraph Avenue.

"The cops are coming," some demonstrators screamed, crushing toward us. "They've got rifles, and they're shooting at people!"

At first I didn't believe it. The gyrations of the mob ratcheted me to the corner. I strained to look up, making out smoke-smeared images of the livid protesters and curious observers who were ringing the rooftops along Telegraph. This time they held the high ground, and some of them were taking aim at the cops with chunks of concrete and debris.

Looking down Telegraph Avenue, all I could see were the uniforms, the men in full riot gear. And sure enough, they had rifles.

I wriggled through the crowd and ran when I could, struggling to get away from Telegraph. When the crowd thinned, I spotted our station car on a small dirt lot a block away from the riot, and Gerd alongside it, his camera out. I snatched up some of his gear, and we headed back into the chaos of Telegraph. I don't think we spoke a word to each other.

Panicked demonstrators were shouting rumors, claims that the police were shooting randomly and that many people had been hit. As we pushed our way toward Telegraph, we spied uniformed officers clad in helmets and gas masks, bearing an eerie resemblance to aliens in a nightmarish science fiction flick. When they faced our direction and knelt, rifles in hand, we ducked into a recessed doorway immediately below street level. Not knowing what was to come, we waited and listened.

The sirens. The shouting. The cursing. The fog of tear gas. The ping of shotgun pellets ricocheting off cars, telephone poles, and buildings. From our vantage point, pinned down, we couldn't possibly determine whether anyone had been hit.

Gerd struggled to capture the scenes, and because I knew that he could only see what was in his viewfinder, I was his eyes for everything else. I leaned out far enough to make sure no one posed any imminent threat. From the others huddled near us, I got what information I could: "Were you on Telegraph when this started?" "Do you know anyone who was shot?" "Are you a student?"—a key question in the political debate about the uprisings.

The events left little time for note-taking. I jotted down names when possible. By this time, KPIX had dispatched other crews to the scene, and every local news outlet had reporters on the ground. I knew this was too big to be only my story, and I couldn't possibly be comprehensive: My job was to provide a detailed piece of the puzzle that my producer would have to assemble later in the day.

I didn't have time to think much about balance—concerns about fairness recede in your mind when one side is shooting at you and the other side is tossing rocks and concrete. What I did keep wondering was why the kids were still out there, in the open, on the street. Some moved past us—some running and some staggering, bleeding, coughing from the gas—but they refused to completely retreat. *Don't they see the danger they are in? If I had a choice,* I thought, *I'd get out of here.*

Of course I did have a choice. I could have called it quits, declared that this kind of journalism was too risky for a mother of two small children. But I knew that in this time and this place, I was doing what it took to be a real reporter. I realized that I had once again crossed over—no turning back.

When Gerd and I observed that the people passing were walking rather than running, we ventured back into the street. Time was running out, so we grabbed more shots and did more reporting on our way to the car; then we dashed for the station to begin editing our raw footage and scripting the story.

At least 110 people suffered significant wounds that day—perhaps more, because some refused to go to a hospital for fear of being arrested. Of the wounded, thirty-five had been pierced by buckshot tough enough to penetrate a steel car door. Buckshot blinded Alan Blanchard, who worked at the Telegraph Repertory Theater, as he stood on the theater's rooftop. Buckshot also struck near the heart of another man on the same rooftop, unemployed San Jose carpenter James Rector. In four days, he would be dead. By most accounts, both men were innocent bystanders.

That night, then governor Reagan ordered in more than two thousand National Guard troops, who bivouacked on the grounds of People's Park. Beyond any doubt, Berkeley was an occupied war zone.

Two months before the People's Park confrontation, Black Panther Party cofounder Bobby Seale had addressed a campus rally and accused the University of helping develop deadly chemical and biological weapons that could be dispersed in tiny droplets. At the time, his fiery speech struck me as farfetched. But it was about to replay in my mind.

On May 20, more than three thousand people held a vigil on the steps of

Sproul Hall to protest the killing of riot bystander James Rector. Suddenly, in the middle of the afternoon, the National Guard formed lines to seal Sproul Plaza at Sather Gate and Bancroft Avenue. The Student Union was emptied and locked down. Then the authorities announced that chemicals were about to be sprayed, and everyone heard the sound of an approaching military helicopter.

People stopped in their tracks. Students, lunchers, employees, and reporters alike were trapped, confused, and captive.

With no further warning, the helicopter swooped down and discharged a white cloud of mystery gas. The recollection of Seale's warning surged through me like an electric shock. What was in the cloud blowing across us? We couldn't possibly escape without inhaling at least some of the gas. We all coughed and wheezed, and some people gagged and vomited. I would later learn that the drifting gas cloud burned the skin of children splashing in Strawberry Canyon Pool, half a mile away. The cloud contained a particularly potent, nauseating form of tear gas. I could hardly believe that the authorities were reacting so recklessly.

But that was the reality of covering Berkeley in the 1960s. Because Bill and I lived close to the campus, we spent many days covering the clashes there. I never again forgot my station-issued gas mask, although Bill's frugal employer, KTVU, required him to share its single mask with another photographer and reporter. Our son Steven was only vaguely aware of the political upheaval underway throughout the East Bay, but he was acutely alarmed that his parents were the only couple in El Cerrito with his-and-hers gas masks.

The tension took its toll on both of us. Bill often worked solo, carrying only a small Bell and Howell sixteen-millimeter silent camera. It enabled him to get in close for great action shots, but he was conscious of being a black man plunging into an unruly mob that didn't immediately know what he was doing there.

While most of my time was spent covering the Berkeley campus, I also covered demonstrations at San Francisco State, where minority students were demanding an autonomous ethnic studies college. The Third World Liberation Front represented an amalgamation of various Asian and Latino student groups, and they joined with the Black Students Union in protests that shut down the university on a number of occasions.

Their struggle would result in two notable national precedents: the merger of minority groups created the first "rainbow coalition," and the struggle also set a record for the longest student strike in the nation's history.

The issue at the crux of the campus confrontations was how much race, color, and culture should matter in shaping students' educational experiences. The confrontational approach that San Francisco State president S. I. Hayakawa took against student leaders, among them future actor Danny Glover, resulted in almost daily rallies. And once again, knowing that possibly some would view my reporting through the veil of my skin color, I was determined that it not appear to be the driving force in my reporting.

I really felt put to the test the day I covered a rally where the Bay Area's most prominent black leaders would be speaking—among them, my old boss Dr. Carlton Goodlett, Assemblyman Willie Brown, Berkeley City Councilman Ron Dellums, and Glide Memorial Church's Reverend Cecil Williams. All these men knew me well. I posed my questions straight and to the point, knowing it was important that my queries not seem biased. While on the job, I was not their friend—I was a journalist. I didn't want them to walk away thinking "There's my old friend Belva," but "There goes a good reporter."

In the end, the university agreed, while retaining control over hiring, to establish the nation's first school of ethnic studies. More than forty years later, College of Ethnic Studies dean Kenneth Monteiro would say, "The determination of the students caused a permanent shift in both the range of voices within the academy and also the range of communities that the university was willing to directly serve."

But it came at huge cost: the student strike lasted five months, it led to the arrest of more than seven hundred people, and it was marked by violent skirmishes between students and police that resulted in countless injuries.

Back at the station, Fred Zehnder pulled me aside to let me know he was shifting me to a new assignment. It appealed to me because I had grown up in the neighborhood with Bobby Seale and Huey Newton. After covering so many violent campus revolts, I figured reporting on the Black Panthers would feel like a vacation.

Graduation, Hoover Junior High School, Oakland, California, June 1947. I am seated first on the left, first row. My best friend, Rose Mary Towns, is at the other end of the row. PHOTO COURTESY OF THE AUTHOR

Aunt Ophelia, my first mom, in her living room, Monroe, Lousiana, 1934.
PHOTO COURTESY OF THE AUTHOR

Sweet 16 party paid for and hosted by me at my aunt Pearline and uncle Ezra's home on Ashby Avenue, Berkeley, California. The floor of the dining room was my bedroom throughout high school. PHOTO COURTESY OF THE AUTHOR

The Belva Davis Show, KDIA Radio, Oakland, 1962. I was a DJ six days a week and scheduled commercials for broadcast throughout the day. PHOTO: WILLIAM MOORE

1964 Republican Convention, the Cow Palace, San Francisco, California. KDIA news director Louis Freeman and I had tickets for seats high in the rafters, but we were driven from the convention by an angry mob of conventioneers.
PHOTO: CORBIS

Klan demonstrators carrying signs supporting Republican presidential hopeful Barry Goldwater outside San Francisco City Hall, 1964. PHOTO: GETTY

Me and my son Steven Davis with Ray Charles and a fan backstage at a KDIA concert, 1963. PHOTO: WILLIAM MOORE

Bill Cosby on one of his frequent visits to KDIA Lucky 13 in Oakland, 1963.
PHOTO: WILLIAM MOORE

Sharon Bailey, producer of Miss Bronze Sacramento,
with regional winner Carolyn Blakey and me, 1963.
Black women were barred from competing in the Miss
America competition, so I joined with Los Angeles
photographer Howard Morehead in producing the
Miss Bronze California Pageant. PHOTO: WILLIAM MOORE

Stepmother Geraldine Melton and father John Melton celebrate my new position as a reporter with KPIX television, the CBS affiliate station in San Francisco, 1967. PHOTO: WILLIAM MOORE

My mother Florence Melton Mays, son Steven Davis, and mentor Miss Anna Dean celebrating Steven's role as an escort at the Links Inc. Cotillion Ball at the San Francisco Hilton Hotel, 1972. PHOTO: WILLIAM MOORE

Female students and supporters confronting National Guardsmen at Sather Gate on the UC Berkeley campus, May 20, 1969. I felt in physical danger as I covered the days-long People's Park demonstration. PHOTO: CORBIS

Black Panther Party cofounder Huey P. Newton talking to reporters at Alameda County Court House, 1979. After two trials ended with deadlocked juries, the state of California abandoned a five-year effort to convict him of murdering a seventeen-year-old prostitute. PHOTO: CORBIS

KPIX noon news team
Ron Magers and me
conducting ceremonies
for the opening of the Bay
Area Rapid Transit
District, September 1972.
PHOTO COURTESY OF THE AUTHOR

Coretta Scott King, widow of Dr. Martin Luther King Jr., being interviewed by
me at an education conference in Monterey, California. PHOTO: WILLIAM MOORE

Wilma Johnson, me, Alex Haley, my husband Bill Moore, and
Vert Smith in front of Haley's boat in Negril, Jamaica, 1976.
The previous evening, I listened to Haley negotiating the final
details of ABC's production of his best-selling novel *Roots*.

Rev. Jim Jones, pastor of the
Peoples Temple, June 2, 1976.
Jones led his San Francisco–
based congregation to Guyana,
where on November 18, 1978,
he and 900 followers took part
in a mass suicide-murder and
killed Congressman Leo Ryan
and four others who had come
to investigate conditions at the
Jonestown camp. PHOTO: CORBIS

Supervisor Harvey Milk, the country's first openly gay elected official, and Mayor George Moscone in the spring of 1978. On November 28, another member of the Board of Supervisors, Dan White, murdered both. The ex-policeman disliked gays and was angry about not being reinstated to the district seat he had resigned. Photo: Corbis

Reverend Jesse Jackson, me, and political reporter Rollin Post at the 1984 Democratic Convention in San Francisco. Jackson would make a strong bid for the presidency in 1988. Rollin and I worked together for more than twenty years. Photo: Jim Dennis

My husband Bill Moore covering the aftermath of the 1989 San Francisco earthquake for KTVU Channel 2 in Oakland. Bill was the first African American news cameraman hired by a commercial television station in California. PHOTO: CHUCK LEIGHTON

With Mayor Willie Brown at a reconstruction ceremony for the earthquake-damaged de Young Museum, San Francisco, 2000. PHOTO COURTESY OF THE AUTHOR

Members of the American Federation of Television and Radio Artists/Screen Actors Guild on strike in 2000. As AFTRA vice president, I joined the picket line. PHOTO: WILLIAM MOORE

Cuba's Fidel Castro greeting me and Congresswoman Barbara Lee at a reception in Havana, 1998. I first met Castro when I was a member of a delegation led by former Congressman Ronald Dellums in 1975. PHOTO COURTESY OF THE AUTHOR

Bill and me with CBS's legendary anchorman Walter Cronkite, his wife Mary Elizabeth (Betsy), and John Martin of ABC News at an AFTRA awards event in New York, May 2003. PHOTO: ANITA SHEVETT

Dr. Ruth Love, Dr. Betty Shabazz, Dr. Dorothy Height, singer Odetta, Dr. Maya Angelou, and me celebrating Angelou's seventieth birthday at a party hosted by Oprah Winfrey in Winston-Salem, North Carolina, 1998. PHOTO: DR. VICKI HUGHES

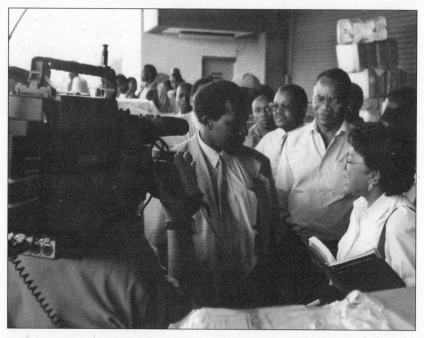

Showdown at the airport in Nairobi, Kenya, over medical supplies for victims of the American Embassy bombing in Nairobi, 1998. When a Kenyan official told the delegation led by Dr. Ramona Tascoe of the National Medical Association that the supplies couldn't be located, I heatedly demanded that they be produced. PHOTO: WILLIAM MOORE

With Oprah Winfrey at a benefit for Glide Memorial Church Foundation's services to the needy and homeless. Photo courtesy of the author

On the set with *San Francisco Chronicle* reporters Carla Marinucci and Bob Egelko, and Paul Rodgers of the *San Jose Mercury News,* during a live broadcast of KQED's *This Week in Northern California.* Photo: William Moore

My daughter Darolyn, myself, mother Florence, and son Steven in 1998 in front of the Monroe, Louisiana, house where I was born. Photo: WILLIAM MOORE

Granddaughters Sterling Alexis Davis and Dava Wilkins at their parents' wedding reception in Montego Bay, Jamaica, December 28, 2009. PHOTO COURTESY OF THE AUTHOR

twelve

...

Ringside
at the Racial Revolution

The first thing I learned about him was that he loved music and played classical piano. We were introduced by his girlfriend, LaVerne Williams, a virtuoso mezzo soprano who would sweep the talent competition at the 1966 Miss Bronze Pageant. LaVerne clearly was smitten with this shy, soft-spoken yet intense Oakland City College student—he possessed a passion for the composition of Tchaikovsky, the poetry of Shakespeare, and the philosophies of Jean-Paul Sartre and Albert Camus. The student had a beautiful face, and in him LaVerne felt she had found a soul mate who shared her artistic sensitivity.

"Belva," LaVerne said, "this is Huey. Huey Newton."

"Hi, nice to meet you," he said.

His name meant nothing to me at first, although I sized him up as well mannered, intellectual, and seemingly a good match for LaVerne. But as we chatted, I eventually placed him as the youngest son of Walter Newton, a devout Baptist who worked several jobs to ensure that his wife remained at home raising their seven children. The Newtons had something in common with the Meltons—both of our families had moved from Monroe, Louisiana, to Oakland and found military jobs during World War II. As I was later to learn, his parents named Huey after Huey P. Long, the cantankerous Louisiana governor whose public racism often masked the good he did for blacks: For example, by declaring it an abomination that white nurses were forced to care for ailing old black men, the governor was able to hire black nurses on the state payroll.

I didn't know then that Huey Newton was on probation, having served six months in Santa Rita Jail for felony assault after repeatedly stabbing a fellow dinner party companion with a steak knife. Nor did I know that he and Bobby Seale had already begun contemplating a bold response to what Oakland blacks regarded as widespread police brutality and oppression. Nor would I have imagined that he would someday prophetically title his autobiography *Revolutionary Suicide*.

But a few months later, in October 1966, Newton and Seale announced formation of the Black Panther Party for Self-Defense. "The black panther is a fierce animal," Newton wrote, "but he will not attack until he is backed into a corner; then he will strike out."

The duo unveiled the party's ten-point platform—an audacious call for radical societal change. Besides demanding that black people receive a decent education, jobs, and housing, the Panthers declared that if the white power structure would fail to provide them, private property and the means of production should be snatched from it. They called for freeing every black man held in prison or jail, reasoning that the all-white juries failed to constitute a jury of the accused's peers. They insisted that all black men be exempt from the Vietnam draft and military service, on the grounds they should not be forced "to defend a racist government that does not protect us." They demanded that the United Nations supervise a plebiscite throughout "the black colony, in which only black colonial subjects will be allowed to participate" to determine their own destiny.

But what became the incendiary focus of the ten-point platform was number seven. Newton had discovered that citizens of California were permitted to carry guns in public, as long as they were not concealed or pointed at anyone. That's it, he thought—a way for us to constitutionally police the police.

"We believe we can end police brutality in our black community by organizing black self-defense groups," read number seven. "The Second Amendment to the Constitution of the United States gives a right to bear arms. We therefore believe that all black people should arm themselves for self-defense."

With that, the Panthers began their own patrols on the streets of Oakland. When they spotted police officers, who were virtually all white, detaining or arresting blacks, they would take up a position about twenty feet away and "observe"—with their weapons in plain view. Their refusal to be intimidated transfigured them into heroes in a community that felt itself oppressed by the Oakland Police Department.

Having grown up in West Oakland, I knew that some of the Panthers' charges were valid. The Oakland force was practically all white, many of them originally from Southern states where running roughshod over the black communities they were supposed to protect was commonplace. We all knew somebody who said he had been insulted, disrespected, or roughed up by the police. Our family history had taught us that the lawman might well be in cahoots with the KKK. We knew that merely because the authorities said somebody did something, that didn't necessarily make it so.

But the Panthers' emphasis on guns was troubling. Seale would later explain how the organization initially financed its operations: He and Newton would go to Chinatown, buy copies of Chairman Mao Zedong's "The Little Red Book" for twenty cents a piece, take them by the boxful over to the UC Berkeley campus, and peddle them to students for one dollar. The profits paid for the Panthers' weapons.

Huey's older brother Melvin thought the gun toting was an ominous idea, and he expressed his reservations—to no avail. "I saw graveyards being dug," he would say, "and I told Huey that then."

The truth was that Panthers on patrol scared the bejeebers out of many people in the black community, because we knew the Oakland cops were as crazy as they were.

A mere three months after I made my debut on KPIX, the Panthers burst into the top of our newscast. It was part of Newton's plan to create a "colossal event" that would intensify the organization's profile. The "powers that be" sought to quash the Panther patrols via a bill introduced by GOP assemblyman Mulford to make it a crime for ordinary Californians to carry a loaded firearm. In brazen defiance, a cadre of thirty Panthers showed up at the state capitol on May 2, 1967, their shotguns and M-1 rifles pointed skyward.

Jaws dropped. People scurried out of their path. California's then governor Ronald Reagan was outside the capitol entrance talking to visiting schoolchildren, but he vanished indoors when the Panthers approached. As they entered the building, anxious security guards huddled, debating whether to apprehend them. Reporters—caught unprepared—began trailing them. With Seale at the forefront, they walked past the sergeant at arms and onto the assembly floor.

Eventually, Seale led reporters into a side chamber, where he read aloud a mandate declaring: "Vicious police dogs, cattle prods, and increased patrols have become familiar sights in black communities. City Hall turns a deaf ear to the pleas of black people for relief from this increasing terror. . . . [So] the time has come for black people to arm themselves against this terror before it is too late. The pending Mulford Act brings the hour of doom one step nearer."

Having made their point, the group departed for the parking lot. A few minutes later, when the Panthers pulled into a gas station, police approached them. One officer asked whether they were a gun club.

"No, we're the Black Panther Party," Seale retorted. "We're black people with guns. What about it?"

KPIX didn't staff a Sacramento bureau, so we were left to chase the story's aftermath. The media lavished attention on the Panthers' stunt, but every story I saw or read focused on the sensational: those gleaming guns. I understood that the group's aggressive tactics were unprecedented and therefore the main story. But in our newsroom, I advocated for something else—a piece that explained what the Panthers were trying to accomplish. In other words, I argued for *context*.

Some facts about my life were unavoidable: Nobody else in our newsroom had grown up in West Oakland. Nobody else had lived in the projects. Nobody else had confronted the senseless discrimination that blacks in Oakland encountered on a daily basis. Nobody else could understand how difficult it was to live in an environment where you had little power and often suffered from neglect or outright abuse. With this explosive a story, how could I hold in check all of my emotions and become, as my first station manager Lou Simon had counseled, a reporter for everybody?

Covering the Black Panthers would become one of the most difficult assignments of my journalistic career, especially in those early years when I was inexperienced and learning my profession live before tens of thousands of viewers. I knew that because I was the only black female TV reporter in the Bay Area, I would be uniquely scrutinized for any sign of pro-Panther favoritism. Yet I also knew the hopes of black viewers that at long last someone with their experiences would be more simpatico to their version of the truth.

While the civil rights movement had made great gains in the Deep South, the decaying urban cores in the North and West were on slow boil. Race riots slammed such cities as Detroit and Newark while devastating the Los Angeles neighborhood Watts, where the cry was "Burn, baby, burn." In 1967, President Johnson's Kerner Commission was at work on a major dissection of the nation's racial unrest. The commission concluded, "Along with the country as a whole, the press has too long basked in a white world, looking out of it, if at all, with white men's eyes and a white perspective. That is no longer good enough." Noting that key segments of the media failed to report on the causes and consequences of racial disorder, the commission said, "They have not communicated to the majority of their audience—which is white—a sense of the degradation, misery and hopelessness of life in the ghetto."

The commission also noted that merely 5 percent of reporters and less than 1 percent of editor/managers were Negro; and it urged the immediate hiring of more Negro reporters to fill the gaping holes in the nation's press coverage. I was pretty sure I was one of those hired to fill that gap.

So there I was, a small, undereducated woman, handed one of life's greatest opportunities and not quite sure I was up to the task.

While the white men in my newsroom could not see beyond the image of Black Panthers as gun-toting thugs, I advocated looking at the story from an alternate perspective. "Look," I said, "if these guys have broken any state laws, then fine, that's the story and nail them. But from what I understand, what they've done is legal. They may have frightened people, and that was wrong, but they didn't break a law. Had they been white cowboys in cowboy hats, would that have made national news and struck such terror?"

The gun angle continued to be the lead story, although the charges ultimately filed against the Panthers were for "disruption of the legislature." I did a secondary piece that aired May 4 discussing the Panthers' ten-point program. I struggled over the script, because the time constraints of TV news of course made it impossible to convey much detail. But my story added a new dimension to the coverage.

This would become my aim and my modus operandi as a journalist: to tell stories that would otherwise go untold, and to put them in context but play it straight—unemotional, factual, and fair.

On the night of October 27, 1967, Huey Newton was in a mood to party with LaVerne. By now the Black Panthers had earned national attention and were clearly a force to be reckoned with; and Newton was beginning to forge ties with white radicals sympathetic to Panther objectives. Newton, however, had a more personal reason to celebrate: his probation for the steak knife assault was set to expire.

But when he arrived at LaVerne's house after ten that night, she told him she was feeling too sick for a night on the town. Instead, according to his fellow Panthers, she handed him the keys to her 1958 gold Volkswagen Beetle and told him to have a good time on his own.

In the predawn hours of October 28—less than five hours after Newton officially went off probation—he was pulled over by a white twenty-three-year-old Oakland officer named John Frey near a strip of Seventh Street in West Oakland known to be hopping all night long. The officer had LaVerne's car on a list of Panther vehicles, and he called for backup. What happened next will forever remain in dispute. Newton would testify that the police, without provocation, shot him in the belly and that he had no memory of what happened afterward. The other officer called to the scene would attest that Newton was the one who opened fire. In any event, by daybreak Officer Frey was dead, the other officer was wounded, and Newton was chained to a hospital gurney facing a murder charge.

LaVerne didn't want to be interviewed on television, and I certainly didn't push her to—particularly given that she had no direct knowledge of what occurred. She stood by Newton and visited him in jail, although the publicity around the case may have been one of the reasons she lost a scholarship to the Metropolitan Opera in New York. Ultimately she left for Europe to establish a successful career as a classical vocalist.

Ben Williams became our lead reporter on the trial, but I took frequent turns reporting daily developments from the Alameda County Courthouse. The landmark case triggered an international "Free Huey!" campaign.

It was the first time I had ever even attended a criminal trial. Apparently, journalism was to be my college education.

Two nights after Martin Luther King's assassination in April 1968, the Panthers and Oakland Police squared off in another fatal shoot-out—this one, located near my old hangout of deFremery Park, lasted an hour and half. The Panthers' chief of staff, David Hilliard, would later recall how their hotheaded minister of information, Eldridge Cleaver, had rallied them by announcing, "I'm launching a counteroffensive against the pigs. . . . It's time to intensify the struggle. We gotta do the dog in Babylon."

Much of what happened that night is in question. But it all reached a crescendo with a wounded Cleaver and the party's youngest founding member, seventeen-year-old Bobby Hutton, barricaded inside a West Oakland house while some fifty armed officers surrounded the structure, pummeling it with tear gas and firebombs. The two Panthers, after stripping off much of their clothing and realizing their situation was hopeless, emerged from the house.

A naked Cleaver managed to surrender, but Hutton ended up with ten bullets in his body. Panthers and witnesses claimed that the cops ordered Hutton, with his hands up, to run toward a police squad car, and then they opened fire on him.

The authorities, of course, provided a far different account to me and to the other reporters gathered behind police lines in deFremery Park early the next morning. I was glad to learn that KPIX photographer Lou Calderon—the cozy-with-the-cops cameraman who had taken me on my rookie police-chase story months before—had picked up the shoot-out on his police scanner and arrived overnight to capture the scene. It seemed that his film could resolve what actually happened to Hutton. But mysteriously, his film continued right up to the moment when Hutton came out of the house, and then the footage abruptly stopped. Lou told producers his camera had jammed.

Reporters who covered only Panther violence, and the readers and viewers who relied upon their coverage, must have been mystified by the respect and popularity the Panthers enjoyed in much of the black community. People certainly felt unnerved to see rows of rifle-toting Panthers—clad in their uniform of black leather jackets, boots, and berets—drilling in unison while chanting "Off the pig!"

To explain the Panthers' appeal, I did several stories on the social services they advocated and provided. Whether it was a calculated ploy or a heartfelt commitment—and it could have been both—Panthers such as Seale wanted to create a free breakfast program for the neighborhood children. The new rector of West Oakland's St. Augustine Episcopal Church, Father Earl Neil, agreed and persuaded my longtime friend Ruth Beckford to help organize it. Ruth, a crackerjack organizer, believed in the importance of giving children the fuel their minds need to do well in school, and she recruited a nutritionist and other health advisors. The program opened in January 1969 with 11 children, and by the end of the week it was serving breakfast to 135 youngsters. The principals of nearby schools sent the Panthers thank you notes. Soon the breakfast program was being duplicated across the country. I interviewed civil rights icon Rosa Parks, who visited the Panther-established Oakland Community School and talked about the importance of educating young blacks.

At the same time, my connections as a "local girl" helped me secure exclusive interviews with Panther leaders, who seemed to be forever in and out of jail—facing trials, mistrials, and retrials. Seale protested at the 1968 Democratic National Convention and ended up, along with seven white leftists, being known as "the Chicago Eight": they were charged with crossing state lines to incite a riot. While Seale was detained in San Francisco County Jail, awaiting transfer to his Chicago trial, I pushed hard for an interview. At last the authorities granted my request. But when I arrived at the jail, a deputy informed me that because I hadn't specifically sought permission for filming, no cameraman could accompany me.

"Isn't it obvious that a TV interview would require a cameraman?" I asked incredulously. "Television without pictures doesn't exactly work."

"Sorry, I've got my orders," he said. "No camera."

I phoned my producer; in desperation we decided that I would get what I could from Seale and return to the studio to be interviewed on the set about what he said.

The guard, instead of escorting me to the visiting room, led me to a holding cell.

"There he is," he said, gesturing to Seale waiting inside. "Go on in if you want to talk to him."

No sooner had I stepped into the cell than the guard banged the door shut—locking me inside—and vanished.

If his intent was to scare me, it didn't work. Seale and I did the interview. I was scribbling notes as fast as I could, but after thirty minutes I knew I needed to get back to the station to make the newscast. Still no guard in sight.

"Hello?" I ventured.

Nothing.

"Hello, I'm ready to go now," I called louder.

Still nothing.

Seale and I exchanged smiles, and he shrugged.

"Can someone please get me out of here," I shouted at the top of my lungs.

At last, a grinning deputy showed up and unlocked the door. I wished Seale a safe trip and rushed back to KPIX.

His case eventually was severed from the case of the other seven, and his outbursts—he called the judge a "fascist dog" for refusing to delay his trial until Panther attorney Charles Garry could represent him—prompted the judge to order him bound and gagged in the courtroom. He was sentenced to four years in prison for contempt of court, although two years later the government suspended those charges and ordered him released. A few years later he ran for mayor of Oakland, garnering 40 percent of the vote.

I never felt afraid of the Panthers, and I never believed either they or the police were trying to unduly influence my reporting. Perhaps I instinctively sensed that I should never let them see my weak side, even if I was only five foot one. I adopted an attitude of bold confidence that seemed to work for me. And truth be told, I think being known in the community as the mother hen of the Miss Bronze girls gave me a lot of passes. Everyone, even callous criminals, seemed to love the pageant girls and the concept of lifting up the black woman—and they seemed to respect me for what I did to create that pageant.

Perhaps that was one reason why Huey Newton, when he was released from prison in 1970, issued me an invitation to his penthouse on the twenty-fifth floor of 1200 Lakeshore Boulevard in Oakland. His conviction in the Frey killing had been overturned, and he was ensconced in an apartment cynics nicknamed "The Throne." The penthouse wasn't actually all that fancy, but it did afford stunning views of Lake Merritt and the Alameda

County courthouse. My cousin Shelby, our Miss Bronze co-producer, had taken an apartment in the same recently integrated building, and Newton called him seeking company. "Bring Belva with you," he said.

This was the first of a handful of sojourns we would make to Newton's place, which was modern, sparsely furnished, and impeccably tidy. He always greeted us warmly, but the apartment itself was like an icebox. I was baffled that he was clad in short-sleeved shirts—I always made sure whatever the season to wear a warm suit coat, which I would never take off.

Newton was a human pinball, bouncing from topic to topic: Marxist theory to Maoist doctrine, Oakland political shenanigans to African coups. The guy would talk and talk and talk and talk and talk. He was charming—and more than a little manic.

Then he would spring up from the sofa and ask, "Can I get you something to drink or eat?"

"No, we're fine," we would assure him. His stream-of-consciousness conversation would resume, but within a few minutes he would be on his feet again. "Are you sure I can't get you something?"

Huey and Shelby often shared a bottle of cognac, but I made sure to never drink anything other than soda from a bottle. I also made sure never to reveal my personal opinions, instead remaining in my default "objective reporter" mode. I never really attempted to extract a story out of the exchanges—Huey's expositions on theoretical dogmas were hardly my area of expertise, nor the stuff of local TV news. Perhaps he saw me as a trustworthy conduit to the establishment; he surely didn't know many people whose jobs required them to regularly question police and district attorneys. Or perhaps he just loved having an audience, any audience.

"Well, we really should be going," I would say, reaching for my bag.

"No, stay, stay, stay, stay, stay," he would implore.

The last time Shelby and I paid a visit to Newton, we took ten-year-old Darolyn along. The fact that I had my daughter in tow is a testament to how safe I felt in Newton's presence—and also how much I wanted a ready excuse to exit. "We really have to go—she's so cold," I said about an hour after our arrival, wrapping my arms around her shoulders and ushering her to the door.

In retrospect, no wonder Darolyn once told me she didn't have to do that well in school: her real life was far more educational.

Most of the good that the Black Panthers did seemed to me to come from the organization's females—women like Ericka Huggins, who directed the Panthers' Oakland Community School for eight years, until 1981. When Newton wound up in prison again, Elaine Brown assumed the party leadership. Years after leaving the party, she would write that a woman in the Black Power movement was considered "at best, irrelevant. A woman asserting herself was a pariah. If a black woman assumed a role of leadership, she was said to be eroding black manhood, to be hindering the progress of the black race."

But what crystallized the party's sexism, to me, was watching Cleaver at a couple of posh fundraisers where he would summon his wife, Kathleen, and insist she taste-test his food to ensure it wasn't poisoned.

I never much cared for Cleaver, who blazed onto the national stage with publication of his memoir *Soul on Ice*, in which he described how he had raped black girls before deciding that raping white women could be an "insurrectionary act." Although he later repudiated such a repugnant thought, he continued to strike me as a bizarre choice to be the party's spokesman, not to mention a downright creepy person. I didn't try particularly hard to mask my disdain of him, and I wasn't surprised that he jumped bail on charges stemming from the shoot-out, got himself kicked out of Cuba, was asked to leave Algeria, and ended up in Paris touting his new invention: pants that featured a visible, exterior penis compartment instead of the conventional "sissy pants" that disguised a man's true anatomy.

He and Newton, both gargantuan egos, struggled over the direction of the party, and Newton ended up kicking him out of the Panthers.

Given our history, I was stunned to discover that Cleaver intended for our lives to intersect once more. Bill and I were on vacation in 1975, sitting at a small beachfront bar in the Virgin Islands, when the island's governor, Cyril King, arrived to deliver a message. Cleaver had decided to return to the United States on one condition: that I be allowed to do a television interview with him before he surrendered to authorities.

So when I returned, Cleaver came to the KPIX studio, and I taped a long interview in which he talked about the shoot-out, life abroad, and his feud with Huey Newton. He then claimed that the FBI had crafted a systematic plan to eliminate the Black Panther Party.

We were editing the interview for our Sunday news program when I got word that some KPIX producers opposed airing that portion of Cleaver's interview. In their view, the station would be irresponsible to broadcast such inflammatory allegations—unsubstantiated at best, reckless at worst—against a revered federal law enforcement institution.

Once again I was reminded of how personal circumstances shape our worldview. Frankly, I didn't find Cleaver's allegations far-fetched—but more to the point, I didn't feel that the station would be right to censor him. By now I had logged almost a decade in television news and had grown surer of myself as well as of my journalistic duty.

So I fought back, fought hard—and after two days I prevailed. The Cleaver interview aired with his accusations intact. The FBI declined our offer for the agency to respond.

Within a year, the country would learn in detail about the existence of COINTELPRO, the FBI's Counter Intelligence Program that engaged in covert—and often illegal—spying on, and interference in, dissident groups. Director J. Edgar Hoover had instructed agents to "expose, disrupt, misdirect, discredit, or otherwise neutralize" the activities of organizations from the Communist Party to the NAACP. Chief among these was the Black Panther Party for Self-Defense, which Hoover labeled "the biggest threat to internal security in America."

The release of COINTELPRO documents indicated that law enforcement agents had bugged dozens of locations, including Huey Newton's penthouse; they created and exploited schisms within the group and forged letters to provoke paranoia and confrontation between Newton and Cleaver. A 1976 investigation by the Senate's Church Committee concluded that "the chief investigative branch of the Federal Government, which was charged by law with investigating crimes and preventing criminal conduct, itself engaged in lawless tactics and responded to deep-seated social problems by fomenting violence and unrest. . . . Although the claimed purpose of the Bureau's COINTELPRO tactics was to prevent violence, some of the FBI's tactics against the Black Panther Party were clearly intended to foster violence, and many others could reasonably have been expected to cause violence."

In short, Eldridge Cleaver was right.

Ron Magers was my KPIX co-anchor at the time, and to this day he says that my battle over the Cleaver interview changed his view of journalism. "I have argued ever since against withholding almost any information from any story. If we know it, we should air it and let it survive or die in the court of public opinion," he recently wrote me from Chicago, where he is a prominent TV anchor. "I can't tell you how many times I've used the example of that show. Times were tense in those days and you argued for what was right—but scary."

Our television audience still was getting acclimated to the idea of seeing black women on the evening newscast—and viewers seemed to find it doubly difficult when I was covering Angela Davis, a Black Panther member stripped of her job as an assistant professor of philosophy at UCLA in 1969 because she was a member of the Communist Party. Davis castigated a judicial system that she said put far too many black men in prison, many of them her Panther comrades, whom she called political prisoners. In 1970 she wound up behind bars herself—charged with being an accomplice to kidnapping and homicide because she had purchased guns used in a violent Marin County courthouse break—but a jury of eleven whites and one Latino ultimately found her not guilty.

As various Panthers went in and out of prison and jail over those years, another African American man remained locked deep inside San Quentin; in fact, since his incarceration in 1928 at the age of nineteen—for receiving two stolen suits—this inmate had logged forty-six years behind bars. His name was Wesley "Bob" Wells, and Panther lawyer Charles Garry dubbed him "the first Black Panther" because his struggles foreshadowed the Panthers' battles against racism ingrained in the justice system.

I became invested in his story because of the penitentiary's warden, Louis "Red" Nelson. One day when I was visiting San Quentin, Nelson asked me to go for a drive around the grounds and began to tell me about this old prisoner, a onetime hell-raiser who had spent his entire adult life incarcerated.

"He's doing life without the possibility of parole," Warden Nelson mused as we took in the prison's sweeping views of San Francisco Bay and its tease of freedom beyond the gates. "He's getting old now, has trouble taking care of himself. I guess I'm concerned about him in here. He still has enemies. I just think it wouldn't be such a bad thing if this guy could see what the outside world looked like before he passed on. And I thought maybe if you wanted to do an interview, I could help make that happen."

I noted the irony: Nelson was known as a hard-nosed warden—hated by many of the inmates for his severity—and yet now, as he prepared to retire from a lifetime of prison work that stretched from Alcatraz to San Quentin, he was acting out of compassion for one of his guys.

I also knew I *had* to do this story. Wells had been a cause célèbre before. He had knifed another inmate in a prison fight, garnering an indeterminate sentence, and later he hurled a spittoon at a guard, hitting him in the face. The assault of a guard landed him on Death Row. After a national campaign for clemency—even conservative columnist Walter Winchell said the punishment didn't fit the crime—then governor Goodwin Knight commuted his sentence to life in prison. But with Garry as his attorney, Wells was the first to raise the issue of the double standard of inferior treatment for blacks in California's penal system.

When Wells first sat down for our interview, he was wiry and wary, as though he were wearing his boxing gloves. My strategy was to make the interview feel like a conversation. Prisoners build up defenses to survive inside, and they need to be brought back to their humanity. I tried to treat him as a person first, not an inmate.

While we talked, I could feel Wells unwind, open up, and talk about what a taste of freedom on the outside world might mean to someone who had spent his life in a cell. He almost laughed when acknowledging that he had more than four decades' worth of the world to catch up on.

We aired Wells's saga on a new KPIX Sunday prime time program called *All Together Now*, a news and public affairs show that was groundbreaking by virtue of being devoted to minority issues. In such a format, I could give him almost half an hour to build a personality. The broadcast helped coalesce efforts to free him, and soon other local and national media were extracting sound bites from my interview to tell his story.

On July 1, 1974, Bob Wells walked out of prison a free man and was met by reporters gathered outside who wanted to know how he felt. "Man, don't my expression tell you how it feels?" he replied with a broad smile. "The power of the people got me out." And with that, he climbed into a Rolls-Royce rented by his jubilant supporters and departed for Delancey Street, the San Francisco residential program that helps former convicts adjust to life on the outside.

But adaptation was far from easy for Wells. He was disoriented by free time and confused by all the choices available once prison regulations no longer dictated his daily routine. "There are just too many decisions to make out here," he told me. "And then, when you make 'em, they don't like what you decided."

He started drinking too much, and over the next year, he showed up at KPIX to see me about a dozen times, whenever anything went wrong. Our station's softhearted receptionist, Lila Mudd, would never let him up into the newsroom; instead she invited him to hang out on the couch in the lobby, where he would watch television until Lila went home.

One day as I was signing off the noon news, Lila took an urgent call from a Muni bus driver. Wells had lain down in front of a bus on the streets of San Francisco and was refusing to budge. Asked if he had any family, apparently Wells gave my name.

I spoke with the driver, who said, "Miss Davis, I don't want to call the cops. I just need somebody to get him out from in front of my bus."

"I'll be right there," I answered.

One of our cameramen rushed me to the intersection, where I found Wells sitting up in front of the bus. When he saw me, he started to cry.

"Hi Bob," I began. "What's wrong?"

He just shook his head and rubbed his face with his fist to wipe away the tears. "Maybe I should just go back to San Quentin," he said. "I don't really know anybody out here."

"Well, you know me," I replied, "and you know the people at Delancey Street. So listen to me: right now I need you to get up and let this bus driver be on his way, and let's get you back home to Delancey."

I thought about how alienating the world must seem through his eyes. All those politicians and activists and reporters who had rallied around him had since moved on to the next big cause—that's what we do. He was left adrift.

A few months later, I learned that he had died: a heart attack. I will always wonder whether, at the end of his life, he found at least some happy moments of freedom.

As the 1970s unreeled, the Black Panthers continued to implode. Increasingly, their exploits resembled those of an organized crime syndicate—overshadowing the valuable social services they tried to provide. They turned on one another. Many members ended up dead or disillusioned. The party was over.

Eldridge Cleaver did an outlandish about-face, announcing he was a born-again Christian, then a Moonie, then a Republican candidate for U.S. Senate. Kathleen Cleaver divorced him, obtained a Yale law degree, and clerked for a federal appeals court before becoming a law professor. Bobby Seale quit the party in 1975 and wound up in academia, and also authored the recipe book *Barbecue'n with Bobby*. Elaine Brown resigned and moved to Europe to kick a Thorazine habit she had developed to deal with the pressure; later she carved out a new life for herself in the nonprofit world in Atlanta.

Huey P. Newton descended into drug addiction and was gunned down by a reputed crack cocaine dealer in 1989, on the West Oakland streets that had once given birth to the Black Panthers.

I had lost touch with all of them except the women. At a reception given by the Congressional Black Caucus to celebrate the Obama inauguration, I saw Newton's widow Fredrika and Elaine Brown. Ericka Huggins operates a meditation program for prisoners; and every time I see her, she advises me that I should take up meditation to relieve my stress.

In hindsight, the Black Panther Party was like a blazing comet, generating so much light and heat that it burned out swiftly. The sabotage of COINTELPRO is much to blame, but so too are the drugs and alcohol that fueled the Panthers' immolation. The distance between their ideals and their actions at last became an unbridgeable chasm.

thirteen

· · ·

Freeze Frames

I really never said no. During my first decade in television news, I agreed to whatever the editors tossed my way. My assignments varied vastly from day to day—as if I might be asked to juggle a whiffle ball, a bowling ball, a porcupine, and a vial of nitroglycerine.

I felt the need to prove, over and over again, that I could handle anything.

Dispatched to cover the Warriors basketball team—at a time when there were no female sports reporters or sportscasters—I tried talking my way into the locker room in pursuit of lively quotes from sweat-soaked, nearly naked players. The team barred my entrance, thank goodness.

So as the other stations' guys waltzed past me and carried on their exclusive interviews inside the locker room, I hovered outside, praying to snag at least a quick comment from a departing rookie—a nearly hopeless effort. Most of the Warriors brushed past me offering nothing more than a disdainful smirk. Even when one did deign to be interviewed, my cameraman could scarcely back up enough to capture us both in the shot, given that the players towered one to two feet over me.

But on my third foray, a man I shall always adore came to my rescue. Warriors star center Nate "The Great" Thurmond took pity on my plight, and as he dressed, he sent word for me to meet him in a specific seating section inside the arena. There I balanced precariously on the seat of a fold-up chair that elevated me to almost eye level with this six foot eleven hoopster. He graciously answered my questions and guaranteed that I would save face with the guys back at my station.

KPIX loved me airborne. The station sent me up in a single-engine hot rod, a vintage biplane, a blimp, and a hot air balloon. I always was willing, even when the balloon hit a downdraft over a small pond of water and almost careened into the side of a hill somewhere over Contra Costa County.

"Don't ask any questions, just do what I tell you," barked the pilot as we drifted downward, sideways. He ordered everyone aboard to hang on tight, dangle our feet over the basket, and shove off the hill. We complied and, fortunately, wafted airborne again. Unfortunately, we had no video because the cameraman, too, had to pitch in to prevent us from crashing.

I also accompanied a pilot in a STOL aircraft, an acronym for *short takeoff and landing*. The pilot sent the plane plummeting earthward in a nosedive and then—just before it touched down—he throttled it upward in what felt like a vertical climb to the sky. My heart dropped into the pit of my stomach with a splat. Actually, I had to endure that stunt twice: the first time, my cameraman threw up all over himself and missed the shot. We cleaned him up and repeated the ordeal.

The Sutro Tower is an orange and white broadcast antenna that resembles a pickle fork and dominates the San Francisco skyline. In an era before cable TV, the tower was designed to remedy the erratic TV reception that plagued the city's hilly neighborhoods. The Sutro rises nearly one thousand feet—more than one hundred feet taller than the city's tallest skyscraper, the Transamerica Pyramid—and perches atop one of the city's highest peaks.

Just before it was completed in 1973, photographer Dave Ambriz and I were sent to do a progress report. Of course, we could have shot that story from the tower's base, but that perspective was too dull for Dave, who asked whether we could go to the top. Turns out there was no elevator. The construction crew jokingly offered to take us up their way, in an open construction basket.

They never expected us to say yes, but of course we did. Before second thoughts kicked in, we clambered into the basket—which had a wood plank floor, metal rods on each corner, and a wire railing. We grasped the wire and asked to be hoisted into the air.

The afternoon winds had picked up and were gusting in off the Pacific Ocean, pushing the basket to and fro as though it were a playground swing. We had to rock in rhythm with the swaying to keep from losing our balance. I glanced down for a moment, caught sight of our station vehicle rapidly dwindling to the dimensions of a matchbox car, and admonished myself not to look down again.

When at last we jerked to a stop near the top, Dave realized we didn't have sufficient space for him to frame a shot of me with the city skyline as my backdrop. "This won't work—all I can see behind you is blue sky," he said from behind his viewfinder. "We've got to get a wider angle."

Which meant only one thing: One of us needed to venture out onto a crossbeam. Our tower guide sized me up and ruled out that possibility. "You're so tiny you'll get blown away," he shouted.

So Dave straddled the beam, scooted himself out until he was several feet away, and hoisted the camera onto his shoulder. I hollered out my narration as he filmed me, the wind whipping my hair into my eyes. "I'm Belva Davis for *Eyewitness News*," I concluded, grateful that at last we could start our descent.

A few weeks later, the guys around my station cackled as they related the tale of another local station's "weather girl," who had attempted a similar feat atop Sutro Tower and panicked so much that she wet herself. I didn't see what was so funny.

While anchoring the noon news, I honed a reputation for being unflappable. I remained unflustered when guest Alice Faye, onetime movie queen and favorite singer of composer Irving Berlin, abruptly demanded that I switch seats with her because she thought my location had more flattering lighting. Apparently she didn't consider that my brighter lighting was calibrated to my skin, which was several shades darker than hers. I moved.

I wasn't fazed when, during a hamburger-cooking demonstration, station personality Rolf Peterson ignited a barbecue grill, which triggered a smoke alarm that persisted even after he tried extinguishing the blaze with beer.

And I remained cool while interviewing William Shockley, the Nobel Prize–winning Stanford physicist who espoused eugenics—the notion of breeding humans to create a superior species. He claimed that intelligence was hereditary, and he noted that blacks scored an average 15 points lower on IQ tests than whites. Most experts repudiated his theory; they noted that poverty, substandard schools, and other socioeconomic factors were the real culprits. Although I would have preferred not to devote airtime to

Shockley's views, which I found repulsive, my job required me to ask thorough questions while keeping my opinions to myself. My feelings for the subject weren't supposed to matter.

Easier said than done when my subject came from outside the human species—I must confess I'm not really much of an animal lover: unable to recover from my childhood encounters with animals, I've been known to shrink in fear in the presence of a Chihuahua. Nonetheless, being a local TV personality obligated me to meet and greet a host of critters.

During a visit to Marine World/Africa USA, I posed with a smile masking sheer terror as a killer whale splashed out of his tank to give my cheek a "kiss." But even that wasn't enough.

One day while I was doing the noon news and we had gone to a commercial break, I was preoccupied with reviewing news copy when a strange movement in my peripheral vision caught my eye. Suddenly, I seemed to be hallucinating: a huge Bengal tiger appeared to be lumbering across the set, headed straight for me. Frantic, I looked for my co-anchor, Dave Fowler, who was missing from his chair. *Where is he? Where is the director? the crew?* In the blinding glare of studio lights, I couldn't make out another living soul—only the unmistakable form of this tiger, body sleek and sinewy, yellow feline eyes focused directly on mine. Paralysis nailed me to my chair. I couldn't shriek, couldn't run. The tiger cocked its head and lifted its enormous padded paw onto the anchor desk.

Everything went black.

When I came to a few seconds later, the studio was echoing with laughter. Dave had his hand on my shoulder; the crew was cracking up; and the tiger's handler had a firm grasp of the chain that I hadn't been able to see around the big cat's neck. Dave liked me, but not as much as he loved the playing of a wicked practical joke.

I had always dreamed of going to the Academy Awards, so I sold KPIX on the notion of sending Steve Paszty and me down to Hollywood for the big night. The station had a miniscule travel budget, but the biggest hitch was figuring out how to get our footage on the air on Oscar night: in 1970, local TV stations did not have satellite feed.

So we executed our "coverage" like clockwork. We would work a regular shift, and then at 4:00 p.m. we would catch a cheap PSA flight to Los

Angeles. I would make a mad dash into the airport bathroom and change from my day suit into my pseudo-glamorous evening gown, while Steve rented us a car. Then we would drive to the Dorothy Chandler Pavilion and secure our place behind the rope lines along the red carpet, which by today's standard drew relatively few reporters.

As the stars stepped out of their limousines and strolled by, I would call out their names in hopes they would stop by and answer a question or two: "Mr. Fonda, just a minute please?" "Miss Dunaway, can you tell us which nominee is your favorite?" "Mr. Nicholson, how does it feel to be nominated?" Sometimes they obliged, although neither my queries nor their answers were memorable in the slightest: the Oscars aren't designed to be profound.

Once the stars were ensconced inside, Steve would frame me in a very wide shot, and I would say, "And tonight's winner for best picture was blah-de-blah. The best actor trophy went to blah-de-blah, and the Oscar for best actress went to blah-de-blah." Then we would rush to LAX, catch the next plane bound for San Francisco, and drive so fast to KPIX that I'm relatively certain our car wheels lifted off the ground. Our goal was to get our film "into the soup," so it would be developed in time for the final segment of the 11:00 p.m. newscast. Then I would pull the names of the actual winners off the AP wire and we would edit them in, and viewers would hear me saying the correct names without noticing that my lips were out of sync. At the time, it didn't occur to us that what we were doing was a bit deceptive—we preferred the term *competitive*.

It worked so well that some of my colleagues at the station never quite figured out how I was able to be in two places at once.

While I found entertainment news endlessly fascinating, I could not have cared less about sports. Local television always devotes a sizable chunk of its newscasts to baseball, football, and the like, but I've always had trouble feigning interest in the ongoing litany of lineups and scores.

One evening during the holidays my mind drifted as my co-anchor Ron Magers bantered on-air with sportscaster Barry Tompkins. I was having at least forty people for Christmas dinner; and knowing that the crew seldom framed me into the sportscast shot, I began drafting my shopping list.

Suddenly Ron leaned over to me. "Belva doesn't share our deep interest in sports, so while Barry and I have been talking, she's been hard at work on something else over here," he announced to our audience, picking up my sheet of paper. "Let's see what she's written: *two 25-pound turkeys, 10-pound sack of potatoes, five heads of lettuce . . .* "

I cracked up, thankful that a red face doesn't show through brown skin. I correctly anticipated weeks of teasing in the newsroom and in the aisles of my grocery store.

One of the fringe benefits of journalism is the entree it provides to meet some of the world's most stimulating people.

After covering Senator Robert Kennedy breaking bread with fasting United Farm Workers union head and civil rights leader César Chávez in Delano in 1968, I shared a helicopter ride with the senator while he sought a firsthand look at the abysmal conditions on a Native American reservation outside Yreka. Fog forced our chopper down, and the reservation visit had to be aborted—but being stranded at a remote Northern California airstrip gave us plenty of time to talk. I marveled that we shared such an intense interest in the plight of Indian people.

Kennedy had been on a national poverty tour and was helping to expose the appalling realities of Indian life: Residents of one-third of California's reservations lacked clean drinking water, and Native Americans here had an average life expectancy of only forty-two years. My reports would be packaged into an award-winning weeklong series in 1969 titled *Nothing Left but Pride*. The story was the sort I gravitated toward because it exemplified my determination to give a voice to the voiceless. Kennedy had somehow acquired the same motivation in politics. While my empathy flowed from my own life struggles, Kennedy attained empathy despite having grown up in posh circumstances.

On other days, after I signed off from anchoring the noon news, I would answer my phone and strain to hear, through the static, a deep voice that sounded halfway around the world—which it was. My caller was Alex Haley, patched through from some freighter traversing the Pacific or the Indian Ocean. I had met the author of *The Autobiography of Malcolm X* at one of celebrity lawyer Melvin Belli's mod bashes, and shortly thereafter Haley had shipped out as the lone paying passenger on a freighter—his favorite mode of travel because it gave him the time and space to finish the novel that had vexed him for years. Soon he began to phone me, first asking for a recap of the day's news, and then talking about his project. He seemed to need to verbalize his manuscript before committing it to paper.

He aimed to trace his own family lineage back to a Gambian named Kunte Kinte, who was kidnapped, shackled, transported across the sea to Maryland, and sold into slavery.

The book, of course, would become an international best seller and win a Pulitzer Prize. Later, Bill and I were guests at Haley's hillside house in Jamaica where we heard his typewriter clacking all through the night, while he finalized negotiations with ABC to produce a miniseries based on the book. By morning the deal was struck, and Haley was beaming as he led the way down to pristine Negril Beach, where his bright yellow seaside home was located and a boat named Roots rested on the sand. He invited us to join him wading waist-high into the Caribbean, and he exulted that he could still clearly see his toes. He had more reason to celebrate than even he knew: the miniseries *Roots: The Saga of an American Family* would shatter viewership records and instill in black Americans a new sense of pride in their complex, valiant history.

When Ronald Reagan was governor, I visited him in his Sacramento home, watching his whimsy as he played with toy trains in his basement. I accompanied Nancy Reagan to his capitol office as she filled a bowl on his desk with jelly beans. I sipped tea at a "ladies only" press event with a white-gloved First Lady Pat Nixon and her daughters. I even chatted briefly with then president Richard Nixon in a receiving line. But I impressed my daughter far more by scoring an interview with five shy brothers who were wrapping up a weeklong run of performances at San Carlos's Circle Star Theater.

The year was 1974, and while the Jackson 5 was still a family affair, the youngest, Michael, already was on the fast track to superstardom with solo recordings of "Ben" and "Rockin' Robin."

"She looks just like Mama, don't she?" he asked his brothers as I introduced myself. And then, more insistently, "Don't she look just like Mama!" as though encouraging each of his brothers to share his vision of a woman exactly like their mother—but the difference was that I was sitting backstage with them at that very moment. I could only imagine how the Jacksons, who were spending their young lives in strange hotel rooms across the country, must have yearned for the presence of their mom.

"Your mother would probably laugh if she heard you say I look like her," I said with a laugh, "because she is much prettier than I am."

I worked my way through a few routine questions, and then I asked whether they had yet visited San Francisco.

"No," one of them replied. "We sure would like to go and buy some jeans, but the stores are always closed when we get off."

I had a brainstorm: Darolyn had just been promoted to assistant manager of Tops and Trousers, a jeans shop on Union Square. The store closed at nine o'clock, but she usually stayed late to close the books. I reached her and explained the situation, asking if she could get permission to reopen the store later so Michael and the other Jacksons could go jeans shopping. She hesitated a millisecond—she was only fifteen and hadn't been truthful about her age when she interviewed for the job, so she was trying to keep a low profile. But the prospect of meeting the Jackson 5 was irresistible.

She agreed. Their limo arrived, and they went on a late shopping spree. She told me later that they couldn't have been more polite.

I got my first crack at interviewing a sitting president when Gerald Ford made a swing through California. The date was September 22, 1975, and security was tight. Less than three weeks earlier, Ford had dodged a would-be assassin's bullet in Sacramento—the bullet fired by Lynette "Squeaky" Fromme, a follower of Charles Manson and his murderous "Manson Family." For Ford's visit to San Francisco, the Secret Service barred reporters and photographers from his proximity.

But KPIX was an exception. It was owned by Westinghouse Electric Corporation, whose executives had already arranged for several of its broadcast journalists to have an afternoon sit-down with the president inside the elegant MacArthur Suite at the St. Francis Hotel. We prepped for days to maximize our thirty-minute allotment with the president, preparing broad-ranging questions: Fromme's assassination attempt, an ill-fated swine flu vaccination campaign, and his appointment of John Paul Stevens to the Supreme Court. Our hope was to prod him into saying something that would give us a scoop. We wanted Gerald Ford to make big news that day.

As it turned out, he did—but whatever he said to us would swiftly be rendered so irrelevant that I don't even recall it.

I do remember that Gerald Ford was exactly what I expected: He looked like an average guy, he sounded like an average guy, he acted like an average guy. We took our places in a semicircle of upholstered chairs, and he sat in front—affably fielding our queries. Next, our photographers moved to shoot cutaways of us over the president's broad shoulders. Then we all stood, and Ford began moving around the room, making his farewells, shaking everyone's hand—*every* hand, that is, *except mine.*

As Ford headed out that door I stood aside awkwardly, my eyes darting around the room to see whether any of my colleagues had noticed the obvious slight. But before he got far down the hall, he seemed to realize his oversight and its potential ramifications: I was the only person of color in the room. The president did an about-face, strode back in, and headed for me with his hand outstretched. I instantly forgave him for what must have been an inadvertent omission, and he gave me a warm smile. A minute later, he walked out of the hotel's Post Street entrance toward a waiting sedan. Watching overhead from the windows of the suite, our KPIX contingent heard the pop of what sounded like a firecracker; we watched as two beefy Secret Service agents and then chief of staff Donald Rumsfeld threw themselves on top of the president and thrust him into the car before it roared away.

In the crowd below was a middle-aged misfit named Sarah Jane Moore, a small-time FBI informant and dabbler in radical politics who felt ostracized by all sides and hoped the assassination of Ford would provoke a revolution. One of her public defenders would later characterize her conduct that day as rather like a to-do list: "Take my son to school, shoot the President, pick up my son from school . . . "

The bullet she fired at Ford from a .38 caliber revolver ricocheted off the hotel entrance, slightly injuring a bystander. Moore was then wrestled to the ground by a disabled ex-marine, Oliver Sipple, who found himself at the epicenter of controversy when press reports noted that he was gay. His sexual orientation came as news to his family, and he later sued—without success—for invasion of privacy.

This second attempt on Ford's life meant we had our big story—but the Secret Service immediately locked down the St. Francis, so we were barricaded inside the MacArthur Suite. Initially the hotel switchboard was shut down, so we couldn't even call KPIX to tell our own newsroom what had happened. We were climbing the walls, but to no avail.

By the time agents finally permitted us to leave, the story was everywhere. We had little to add. My coworkers joked that perhaps I was Ford's talisman: Had he not returned to shake my hand, Moore might have had a clearer shot and hit her mark.

Later I was among the first reporters to garner an interview with Sarah Jane Moore, who would end up spending more than three decades behind bars. Nothing she told me made it any easier to decipher her convoluted motive.

The national president of Westinghouse Broadcasting, Don McGannon, was an advocate for diversity and astute news programs. During the Vietnam War, he even flew there personally to get a look at life on the ground. On his return, he had a long layover at San Francisco's airport, and KPIX dispatched me to talk to him about his trip. I was nervous about interviewing the corporate overlord of my TV station; but I discovered him to be a pleasant man who knew more about me than I could have imagined. Yet I was so unsophisticated that I soon found myself confessing to him how inadequate I felt because I lacked a college education.

"What in the world was I thinking?" I reproached myself later that night. "I think I just committed career suicide."

To the contrary, a few days later I received a cordial, handwritten letter from McGannon. In it, he included a veritable honor roll of accomplished, famous Americans who had not finished college. I almost wore the paper out from reading it over and over.

Our tiny KPIX newsroom was a cluttered agglomeration of shared desks, battered typewriters, clattering wire machines, reams of paper files, and newsmen who were walking clichés—cigarettes dangling from their sardonic mouths. Any class it lacked, we absorbed from our masters: As a CBS affiliate, our station received annual visits from venerable network anchor Walter Cronkite, aka "the most trusted man in America." These visits were a point of pride for him—he'd talk with local reporters and anchors, not only about news values, but about personal matters, such as how to parent in our high-pressured world and the importance of never taking ourselves too seriously.

One day my young co-anchor Ron Magers wistfully said to me, "It's kind of awful to think you may be working at the best place you will ever work in your entire life, and you're only twenty-three years old." I don't know if that proved to be the case for him—Ron went on to become the most popular anchor in Chicago. But those years at KPIX were something special. I know in my case, he was absolutely right.

fourteen

. . .

A Woman's Touch

Television still was very much a boy's club at the dawn of the 1970s. Network and local TV executives were virtually all male. Three-quarters of the characters on prime time dramas were men. And males held more than 85 percent of on-air news jobs.

Frankly, the guys calling the shots had trouble figuring out what to do with women: NBC censors ruled that *I Dream of Jeannie* star Barbara Eden's midriff costume could never reveal her navel; CBS executives insisted that newswoman Mary Richards on *The Mary Tyler Moore Show* could not be divorced; and at least thirty TV stations dropped the sitcom *Maude* when its lead character had an abortion.

Nor did TV news tend to tackle serious subjects that were considered "women's issues." Childcare, health, education, reproductive rights, and other topics of pressing concern to women probably would have been rejected as unworthy of much coverage in a serious newscast, had women been enough of a force in the newsroom to suggest them.

"Other institutions push envelopes," Syracuse University pop culture professor Robert Thompson once keenly observed. "Television licks the envelope only when it's safe to do so."

In this milieu, I took a call one day from Rhoda Goldman, great-grandniece of Levi Strauss, and one of California's most prominent philanthropists. She said she had something important to discuss and wanted to meet for lunch. My schedule was crammed that week, but I proposed that we meet at the station instead.

What I did not know at the time was that Rhoda had battled breast cancer and had a mastectomy; the experience left her appalled at how oblivious the male-dominated medical establishment often was to the psychological toll the disease and its treatment takes on women. She had cofounded the

San Francisco branch of Reach for Recovery and had become its first volunteer—determined that no woman should face the disease alone.

She told me how she would meet with women diagnosed with breast cancer, and she would share her experience and counsel them about their options. If they needed a mastectomy, she would visit their hospital rooms after the surgery—in she would come, toting small rubber balls they could squeeze to exercise their muscles for faster and more complete healing.

"Our greatest need is for better education," she said. "If you could give people information about early detection and the value of treatment, you could help erase the awful stigma around breast cancer. You could literally save lives."

I was acutely aware of the stigma, and I wondered aloud whether we could ever convince women to talk on-camera about having their breasts surgically removed. Rhoda Goldman promised to serve as a liaison to patients and help persuade them to go public with their stories.

As co-anchor of the noon news, I pitched the story to my producer, Roxanne Russell. Granted, when KPIX first hired Roxanne fresh out of the UC Berkeley School of Journalism, I took one look at her sitting in the editing bay in her miniskirt and flatly rejected my boss's brainstorm to team us together. I was wary of the station creating a "girl's ghetto"—sticking its only female reporter with its most inexperienced editor for no reason other than our sharing the same gender. But my first impression was dead wrong: Roxanne was sharp as a stiletto and had excellent news judgment. Her fast promotion to producer of KPIX's *Noon News* was only the first of many career advancements for a woman who would eventually produce for every CBS Network news program.

The two of us readily agreed: breast cancer is one of the top killers of women. It didn't merely deserve a story; it deserved a weeklong series and ongoing coverage.

Through Rhoda Goldman, I contacted and interviewed a thirty-two-year-old woman who had left her family in the Midwest and moved alone to an apartment on the edge of Pacific Heights in San Francisco; she had no one close to confide in when she'd received the diagnosis, and she opted against telling her family. Her doctor warned her that removal of her breast via a radical mastectomy might be the only way to save her life.

Her reaction embodied everything Rhoda Goldman had warned about.

The woman told me, "I want to fall in love. I want to get married. I want to have children. And I feel like if I agree to this surgery—if I let them disfigure me—I'll never have any of those things."

We reporters train ourselves to detach emotionally from our subjects, but sometimes it is impossible to do. This was one of those times. I couldn't get this woman out of my mind. I talked to her about the medical consequences of refusing surgery; I passed along written material; and I tried to make her see that she could have a rich life without her breasts.

She refused to believe it, rejecting a mastectomy and even the less invasive lumpectomy. Vitality drained out of her day by day.

In a matter of months after our interview, she was dead.

Her death haunted me—and gave me more resolve to tackle the taboos of breast cancer.

My reporting persuaded me that self-examination was an important key to early detection, but that most women didn't know how to properly examine their own breasts for telltale lumps. Clearly, one part of our series should include a straightforward depiction of a self-exam. But how to show that on television?

The most obvious option was no option at all: nudity on the newscast was a no-no. We tried filming a woman doing an exam fully dressed, but that didn't work—viewers wouldn't be able to really see what she was doing beneath her clothing. Then we got the idea to dress her in a leotard: the outlines of her breasts would be visible, and viewers would receive a relatively clear how-to demonstration, but all done in good taste.

Some of the men in the newsroom were already skeptical of our plan for a "booby series." When the news director got wind of our leotard idea, he was horrified. Film a woman squeezing and massaging her breasts, and air that on the local newscast? He balked.

But Roxanne and I fought back. This was *our* story. *Our* newscast. *Our* bodies. *Our* lives. We weren't willing to let squeamish men overrule us. "Don't you realize," we demanded, "that this is tasteful? Don't you realize that this is important? Don't you realize that this is news?"

To his credit, the news director decided to seek a second opinion, that of station general manager Bill Osterhaus. As Roxanne and I hovered anxiously outside the door, Osterhaus strode into the editing room and ordered the editor, "Roll it."

We could hear the clicking of film moving through the viewer. Roxanne and I exchanged looks, both of us secretly noting the irony that the fate of this critical "women's issue" rested with men.

Then Osterhaus emerged into the hallway and shot me a smile. "Run with it," he said.

Our series generated a huge response, particularly from women, and it went on to win a local Emmy. For the first time, a "women's issue" story had garnered the award.

Breast cancer, of course, is not just a women's issue, although it is a hundred times more common in females. Our series also broke the even greater taboo of male breast cancer.

To do so, I interviewed a man who talked about how his diagnosis had affected his life. He stressed that men also should pay attention to their bodies—for example, feeling in the shower for any unusual nodules in their chests.

At the man's request, we filmed him in silhouette and slightly altered his voice. He had agreed to the interview on condition that I keep his identity a secret. Viewers might have wrongly presumed that the man sought anonymity because the disease embarrassed him. Actually, he feared that going public with any potentially life-threatening cancer might scare away the investors so necessary to the success of his new business venture, which was on the verge of going public: a chain of jeans stores named Gap.

Don Fisher went on to live thirty-seven very full years after my series aired. He became a legend in retailing, developing companies including Banana Republic and Old Navy—he was the first retailer in history to reach $1 billion in sales in less than four years. Since its initial offering in 1973, Gap's stock has split nine times. After he died in 2009, I ran into his widow, Doris. She thanked me for keeping his secret all these years, and we agreed that he would want his full story told now.

A retired beer salesman and civil service commissioner named Dan Casentini phoned KPIX asking for me one afternoon in 1976. He was a regular viewer, noticed that I often contributed health reports to the daily newscasts, and wanted to know whether I had ever done a piece about heart bypass surgery. I hadn't and asked what prompted his call.

"It's my heart," he said. "I'm fifty-five years old, and my doctor says if I want to live to see fifty-six, I need to have this operation. But let them cut me open like that? I just don't know. What do you think, Belva—what should I do?"

What he didn't know was that I had suffered from hypertension since I was nineteen years old—and it had kept me hospitalized and sedated for a week after the birth of my son. My heart went out to this man. I was touched that he had such faith in me, but I wasn't qualified to give anyone medical advice. Before I knew it, I heard myself offering to call his doctor and do some research into his condition.

When we spoke again, I told him that the decision was his. "But," I said, "Mr. Casentini, if I had your prognosis, I would absolutely have this surgery."

"I really do want more time with my children and my grandchildren," he mused. "And my dream is to return to Italy—to Lucca, where my father, Guido, was born . . ." His voice trailed off, leaving silence on the other end of the line.

At last he spoke: "I'll do it under one condition: You come into the operating room with me. And bring your TV camera with you—that way I know they're gonna do it right."

I was intrigued, although I knew this wasn't going to be easy. I needed to secure the approval of Casentini's family, his health insurance company, his personal physician, and the surgical team, not to mention the hospital administration at St. Mary's Medical Center in San Francisco. But Dan Casentini was so adamant that they all acquiesced to his wish.

While he prepared for the operation, I assembled the other components of a series to educate viewers about cardiac health. I learned that one out of every ten Americans at that time suffered from high blood pressure, and that its death rate for blacks was from three to twelve times higher than for whites. I included a list of local spots offering free blood pressure screening. I interviewed surgeon Elias Hanna about the procedure, which involved taking a vein from Casentini's thigh and using that to repair his heart. My report even incorporated an excerpt of a public service film in which the Supremes, in sparkly beaded evening gowns, harmonized about hypertension:

It hits the sisters and it hits the brothers,
Black folks seem to get it more than others . . .

On the day of Casentini's surgery, my cameraman and I donned surgical scrubs and masks, and we followed Dr. Hanna into the operating room. I sucked in my breath when his scalpel slid neatly down the patient's chest in its initial incision. But I didn't flinch throughout the procedure, not even when they lifted the heart from its chest cavity. I was surprised by the piped-in jazz music and the chatter as doctors talked about the weather and their golf games. *ER* and *CSI* weren't around yet, and suffice it to say, they never showed anything this realistic on *Marcus Welby, M.D.*

Two days later, I returned to St. Mary's to interview a recuperating Casentini. He acknowledged his habits of smoking three packs a day, drinking more than he should, and carrying around too much stress—all confessed in hopes that others could learn from his mistakes. "I feel like I've come back from the dead . . . I mean it, Belva," he told me.

The final step before broadcast was to edit all these pieces into a coherent series. Producer George Osterkamp and I knew that some people in the newsroom were highly skeptical about airing graphic film of an operation in living color, particularly during the dinner hour. We wanted to demystify this relatively new medical procedure, but we also knew that much of the footage we shot could never be broadcast.

As we went to work in the editing bay, we were mindful of one question: How far can we go without going too far?

Curiously, watching some of the raw footage was more disturbing to me than being physically present in the operating room. In fact, while reviewing the film in the editing room, I started to get woozy. A cold sweat crept over me, and I had to excuse myself to the ladies' room and dab at my face with damp paper towels to tamp down the nausea. Ultimately, we selected our footage with discretion and omitted anything our news director felt was too edgy. On the night the surgery footage aired, I also appeared at the anchor desk to warn viewers that anyone troubled by the sight of blood might not want to watch.

While KPIX fielded some complaints, they paled in comparison to the positive response from those in the audience who found the series informative and even potentially life-saving.

Casentini's daughter Donna Ames-Heldfond later told me how much Casentini enjoyed the extra years he had with his children and grandchildren—and how grateful she was for the opportunity she was given to let her father know just how much she loved him.

A couple of years after the story aired, I received a package from Dan Casentini himself, and it provided unmistakable proof that he had fulfilled his dream. Inside was a gold locket in the shape of a heart, delicately inscribed with the word *Lucca*.

Another consequence of the addition of women in the newsroom was the stunning revelation that parenting issues could be newsworthy. One of my contributions was inspired by my daughter being diagnosed with dyslexia.

Darolyn had been struggling at her El Cerrito elementary school. At first we attributed this to the school district's undergoing busing to achieve racial balance in its classrooms, which put stresses on teachers and students alike. But she described her effort to read as a battle in which she strained to decipher words and sentences from letters that floated around on the page. We were fortunate that her regular pediatrician at Kaiser Permanente in Oakland, Dr. Joseph Rosenthal, also specialized in learning disabilities and could correctly assess what she needed.

Our family's experience prompted me to push KPIX to devote fifty minutes of airtime over five nights in 1973 to a series we called "It's a Shame . . . He Just Can't Read." With George as producer and Steve as my cameraman, I reported and narrated an in-depth look at learning disabilities that targeted the many children who had never been properly diagnosed or received the treatment that would enable them to read.

By relating my own experience as a mother, I persuaded other parents that I would tell this story with sensitivity and respect. At one point in the series, I appeared in a stand-up and got personal: "Like many parents, we didn't discover that our child had a reading problem until late in elementary school—just about the time she was finishing the sixth grade . . . "

The piece included scenes of Dr. Rosenthal coaching other children and admonishing them to remember that, no matter what, they were not "dumb." It featured interviews with psychiatrist Robert Ornstein of the Langley Porter Psychiatric Hospital and Clinics, who performed an on-camera EEG of my skull to illustrate which parts of my brain activate when performing different tasks such as writing a letter and building a pattern with blocks.

But the core power of the series emanated from interviews with dyslexic patients themselves. One cherubic girl with blonde curls explained her frustration that other children in her class read "smooth," while she read "jumpy." A dyslexic adult, filmed from behind, over her shoulder—because she was too embarrassed to be identifiable—talked tearfully about her shame at being unable to ever read. And a brilliant man who had designed the geodesic dome inside San Francisco's Exploratorium science museum discussed how difficult it had been for him to land a job because his dyslexia sabotaged his attempts to complete written job applications.

The series garnered my third Northern California Emmy, edging out more traditional reports about crimes, fires, and violence. But it did something more important.

Women like me were bringing the concerns and passions of our everyday lives into the newsroom, and we were demanding that attention be paid. We were ready to stop licking envelopes and start pushing them. In so doing, we would expand and enhance the very definition of the word *news* forever.

fifteen

. . .

When Work Hits Home

We felt fortunate that our family emerged relatively unscathed from the 1970s—which is rather ironic to say, considering we were driven from our home after a biker gang of white supremacists plotted to kidnap our teenage daughter.

Nonetheless we fared better than many others in the San Francisco Bay Area who paid a far greater price during what was to be a harrowing decade, drenched in a senseless violence that seemed to seep toward the edge of apocalyptic: The Zebra murders. The Symbionese Liberation Army abductions, armed robberies, and shootings. The cult exodus and mass suicides of Jonestown. The assassination of San Francisco's mayor and first openly gay supervisor. Real life too often resembled the melodramatic movie trailer "In a world gone mad . . . "

For six months beginning in the fall of 1973, San Francisco and its environs were unnerved by faceless assailants who unleashed random yet deadly attacks on everyday people doing everyday activities. Homicide inspectors who worked the case would characterize it as "the opening of the gates of hell"—it was, indeed, one of the most ruthless and prolonged cases of domestic terrorism in U.S. history.

The Zebra killers first struck one October evening, targeting a young white couple strolling hand in hand down Telegraph Hill. Two young black men in business attire forced Richard and Quina Hague into a white utility van, ordered them to lie down face-first on furniture pads and bound their hands with twine, while a third man drove the van to a relatively deserted section of Southern Pacific Railroad. Then, dragging them to the tracks, the men attacked with machetes, leaving Richard for dead and all but decapitating Quina. He barely survived, but she did not. In fact, in the words of San Francisco Homicide Inspector Earl Saunders, she looked like "a painting hacked at by some madman." Saunders, who would someday become the city's first African American police chief, examined her wounds during the autopsy and concluded that they bespoke "a hate beyond reason."

In the following weeks, victims were shot in a pay-phone booth, at a Laundromat, Christmas shopping. One day in January, five random shootings occurred in a single day. Now on high alert, baffled police designated a special radio frequency, the Z band, for the case—Z as in *zebra*, giving the case its tabloid-worthy tag.

But the name zebra conjured up an image more chillingly precise: black against white. For as the killings piled up, each echoed the pattern of the Hague incident: every victim was white, and the killers or would-be killers were invariably described as well-dressed young black men.

As anxiety mounted, San Francisco's mayor at the time, Joseph Alioto, authorized police to stop and search all young black men who stood more than six feet tall with a short Afro and a narrow chin—a description that fit thousands of local blacks, including our son Steven, whom we told not to travel from our El Cerrito home to San Francisco. In fact, roughly five hundred African American men unconnected to the attacks were detained before U.S. district judge Alphonso Zirpoli ruled the dragnet unconstitutional.

As two of the few African Americans working in the local news media, Bill and I waged an ongoing debate about the personal and professional complications of the Zebra story. I was in a position similar to that of Southern white reporters who covered the civil rights demonstrations in the 1960s— always mindful that my color would determine the trust some would place in my reporting. Bill displayed laminated press placards across his windshield; he mounted several radio antennae on his car; and he draped his two-way-radio microphone over the arm of the rearview mirror, as police were known to do. The purpose, he explained was "to let the cops know I'm not a crook, and let the crooks know I'm not a cop!"

Moreover, what the police had anticipated finally happened: the murder of a young black man by two whites driving by in a pickup truck—a random reprisal for the Zebra rampage.

At least fifteen people would die and eight others would be seriously injured before police cracked the case with the help of an accomplice-turned-informant. They traced the methods behind the madness to a renegade group of local Black Muslims calling themselves "Death Angels." These cold souls didn't consider their victims human beings—they simply called them "blue-eyed devils"—and their aim was to kill as many as possible to earn more points toward paradise.

Among those arrested was Larry Green, who hailed from a respected family a few blocks from my mother's home in Berkeley. He and three code-fendants faced a trial that lasted longer than any previous trial in California history; but after a year and six days, a jury found them guilty on all counts and they were given life sentences.

The police had not been so successful at capturing a serial killer known as the Zodiac. That case, in which the killer tauntingly sent coded crypto-grams to the news media, remains unsolved. At least seven people lost their lives in that rampage, which also contributed to the climate of dread that shrouded the city. But while the Zebra and Zodiac killers were still running amok, another brutal murder would shake me more personally.

I had met Marcus Foster in 1970 while covering his hiring as the first African American superintendent of the Oakland Unified School District. A respected Philadelphia educator who'd earned his doctorate from the University of Pennsylvania, he soon impressed Bay Area academics and par-ents alike. He possessed an unwavering determination to motivate students, particularly the underachieving ones.

To me, he represented the fruits of the civil rights struggle.

We'd met as professionals but parted from our first interview as friends. That's why I felt comfortable calling him months later to seek his advice about Darolyn. I was concerned enough as a mother to not worry too much about whether I was crossing some journalistic line.

My daughter was a slim girl with nutmeg-colored skin and big brown eyes, who had inherited my trademark thick, curly hair and inextinguish-able curiosity. Although bright and well-spoken, she was floundering in sixth grade. We didn't know whether to blame the dyslexia or the racial ten-sion, but we knew something had to be done.

"From what you've told me, Darolyn needs to be in a very different school," Foster said. And he had just the place: Lakeside, a small, racially diverse private school in the hills above Oakland that followed a creative, free-form curriculum.

I hesitated. "I'm away all day, and I know Oakland is close by, but she'd be pretty far from home."

"Darolyn will be fine, Belva," he assured me. "And how about this? I'll keep an eye on her progress myself."

It was a promise he was unable to fulfill. Early on the evening of November 6, 1973, when he and assistant superintendent Robert Blackburn were leaving a school board meeting, three men emerged from the shadows and opened fire. In seconds, they pumped eight cyanide-tipped bullets into Foster's body. Blackburn was shot four times but lived—saved by the skill of a young black resident at Highland Hospital named Coyness Ennix, who worked through the night to save Blackburn's life.

Foster was dead on arrival.

Again, I felt as though the world was slowly loosening its grip on sanity. Who could have done such a thing?—and why?

The answers served only to raise more questions. An obscure cadre calling itself the Symbionese Liberation Army issued a communiqué taking credit for Foster's killing. The group offered the explanation that he deserved to die because he had supported police patrols on Oakland campuses and the issuing of photo ID cards to high school students. What proved to be a defining characteristic of the SLA was that the group bungled its mission: Foster had actually withdrawn support for the IDs and had stated that he would not allow police on school premises.

Within two months, authorities arrested two white SLA members who would ultimately be convicted of Foster's murder. The SLA itself, which claimed to be at the vanguard of a black revolution, actually consisted of a small band of white self-styled guerrilla warriors and one black spokesman, a prison escapee named Donald DeFreeze who demanded to be addressed as "General Field Marshall Cinque" after the African leader of the historic *Amistad* slave ship revolt.

With an obtuse logic typical of the times, the SLA's manifesto declared, "Our name 'symbionese' is taken from the word 'symbiosis' and we define its meaning as a body of dissimilar bodies and organisms living in deep and loving harmony and partnership in the best interest of all within the body."

On the day of Foster's funeral, I dragged myself home, struggling to resist the pull of a vortex of despair. I couldn't comprehend how the muddled thinking of these militants had, in one erratic burst of violence, cost the children of Marcus Foster their father, and the children of Oakland's public schools the opportunity to benefit from his inspiration. The SLA's other victim, Assistant Superintendent Blackburn, would characterize the army as "a pathetic, mediocre sort of after-spasm of the best part of the 60s." But racial tensions were escalating, and the SLA's recklessness would soon ricochet at angles no one could have envisioned. Among those at risk would be my own daughter.

Many Californians in 1974 regarded heiress Patty Hearst as the embodiment of an American princess. With an aristocratic voice and poised bearing, she hailed from a publishing family of billionaires. Her eccentric grandfather William Randolph Hearst was the inspiration for the film *Citizen Kane*, and he had built San Simeon, a coastal palace so outlandishly lavish that it became a state landmark and top tourist draw. The Hearst family, publisher of the *San Francisco Examiner*, owned one of the largest diversified communication and real estate corporations in the world.

As for Patty, she had left her elite hometown of Hillsborough, on the San Francisco Peninsula, to enroll at UC Berkeley—a campus studded with stately buildings made possible by her family's largesse. At nineteen, she was living in an apartment she shared with her fiancé, graduate philosophy student Steven Weed.

Her family's prominence brought Patty into the crosshairs of the SLA, which concocted a daring scheme to accomplish three goals at once: (1) propel itself to international prominence, (2) lay siege to a family fortress of capitalism, and (3) garner a hostage who would serve as leverage to negotiate the release of the two SLA members in custody over the Marcus Foster slaying.

So on the night of February 4, 1974, two men and a woman knocked on Patty's apartment door and forced their way in. "Bitch," one of them spat out, "better be quiet or we'll blow your head off." Bludgeoning Patty's fiancé with a wine bottle and spraying the apartment with gunfire, they bound, gagged, and blindfolded her in her bathrobe, and shoved her into the trunk of their getaway car.

In the Bay Area, the ongoing kidnap story was big enough to compete with the nation's other top story: the Watergate scandal's unraveling of Richard Nixon's presidency. Patty's father, Randolph Hearst, signaled that he would meet the demands of his daughter's kidnappers.

Quickly abandoning its preposterous hopes for a prisoner swap, the SLA instead ordered the Hearst family to spend its fortune feeding California's poor. Patty's father may have had the will and the wallet to comply—the family launched a $2 million food giveaway program—but fights broke out at some distribution points and Cinque dismissed the effort as "crumbs."

As a mother of a teenage daughter myself, I empathized with Mrs. Hearst's anguish. I made a deliberate effort to distance myself emotionally when, in an exclusive interview with my co-anchor Dave Fowler, she broke her silence and pled for her daughter's life. But I also knew that the black people lining up for free food were no different from the relatives who once joined me in sharing a basement floor for a bed. My life as a television anchor was eons away from my impoverished past—but that past continued to inform my work. While KPIX and the rest of the media chased daily developments, I became acutely aware of how the saga refracted race and class: the black figurehead Cinque issuing communiqué demands to the rich white parents; the poor blacks who gathered at the food giveaways, sometimes desperate for anything they could grab; and the Hearsts suffering in silence as squadrons of reporters camped outside their elegant estate. Our station closely followed the story, first with the noon news and often with live updates on developments.

And then, a jaw-dropping twist.

The SLA released an audiotape that featured the previously apolitical Patty brusquely scolding her parents, criticizing "fascism in America," and declaring that "The SLA is very annoyed about attempts by authorities to turn this into a racial issue. It's not. This is a political action they have taken." Next she walked into a bank in San Francisco's Sunset District brandishing a carbine rifle during an SLA holdup—and, although she didn't fire any shots, two bystanders were wounded before she and the robbers fled with ten thousand dollars.

Her parents' insistence that she had participated under duress was undercut when a photograph showed up that displayed Patty toting a rifle beneath the seven-headed cobra symbol of the SLA. The evidence also included a recording in which she declared that she had joined the SLA and taken the name Tania in honor of an ally of Che Guevara.

The attorney general deemed her a willing participant in the bank robbery and issued a warrant for her arrest. Next, "Tania" went on the lam.

And then suddenly and insidiously, the distance between my emotional and professional lives constricted further.

A Richmond police officer phoned me at KPIX, vaguely warning me to be vigilant about Darolyn's safety. He said the police would be back in touch if they could substantiate a specific threat.

Although Bill and I alerted teachers and neighbors—and we ourselves lost some sleep—we continued life as usual.

A few weeks later, the bell rang just before I left for work, and I opened our front door to find an El Cerrito policeman on my porch. At first I thought he was passing along information for some story. But then he posed a question that made me feel as though he were plunging my head into a bucket of ice water.

"Do you have a daughter that attended El Monte School?"

I passed into that panic-induced time warp where everything slows down. Part of my brain realized I was inviting him inside, but another part strained to pick up confirmation that Darolyn still was safely down the hall. I felt a surge of relief when I heard her singing—obliviously off-key as usual. I imagined her primping at the bathroom mirror before racing to gather her books. In a moment, she'd rush in, kiss me good-bye, and dash off to meet her best friend, Roberta, for some gossip before school. Only that wouldn't happen that morning: her young life was about to change. "We have reason to believe that there is a credible threat against your daughter," the officer was saying. "She may be marked as a target for kidnapping."

My hands began to tremble. I had prided myself on standing strong even in the crucible of riots, but now I felt my courage evaporate.

Darolyn rounded the corner and gave the policeman sitting on the white velvet living-room couch a friendly, inquisitive smile. I reverted to autopilot, adopting an air of assurance even amid chaos. Offering an upbeat smile, I introduced them without offering an explanation, allowing her to believe we had been discussing news business. She wasn't ready to hear the truth, and I wasn't ready to tell it to her.

"Dee Dee—," and seeing her frown, I broke off. For the past few weeks, she had been reminding me to drop the nickname; she was too grown up for that now. I started again.

"Darolyn, I'm going to drive you to school today. We'll have some girl time."

Her face twisted in annoyance. "But I have to meet—"

"Darolyn," I interrupted in a sharper tone, catching her eye. Surmising that further argument would be futile, she stomped back to her room and shut her door.

I returned my attention to the policeman in my living room and dropped my voice. "Who on earth would want to kidnap my daughter?"

He toyed with his cap, running a finger inside the band. "As far as we can tell, the threat is coming from members of a faction of the Hell's Angels."

"The Hell's Angels? The motorcycle gang?" I was incredulous.

When he nodded, my questions tumbled out. "Why would they go after my daughter? I haven't ever even done a story about them."

The officer's gaze signaled that I needed to let him finish. "As far as we can pick up, this would be in retaliation for the Patty Hearst kidnapping."

"Why—" I halted, flabbergasted. But if the past few years on the job had taught me anything, it was that rational explanations for mayhem were hard to come by.

"Ma'am, these guys are thugs," he continued. "They're pretty angry about a white girl being kidnapped by this black SLA radical who calls himself Cinque, and they've been talking about wanting to 'even the score' by taking a black girl. Also, they think you're Angela Davis's sister."

I blinked in disbelief. This scene would have been farcical had it not been so frightening. Did these faceless bikers really think Davis was such a rare surname that the mere fact that Angela and I shared the name and dark skin was proof that we were sisters? The Marxist academic with the signature Afro had, of course, become one of the most controversial women in the world when, after a dramatic FBI capture in 1970s, she was tried and acquitted on kidnapping and homicide charges stemming from the Marin County shoot-out in 1972. The noon news that I anchored had become a main source of daily developments on that story too, and I had interviewed her—but that was the extent of our connection.

The officer promised to monitor our home and Darolyn's school.

For the next few days, I tried to convince myself that the threat wasn't real—that someone had overheard a bunch of redneck drunks muttering threats into their beer and had overreacted by contacting the police. Seeking a second opinion from the savvier cops in San Francisco, Bill and I contacted Inspector Saunders, a personal friend who had helped wrap up the Zebra case.

He promised to look into it, and he soon called back to say that whether the source of the threat was the Hell's Angels or the Aryan Brotherhood, the threat was indeed real. "I'm not going to tell you everything I discovered," he began. "You don't need to hear it all. But believe me when I say that there's real reason to be careful."

"What do you mean by careful?" Bill asked warily. "The police are keeping an eye on our house; her brother's watching her every step. Belva and I are getting home from work earlier. You're saying we should be more careful than that?"

"Yeah, more careful than that. You'll never forgive yourself if . . ."

My mind was racing. What should we do? Where should we go? Earl suggested he could arrange better protection if we relocated to San Francisco. When the conversation ended, Bill hung up the extension and joined me in the kitchen. "Can I get you something?" he asked, wanting to soothe me and not yet realizing I was beyond that possibility.

"How about tea?" I said, and then buried my face in my hands. "It's my fault, you know. This would never have happened if I wasn't on TV."

"Stop it!" Bill ordered, pointing his index finger at me. "You do your job well, and that's what you're supposed to do. That's why you're a symbol. This is not your fault."

He wrapped his arms around my shoulders, and just as quickly released me and began pacing the floor, growling under his breath. "Racist bastards—who the hell do they think they are?"

The more we talked it through, the more we decided we should get out of El Cerrito. If a bunch of bikers had their sights on Darolyn, we'd make it harder for them to find her.

I didn't need to look around the kitchen and dining room—the scene of so many late-night family suppers—or the living room, where we always decorated our Christmas tree. I didn't need to admire the view from the deck my father had built for us. I needed nothing to remind myself that a house is simply a building. The folks who live within are what make it a home.

We discreetly rented a house in San Francisco three blocks from KPIX; the gorgeous home was on Russian Hill near the city's famous "Crooked

Street." More stylish than our old place, it featured spectacular views and bedroom walls adorned with silk fabrics. But none of this impressed Darolyn.

"Moving? What do you mean, *we're moving*?" she asked, opposition hardening in the pupils of her eyes. "*I'm* not moving."

I arranged for us to tour the exclusive private high school that Inspector Saunders recommended Darolyn attend for her upcoming sophomore year. The alumni of Convent of the Sacred Heart included a roster of influential socialites and future San Francisco mayor and U.S. senator Dianne Feinstein. Among the 120 girls currently attending were then-current mayor Alioto's grandchildren and future mayor George Moscone's daughters—all under the watchful eyes of the SFPD.

When we completed our tour of the school, housed in a Pacific Heights mansion where the students' steps were cushioned by Persian rugs, my daughter turned up her nose and shook her head. "I do not want to go to school with just girls."

Bill and I continued to withhold the full story from her, not wanting to alarm her with details about the kidnap threat. She automatically assumed I was selfish, ripping her away from her childhood home, friends, and boyfriend in El Cerrito simply for the convenience of living closer to my station.

On our last day in El Cerrito, with the moving van loaded and already westward bound across the Bay Bridge, we stepped out of our home and I shut the door. Bill drove our old Mustang convertible downhill, taking his time as we rolled past the neighborhood we loved. We had rented out our house, not knowing whether we were leaving for a short time or forever.

I stole a glance at Darolyn. She tilted her head back to keep from crying. I wanted to apologize for hurting her, and to explain that I was willing to do whatever it took to keep her safe, but my thoughts remained unspoken. Nor could I tell her that, at her age, I would have given anything to hear those words from my own mother's lips. I had never been able to share with her the raw truth about my childhood—our family's curse of noncommunication was passing like an unshared secret from generation to generation.

Besides, my daughter was in no mood to be comforted.

Darolyn would always say that she practically raised herself—an exaggeration encasing a core truth. She was one of those children who seemed like an adult in miniature—mature and capable. At the age of fourteen she secured her first job, working in a Doggie Diner hot dog stand. And she went on to jobs at the St. Francis Hotel, Budget Rent a Car, a men's clothing shop, and Tops and Trousers as assistant manager—all before she graduated from high school. It wasn't that we needed the money; she needed the independence.

Never once did she ask me for a reference—to the contrary, she preferred that her friends and their parents not know she was related to me. Insisting that I park a couple of blocks away when dropping her off at school, she told other people that her mother was a schoolteacher who worked unusually late hours. She made it a point to never watch me on the news. When my face appeared on TV at her friends' houses, Darolyn would pretend she didn't know me.

I knew that she occasionally paid a price for my career, but I told myself that whatever the costs, they were offset by the benefits. How many teenagers had a private meeting with the Jackson 5, or free tickets to any performance they wanted, or the chance to meet newsmakers like Muhammad Ali, Congressman Ron Dellums, and Huey Newton? Steven has always said it was worth it. Darolyn has felt otherwise.

Uprooted from the home she loved, she now smoldered in silent fury. One day I returned to our new home and was aghast to discover that she had taken a tube of red lipstick and scrawled all over the silk wall covering in her bathroom.

We were like two locomotives on course for a head-on collision—and the impact was about to hit full-force. My daughter hurled years' worth of suppressed resentments, recrimination after recrimination flying at me like shards of steel: I never played with her. I never showed up at her school plays and events, but sent surrogates such as her godmother Rose Mary while I chased the next big story. I left in the middle of every holiday celebration to go do a stint at the station. Her friends' mothers stayed home and cared for their children, but I wasn't that kind of mother. She knew Bill would always be there for her, but not me. With me, it was career first—never her.

By the time my daughter reached the end of her indictment and the flying debris had settled, my soul was stinging from fresh perforations. As she stood before me reeking of teenage righteousness, I couldn't even reply—I was too hurt to speak, but too furious as well.

Part of me felt unjustly maligned. I had given Darolyn the kind of enriched, cultured, secure lifestyle that I could have only dreamed of at her age. I had created a warm home, modeled on the archetypes of *Better Homes and Gardens* magazines and *The Donna Reed Show*. My daughter had a beautiful room all her own, with fluffy pillows and a closetful of fashionable clothes. I made sure that we ate almost every dinner together as a family— on real china with cloth napkins—even if occasionally that meant supper so late that I had to wake my children from their beds to bring them to the table. We had storybook holidays: Christmas gift exchanges among the four of us, followed by huge celebrations for relatives and coworkers who were far from home, and sometimes a side trip to Glide Memorial Church to help serve turkey to the homeless. Having lacked holiday celebrations when I was growing up, I was devoted to making them memorable for my children while also instilling in them the importance of sharing our blessings with others.

We had enrolled Darolyn in the toniest school in the city. We escorted her and her friends to concerts and Disneyland, and we took exotic family vacations to the Caribbean. And most important of all, I had found a second husband who was kind and loving and had become a true father to my children.

As close as Bill was to perfect, he wasn't exactly Mr. Aggressive about his career. With my anchor salary, I was our primary wage earner, and I felt the weight of my immediate and extended family economically depending on me. Besides, I hardly think my children would have benefited by my remaining a Clerk II typist.

To add insult to injury, hadn't the thing that so upset Darolyn—this move—been all about her and our willingness to protect her at all costs?

Against all odds, I had somehow managed to provide Darolyn with the kind of life that would have been beyond the wildest fantasies of a girl in the projects, like Belvagene Melton. My own mother never cuddled me, read me bedtime stories, or played house with me—yet I trusted that she loved me. Never had I possessed the sense of entitlement that would lead me to judge her as harshly as my own daughter was now judging me.

But another part of me was willing to consider the possibility that Darolyn was right. With no example of an intimate mother-daughter relationship to follow, I probably had kept my children at arm's length. Although I was compassionate, I didn't have much instinct for intimacy. And given the relentless demands of proving myself as the first black woman in a white man's world, I certainly had erred on the side of compulsive overachievement at work, probably shortchanging my family in the process.

Bill had become my children's prime nurturer. He attended school events, took the children to their doctor's appointments, and drove to pick up their friends and take them all where they wanted to go. He also possessed a natural gene for play that simply was absent from my DNA. Bill and Darolyn gleefully invented a game they called "Ready, Roll": Darolyn would go to bed Friday nights in fresh clothes; and then the two of them would slip out of the house early Saturday morning, leaving me to rest for the day while they drove up the coast to Mendocino or across the bay to the zoo. Another game they called "Hour of Power": Bill would give Darolyn authority over him for an hour, during which she would dream up crazy stunts for him to perform. Once she demanded that he dress up in clothes from my closet and go ring the doorbell of our next-door neighbor—and Bill actually did it!

I would learn later of their co-conspiracy on the rare occasions when I decided Darolyn deserved a spanking. Bill would take her somewhere out of my line of sight and smack his hands together a few times, while she offered up phony cries and cupped her hand over her mouth to suppress the giggles.

Bill and I flipped many of the conventional gender roles, and it more or less worked. I readily acknowledged that I could never have accomplished what I did without his support.

Now I also had to admit to myself that my children had paid a greater price than I ever realized for my journalistic trail blazing. Nor could I expect them to fathom my behavior, considering that I had withheld from them all the emotional trauma of my past.

My key to survival always had been to keep moving forward—fast-forward—stopping only long enough to close doors behind me. I hoped that someday my children would understand.

In the fall of 1975, a tip led police to swarm around a safe house in San Francisco where Patty Hearst and her SLA comrades were living. A KPIX cameraman and I staked out the house, but authorities arrested her a few blocks away when she went out jogging.

She was convicted despite her defense that the SLA brainwashed her by keeping her locked in a closet and repeatedly raping her; her case became one of the most public examples of so-called Stockholm Syndrome. She would serve twenty-two months of a seven-year sentence for armed robbery before then president Jimmy Carter commuted her sentence. Later, on his last day as president, Bill Clinton granted her a full pardon, and the Hearst family's long ordeal at last was over.

Our family heard no more about beefy bikers plotting against my daughter, and we never learned what became of them. Darolyn graduated from Convent of the Sacred Heart, although she never lost her rebellious streak and persisted in rolling up the pleated herringbone skirt of her school uniform to make it a miniskirt the minute she stepped off campus. She did well there and made lasting friends, among them Rebecca Moscone, whose father George had just been elected mayor of San Francisco.

One day CBS called me and invited me to stop in and talk about a possible network job in New York. My old KPIX boss Dave Horowitz by then was working on the network's evening news, and he had recommended me. The first round of interviews went well, and I was to return the next day to discuss a contract offer.

Instead, I boarded a plane with Bill, flew home, and called CBS to say I had decided to stay in San Francisco. Bill and I had put down roots, and we agreed that the life we wanted and loved was here.

My ambition knew bounds after all.

Steven was more forgiving of my career, but it exacted a toll on my son's life as well. Reverberations shook him even after he reached adulthood, when I tackled the most controversial story of my career.

My childhood hometown of Oakland had made progress in the years since the Black Panthers labeled it a bastion of racism: By the mid-1980s, both the mayor and the city manager were African American, and the police force had recruited and promoted more black officers. Yet my sources in the NAACP and the community insisted that the police still applied a double standard in the way they treated white and black citizens—that the blacks were more likely to be stopped, questioned, harassed, and in some cases, beaten, because of the color of their skin.

The term *racial profiling* had not yet burst into the cultural Zeitgeist—in fact, it wouldn't make its appearance in the *New York Times* or *Los Angeles*

Times until the 1990s. But that didn't mean the phenomenon didn't exist; I know, because I was part of one of the first news projects to investigate it.

In the spring of 1984 I had moved to KRON-TV, San Francisco's NBC affiliate. I pitched the story to the news desk, and an editor referred it to our investigative unit. I was paired with a young, high-octane producer named Jon Dann, whose father was a network news executive. Jon was fearless—a guy who felt endowed to crack open the earth if necessary to get the news.

Our collaboration would lead to a three-part series set to air in mid-May. "Stopped for Questioning" reported that Oakland Police were following an aggressive practice of "proactive policing" that included writing tickets for minor offenses and randomly stopping citizens to ask for IDs. While backers said it deterred serious crime, critics said it led to harassment, particularly of blacks. I also reported that five African Americans, represented by attorney Oliver Jones and backed by the NAACP, filed lawsuits claiming Oakland police had beat them without provocation—in the first case settled, the department admitted wrongdoing and paid the victim twenty-one thousand dollars.

But perhaps the most powerful segments of the story were my interviews with a handful of black Oakland Police officers who backed up the claims of a double standard. They told me they were willing to violate the unwritten code of silence among the "blue brotherhood" because some of their fellow officers needed to be reined in. "I have all my brothers and sisters living in Oakland, and I'm afraid for them making a vehicle violation," said then officer Theresa Jeffrey. "Hey, if they run a red light, they might get beat up."

Oakland Police brass was reluctant to speak to us, but we were persistent. Our report included interviews with then police chief George Hart defending his department's policies as fair and effective, and with a black community organizer who supported the police.

The weekend before the series was to air, KRON began running "film noir" promos in which I was shown walking up a deserted alley, the ghetto in shadows behind me, while I talked about potential dangers of unjust policing. In retrospect, I should have insisted that the promos opt for a straight, less sensational tone.

Suffice it to say that when Hart caught the promo, he was so livid he phoned the station's manager at home on Sunday afternoon. By Monday morning, the chief was at KRON demanding that the series be modified or killed before the public could see it—even though *he* hadn't yet seen it. Our meeting was tense, but the station stood by our series and proceeded to broadcast it.

✓ I had underestimated the blowback.

When KRON's staffers made their daily dinner-hour stop at Tommy's Joynt, a hangout near the station, they encountered the cold stares of a large contingent of Oakland cops who had descended on the hofbrau. My colleagues returned grim and grumbling. "Thanks a lot, Belva," one cameraman told me. "We're gonna get the crap beat out of us on any crime story out of Oakland."

The Oakland Police Officers Association called a news conference lambasting our series as "purposely inaccurate, slated and prejudiced," while the Oakland Black Officers Association erupted in civil war between critics and proponents of our reporting. Two UC Berkeley professors wrote an op-ed piece critiquing "Stopped for Questioning" in detail, concluding that the report "did not fully present both sides of this divisive and complex issue." But their critique had flaws of its own, prompting KRON news director Mike Ferring to take the unusual step of writing a point-by-point op-ed rebuttal.

I took pride in my reputation for fair reporting, and I'd never before faced such accusations of bias. Oh, on occasion a crank would write, "Why don't you go back to Africa where you belong?" I didn't give those notes a second thought. But this sort of sustained attack on my journalistic integrity was different. One day after an Oakland police officer was shot and killed in the line of duty—a tragedy that had no connection to our series—someone anonymously mailed me a strip of fabric stained with blood, and a note blaming me for the officer's death.

Fellow cops ostracized the critical black officers interviewed in "Stopped for Questioning." Some of my sources already had sued the department: they claimed they had been wrongly disciplined as "lackadaisical" for writing too few tickets or making too few "suspicious person" stops in what amounted to an illegal "quota system." Five months after the series aired, the U.S. Equal Employment Opportunity Commission ruled in the suing officers' favor.

But that was not to be the end of the story for two of my key sources. Six months before the series had aired, police officers Theresa Jeffrey and John Clark made a foolish mistake: falsely phoning in a sick day immediately before a week's vacation. They both claimed—Clark in his EEOC complaint, and both officers in the course of sworn depositions during a later federal discrimination suit—that they had, in fact, been ill that day. After city attorneys produced phone records showing that both sick calls were made from Iowa, near where the couple went on vacation, a federal judge dismissed their lawsuit. And they were fired, convicted of perjury, and forced by the judge to publish a humiliating public apology. Their attorney John Burris called it "astonishing" that the minor issue of a fudged sick day triggered such an overkill reprisal.

My colleagues at KRON complained to me that police sources were freezing them out, and that they had to remove their KRON press placards from their windshields because they'd become targets for parking tickets.

And I will always believe that someone else was punished as a result of "Stopped for Questioning"—my son.

In the upheaval after the series aired, Steven happened to be driving through Oakland one evening, and he was pulled over by Oakland cops. About thirty years old at the time, he was working in the real estate business and had never been in any trouble with the law.

"What did I do wrong, officers, what did I do?" he kept asking, handing them his driver's license and feeling his nerves fray when they refused to give him an answer. Instead, they handcuffed him and took him to jail. I was at KRON a few hours later when I learned where he was, and I frantically called Bill at KTVU in Oakland to go get him.

When Bill arrived and asked what Steven's offense was, he was told that our son had made an illegal right-hand turn. No charges ever were filed. Later we weren't even able to locate any record of the incident.

Although I have no way to know for certain what to make of the curious stop, I interpreted it as a retribution and a warning. Inside KRON, a debate ensued about whether we should do a follow-up story exploring whether Steven's experience constituted payback for our reporting.

I wasn't about to let one of my children become a pawn in a story this potentially treacherous. My maternal instinct overruled my journalistic one. "No way," I said firmly. "Let's move on."

sixteen

· · ·

White Night and Dark Days

We knew her only as Miss Glover, a heavyset middle-aged woman with cropped hair and ebony skin—but what distinguished her from our previous housekeepers was her ability to move throughout our house without making a sound. She left our rooms spick-and-span. But in retrospect, her stealth should have been a clue that there was more to Miss Glover than met the eye.

I always made a point of establishing a rapport with anyone who worked for us. Miss Glover was my greatest challenge. She kept herself tightly buttoned up and answered my questions with trepidation, as though she suspected my innocuous chatter concealed traps.

Over time, I learned that she had no family left and was selling the house she once owned in California's Central Valley. "Are you sure you want to do that?" I asked her. "You know, it's always good to have a place of your own to go home to someday."

"No ma'am," she said firmly. "We need the money for the work of the church."

Her church was called Peoples Temple, and by the mid-1970s it was attracting hundreds of followers. Its leader was a charismatic reverend who preached an amalgam of utopian Christianity, racial harmony, communal socialism, megalomania, and paranoia. Temple members called him "Father." To the rest of the world, he was the Reverend Jim Jones.

I had first met Jones the day I anchored a KPIX noon news report about an impoverished Mexican boy journeying to the Bay Area for surgery on his cleft palate. Before our program was even off the air, Jones and a coterie of followers materialized in the station lobby with a check for the boy's medical expenses. Jones hoped to present the donation on-air; but I balked, uncomfortable with the idea that I, as a reporter, would become an intermediary for any monetary exchange.

Nonetheless I did meet briefly with Jones, who was so smooth and slick he was almost oily, and his eyes studied me from behind tinted glasses. "We watch you on the Noon News every day, and we have so much respect for what you do and for how well you do it," he gushed. "So we were watching you today, and when you shared the plight of this poor Mexican boy—well, we knew we had to do something to help."

From then on, Jones made himself a regular correspondent of mine, sending frequent notes about newscast reports that he said moved him. He was generating ripples in religious and political circles throughout San Francisco—a mystery man who was siphoning off scores of parishioners from black churches while ingratiating himself to white liberals including mayoral candidate George Moscone. A white preacher who had adopted children of various races, Jones often said, "I'd give anything to be black." Nobody knew quite what to make of him, but nobody was eager to cross him, either.

Curious, Bill and I attended a service at the Peoples Temple on Geary Boulevard, and we were flabbergasted by the church's obsession with security. I watched while members and guests alike were subjected to searches—including a mother who had to open her baby's diaper for inspection. The scene was bizarre, and I murmured as much to a church member standing in the line behind me.

"Well, remember what happened to Brother Malcolm," she said, referencing the Black Muslim leader who was gunned down before a crowd in New York's Audubon Ballroom a decade earlier. "You just can't be too careful anymore."

Bill and I left the Peoples Temple that day with no desire to ever return.

So when Miss Glover told me that she was liquidating her meager assets to give to Peoples Temple, an alarm went off in my head. But I didn't know whether Jones was just a swindler of lonely older women, or something more sinister.

In November 1975, I was among the speakers at the tenth-anniversary celebration of the Reverend Cecil Williams's ministry at Glide Memorial Methodist Church. A dashiki-wearing dynamo who put the social gospel into practice, Williams headed a vibrant, hip congregation in the city's tattered Tenderloin district. Willie Brown, then a state assemblyman, was emcee of the tribute, which also featured Moscone, Angela Davis, then state senator Milton Marks, and Margo St. James, a prostitute who had founded a lobby to legalize her trade.

But the man who stole the show was Jim Jones. Escorted to the dais by bodyguards, Jones knew that Williams had received a death threat that day; and Jones even had proposed having Temple members frisk guests—an offer Williams declined. Now Jones upstaged Williams at his own event. The Peoples Temple leader told the rapt crowd that he was asked to wear a bulletproof vest because he had, that very day, received not one, not two, but *three* assassination threats on his life. "As of today, Jim Jones and the thousands of Peoples Temple are still peaceful activists," he said. "But change, America! There's one thing we want to tell you, and I think we speak for more than Peoples Temple: If you come for one of us, you damn well better come for all of us!"

The crowd burst into the longest ovation of the night—Jones had ensured that Glide's pews were packed with hundreds of Peoples Temple disciples who could be counted on to hang on his every word. Among them was Miss Glover, who had looked right past Bill and me there as though she didn't recognize us.

Afterward everyone filed out and boarded buses to attend the culmination of the event—a Glide-sponsored concert at the Cow Palace featuring Marvin Gaye and Quincy Jones. Organizers were nervous about filling the vast arena, but Jones had assured them they need not worry, and he proved correct. Peoples Temple had paid five thousand dollars to reserve a huge bloc of seats. The rest of us watched in amazement as women in starched white uniforms directed and seated row after row of their fellow Peoples Temple members. Our Miss Glover was in charge of these ushers.

But the show wasn't over yet. Not long after the concert began, the Reverend Jones signaled his contingent to rise and, in the middle of a musical number, they abruptly trooped out en masse. Their departure left a huge and embarrassing gap in the front of the auditorium, as though the audience just had a front tooth knocked out. We heard conflicting explanations for the exodus: It may have been because Gaye, who suffered from stage fright and was habitually tardy, arrived late and ran afoul of the Peoples

Temple's tightly regimented schedule. It may have been because orchestra leader Quincy Jones rebuffed Peoples Temple requests to give the church an onstage plug. Or it may have been yet another stunt of one-upmanship over Cecil Williams.

Regardless, everyone left with a heightened appreciation for the raw power the Reverend Jim Jones had at his disposal. Throngs of people appeared completely under his control, as though they would do his bidding at all costs. Ultimately, we would discover that's precisely what they would do.

The potency of Peoples Temple grew. The most gullible fell for preposterous "healings" in which Jones claimed to reach into the bodies of the sick and snatch out their cancers—sometimes dangling raw chicken livers and gizzards from his fingers as evidence. The more sanguine recognized such charades as deceptive but were willing to overlook them because they admired the church's engagement in charitable work—a dining hall, drug treatment program, escort service for senior citizens, free physical therapy, even a funding drive to save an endangered pet clinic. The cynical were blasé about the church's theology but calculated how to capitalize on its ability to mobilize shock troops for political gain.

By the time Moscone was elected mayor on a small margin of victory that some credited to Peoples Temple, Jones had the clout to receive—and reject—the mayor's initial appointment of him to the city's Human Rights Commission. Instead he insisted on what he saw as a more prestigious appointment and became chairman of the San Francisco Housing Authority Commission. Within a few months, he had finagled a private tête-à-tête with the woman who soon would be First Lady, Rosalynn Carter.

Beneath the facade, however, the foundation of Peoples Temple was starting to crumble. A small number of fearful Temple defectors began to describe the inner workings of a twisted cult. They told of sleep deprivation and emotional abuse, of manipulation and fraud, of sexual depravity and beatings—all masterminded by a messianic reverend who was losing his mind.

The story was difficult for investigative reporters to corroborate. One reason was the vehemence of the Temple's attacks against those who probed its operations: *New West* magazine reported receiving as many as 100 phone calls and 140 letters a day, from the lowliest Temple member up to Lieutenant Governor Mervyn Dymally, urging the magazine to abort a critical exposé. And another reason was the difficulty of reconciling the defectors' damning tales with the contrary witness borne by the then thousands of Temple faithful who rhapsodized about Jones.

Miss Glover never wavered in her praise of her church or its "Father"— not even when she would appear on our doorstep exhausted, her shoulders sagging and her eyelids heavy from lack of sleep. The Temple often would load members on its fleet of buses and send them through the Central Valley or Los Angeles all weekend, collecting new members and financial donations.

"Miss Glover," I would say as gently as possible, "doesn't your minister understand that you can't be doing this? You can't be working for the church all day Saturday and Sunday, and then ride the bus all night, and then do a good job at work on Monday? You've got to take care of yourself."

"No, it's all right, I'm fine," she would say, "I slept on the bus. Father takes good care of us, don't you worry."

Then one day Miss Glover failed to show up to clean our house, and we never heard from her again. At the same time, Jones joined hundreds of his followers in leaving San Francisco for the South American tropics of Guyana, establishing an agrarian commune named Jonestown.

Defectors and relatives of Temple followers ratcheted up pressure on government officials to investigate claims that Jim Jones had degenerated from a con man to a madman and was either brainwashing people or holding them against their will, or both, at Jonestown. In November 1978, U.S. Representative Leo Ryan announced he was leading a fact-finding mission to determine whether any of the Temple members in Guyana wanted out.

Among those who would accompany him was Bob Brown, an NBC cameraman who had worked alongside my husband, Bill, and had become such a close friend of our family that Darolyn called him "Uncle Bob." Shortly before he left for Guyana, Bob stopped by our house to say good-bye. I told him about how Miss Glover had vanished, and he agreed to keep an eye out for her there and return with whatever he found out.

But Bob never came back, and neither did Congressman Ryan. As the Ryan party and fifteen defectors were boarding a Cessna for their return home on November 18, a gun-toting squad of Temple henchmen dispatched by Jones staged an airstrip ambush. They shot and killed Ryan, the only member of Congress ever killed in the line of duty. Their bullets also claimed Bob, as well as NBC reporter Don Harris, *San Francisco Examiner* photographer Greg Robinson, and Temple defector Patricia Parks. And Ryan aide Jackie Speier and others were wounded by gunfire as they fled for their lives into the jungle.

Knowing that his cult was collapsing, Jones immediately called a "White Night," ordering his followers to join him in a "revolutionary suicide"—a bastardization of Huey Newton's original idea. Adults first squirted bitter cyanide down the throats of babies and children and watched them convulse and die. They themselves then drank from a giant galvanized vat in which the poison had been mixed with Grape Flavor Aid—perishing one by one under the watchful eyes of armed guards and Jones himself, before he died from a gunshot.

A total of 909 people died at Jonestown, prompting some to label it the largest mass suicide in human history. Others stressed that, given the repressive circumstances, *mass murder* would be a more accurate descriptor.

The footage of Guyana, retrieved posthumously from Bob Brown's camera, made my blood run cold—it captured scenes from the Temple's compound and the airstrip. Later other footage hit the airwaves, depicting from overhead the site of the massacre itself, which showed hundreds of bloated bodies wrapped around one another in a final, macabre embrace.

I never did learn what became of Miss Glover, if that was indeed her real name—the State Department did not list anyone named Glover among the Jonestown victims. But as I interviewed Temple survivors, including Jim Jones's son Stephan and attorney Tim Stoen, I discovered that Miss Glover probably was doing more at my house than dusting my furniture and cleaning my floors.

Many Peoples Temple adherents worked as domestics or clerks in the homes and offices of politicians, reporters, bureaucrats, and influential people—an opportunity that Jim Jones never failed to exploit. I was told he would have had Miss Glover reporting back about goings-on in my household; searching for any compromising details; and even delivering my trash to the Temple so members could sort through our papers to glean useful intelligence. I could scarcely believe it: Jim Jones had a spy in my house.

As more information surfaced about Peoples Temple operations, I learned that this was, indeed, a typical technique. Knowledge was power. Jones could use it to bolster his claim of being a psychic with supernatural insight. He could use it to anticipate and extinguish potential Temple criticisms before they became public. And he could, if necessary, use it to blackmail people to get what he wanted. He had an uncanny ability to ascertain the precise contents of a journalist's story days before it was printed or aired, as *Chronicle* reporter Julie Smith once discovered when she attempted a Temple article—Jones somehow learned the exact wording of her draft although it still was in her desk drawer.

I doubt that Jones ever deployed any inside information emanating from my home. I was friends with some of his cherished allies—including Willie Brown and Carlton Goodlett—but I can't imagine being the unwitting conduit of any useful information about them either.

The entire episode remains a mystery. All I know for certain is that Miss Glover's reports about us must have been dull indeed.

The cataclysm of Jonestown shattered the city of San Francisco. Powerful people who had defended Jones walked around stricken. But San Franciscans had no time to regain emotional equilibrium before a second tragedy knocked the wind out of us again. This crisis didn't unfold in some faraway jungle; it struck the very heart of San Francisco—inside City Hall.

On the morning of November 27, 1978, I was at home finishing my makeup when the phone rang. I answered and heard Darolyn's voice, hysterical.

"Mom, mom, the mayor's been shot!" she cried. "Oh God, it just happened. He's dead—the mayor is dead."

I tried to keep my voice steady.

"Are you OK?"

"Yes, I'm fine, but they're trying to get us all out of here because they think he's still in the building."

In the confusion of the moment, I had no idea who *he* was, but I presumed that Mayor Moscone's killer was at large inside City Hall, still armed and dangerous. And my daughter was trapped inside.

Darolyn had graduated from high school only six months earlier, and she eagerly had taken a job working for the mayor. Her immediate boss once was the city's first black homicide inspector, Rotea Gilford, who now headed the mayor's commission on crime and recidivism. Darolyn knew the Moscone family well—she had even danced with Rebecca's debonair dad at their school's Father-Daughter Dance.

"Are you safe?" I asked.

"Yes," she said, and then I heard talking in the background. "They're saying they just arrested the guy who did it."

"Stay put, Darolyn, I'm on my way."

We lived only a short distance from City Hall; so I raced there, abandoned my car somewhere on the street, and rushed in. Under the rotunda, all was in pandemonium: people were wailing and crying, either scurrying to and fro or standing numb in a daze. With the horror of Jonestown still fresh on my mind, I worried that the death squads about which Jones had rambled in his final days were being unleashed in San Francisco.

But the killer proved to be a lone individual with a petty political grievance and an unstable temperament. He also had been a San Francisco county supervisor.

Dan White was a square-jawed, straitlaced former firefighter and policeman, emblematic of an "old San Francisco," whose socially conservative Irish and Italian citizenry were losing their grip on the city. A rainbow coalition of minorities and the left had elected the liberal Moscone as mayor, and newly instituted district elections had enabled the city's Castro District to elect the first openly gay man to public office in California. White perceived Moscone and Supervisor Harvey Milk as threats to the old order; but perhaps more tellingly, he believed both men had personally double-crossed him. In a fit of pique, he had resigned—and then regretted his decision and asked the mayor to reappoint him. Moscone was not going to do that.

So, after a sleepless night, White had dressed, fully loaded his old police revolver, stuffed ten extra bullets into a pocket of his tan three-piece suit, and walked into Moscone's City Hall office to confront him. After the mayor turned to fix him a drink, White fired two bullets into Moscone's torso and two more at point-blank range into his skull.

Then he reloaded.

Supervisor Milk was in his office. Within minutes, White cornered him and reenacted the ritual of execution: this time, three bullets to disable his victim and two more into his brain. White then fled past a row of fellow supervisors' offices. One of them, Board of Supervisors president Dianne Feinstein, heard the shots and was the first to discover Milk's body. When she checked for his pulse, her fingers slipped into the gaping bullet hole in his wrist.

I found Darolyn in her first-floor office. My usually fearless daughter still was trembling. I held her close, not only to console her, but also to affirm for myself that she was safe and sound. Then I had to get to work.

Before long I'd confirmed the rumors. By the time a traumatized Feinstein stood on marble steps to deliver a press announcement, her skirt still stained with Milk's blood, I already knew what she had to say: "As president of the board of supervisors, it is my duty to inform you that both Mayor Moscone and Supervisor Harvey Milk have been shot and killed."

Reporters gasped, and someone shouted "Jesus Christ!" before they quieted enough for Feinstein to complete her terse statement. "The suspect is Supervisor Dan White."

Turning on my heels, I headed for my car. As I crossed the sidewalk and looked back at the dome of City Hall against the gray sky, my cosmopolitan metropolis suddenly felt fragile. How much more violence and pain could one city absorb?

A stopwatch was ticking in my head: only five hours until the evening newscast would go live. I was about to anchor the most difficult broadcast of my career. And I knew it was vital to do this right.

A year earlier I had made a professional switch. After a decade of reporting and anchoring at KPIX, I had moved to KQED, one of the most watched and respected PBS stations in the country. The switch meant a huge pay cut. But it also meant the opportunity to become the sole anchor of a primetime newscast.

My new job allowed me to reunite with former colleagues who had preceded me to KQED: people I respected and loved, including Bill Osterhaus and George Osterkamp, who offered me the job; Bill Hazelwood, the former producer of our weekly minority-affairs program *All Together Now*; and my fellow KPIX reporting colleague Rollin Post. Producer Roxanne Russell signed on soon afterward. KQED hired astute news producers, including John Roszak, and also reporters who specialized in law, science, politics, entertainment, and health and would leave their mark on journalism: Phil Bronstein, who would become executive editor of the *San Francisco Chronicle*; Randy Shilts, who would author best-selling books on Harvey Milk and the AIDS epidemic; and Bill Skane and Bill Whitaker, both of whom would become CBS network correspondents.

KPIX was gracious to me, permitting me to continue as paid anchor of *All Together Now.* By working a twenty-hour week at KPIX on top of my forty-hour week at KQED, I was able to financially break even.

As I made my way to KQED the day of the City Hall assassinations, I was mindful that my new station had a tight budget, a small staff, and very limited resources. The city's commercial stations would be able to go all out on this story in a way that our public station could not. But as soon as I arrived at KQED, I could see our staff working together like a finely tuned machine. We held an impromptu news meeting to discuss how to best cover the day in a way that played to our strengths.

The answer was self-evident. Our newscast, *A Closer Look*, needed to deliver exactly that—thoughtful coverage, insiders' analyses about the emotional and political ramifications of events, and a tone that served to inform and calm viewers amid the turmoil. We decided to expand our broadcast to a full hour that night.

My first booking call went to my old friend Willie Brown, who had been in the mayor's office only minutes before his fatal rendezvous with White. There was no quicker political mind or sharper strategist than Brown, who was the first to consult the city charter to ascertain the line of succession. He recognized that George Moscone's legacy was at stake.

But he also loved the mayor like a brother. I had never seen my usually ebullient friend so sad. Asked by reporters how he would remember Moscone, his disbelief was apparent. "I will remember George Moscone as . . . how can I forget George Moscone? I don't think he's dead."

Even so, Brown agreed to appear live in our studio. So, too, did the man who discovered Moscone's body, his press secretary Mel Wax, whom I had replaced as KQED's anchor when he left the station. Of course every journalist in town wanted Feinstein, who was now officially acting mayor. I did not push her to come to our studio: I knew too much about the ordeal she had been through to impose upon her further.

But she did consent to a live audio interview from her home. The station set up a remote link; however, it was beset by technical glitches that threatened to doom our interview. Finally Feinstein said, "Well, why don't you just call me back on my regular phone?" and we did the interview that way, holding a mike to the receiver so viewers could hear her words.

As the program continued with a roundtable discussion, I turned to Wax. "Was there ever any indication, anything that would have caused those in your office to worry about such an event?" I asked.

"No," he answered. "As the archbishop said, you can't explain the unexplainable."

Jonestown was mentioned, and Rollin said people must not succumb to paranoia. When another panelist interrupted with, "I think we have a right to be paranoid," Rollin replied, "Yes, but it's not healthy."

After we finally signed off, I sighed with relief and, despite the sound snafus, felt a professional pride in our newscast. The program would later receive the Corporation for Public Broadcasting's award for Best Local News Program and a certificate of excellence from the California Associated Press Television and Radio Association for best live coverage.

Knowing that Bill had driven Darolyn home that evening, I made my way back to City Hall, where thousands of citizens had gathered for a vigil, a stream of twinkling candles illuminating the cold night. Feinstein spoke with somber dignity, seeking to soothe the collective anguish—functioning, as one reporter noted, like San Francisco's "civic widow." Then Joan Baez began to sing "Amazing Grace."

I mentally clocked out as a journalist and let myself feel like a human being. And then I couldn't stop crying.

seventeen

· · ·

Diversified Interests

I'm sometimes astonished to remind myself that I grew up in an era before colorization, when not only were television and movies almost exclusively black and white, but the people who starred in them could more accurately be characterized as white and whiter. On the rare occasions that I did see black people on-screen, they were playing sidekicks, servants, or slaves.

Back then—except for films made by pioneering black filmmakers such as Oscar Micheaux—the media gave me no black heroes or heroines, no depictions of black family life, and of course, no black journalists telling the stories of my community.

After I broke through one of those barriers and into the business, I felt obligated to help tear down other obstacles and make way for more people of color, so that we could transform the face of news and entertainment. Over the years, I've tried to mentor, support, and encourage dozens of young journalists and performers. But I also tried to advance the cause in a more systematic fashion, starting with my union.

I must confess that I didn't grow up with an inherent affection for unions. In my family, we knew that union shops were the gatekeepers and that they looked out for their existing white members at the expense of minority new-comers. Unions made getting work harder for the men in my family—my father, uncles, and even my husband. They couldn't get a high-paying union job without union membership; and they couldn't obtain union membership unless a certain number of white members were willing to withstand rebuke from their fellow journeymen and vouch for the newcomers.

But in 1967, when I joined the staff of overwhelmingly white TV sta-tion KPIX, the station's union contract required that I become a member of American Federation of Television and Radio Artists (AFTRA). My attitude about unions was about to change.

One day my shop steward, studio announcer Bill Hillman, dropped by my desk to ask about my workload. I was so thrilled to be a TV reporter that I'd never stopped to question whether my station might be taking advantage of me. But in that past month alone, I had worked twenty-nine consecutive days without one off.

Was it because I was black? or because I was female? or simply because I was naive and compliant? I didn't know, but I did know that my steward had a point. "That's just not right," he said with a shake of his head. "It's just not right." Years later at Hillman's request, I gave permission to the union to use copies of my time cards as ammunition in its battle to establish a forty-hour workweek for TV reporters. In so doing, I unwittingly thrust myself into the crux of a bitter debate and made myself unpopular with managers and even many of the old newsmen.

One of those was George Herman, who had covered the Korean War and the White House for CBS. We had never met before when he asked Hillman to invite me along for drinks at the Fairmont Hotel bar. But no sooner did we sit down than he lit into me. "You're about to ruin my career," he said. "I can see it now—I'm on a stakeout, and when my eight hours are up, I'll have to turn my notes over to some yokel so nobody has to pay me overtime. No good reporter should work on the clock."

Nonetheless, AFTRA prevailed, guaranteeing that my fellow unionized broadcast reporters who worked more than a forty-hour week were entitled to overtime pay. And Bill Hillman and I forged what would be a lasting alliance. Hillman—a white man who worked in a dim sound booth doing live station and public service announcements and spent his downtime reading intellectual journals—was determined that his union reflect the diversity of the country in general and the Bay Area in particular. He became president of our local and then invited me to my first union convention.

AFTRA in those days represented forty-five thousand radio and television artists, but only a few dozen minority members. I stepped into a convention hall full of white men; I felt many of them eyeing me quizzically or resentfully and asked myself why I had come. I was sorely tempted to just sit quietly through the meetings and then retreat to my hotel room service in solitude. But I forced myself to not be invisible—to strike up conversations and join group dinners, exposing myself to the entrenched union leadership. With Hillman's help, a handful of female and minority members developed enough critical mass to activate within the union an Equal Employment Opportunity committee.

At first AFTRA's leadership could never seem to squeeze our committee onto the agenda or accommodate us with a meeting room. We were a small nucleus, so we would end up clustered in a coffee shop or convened on turquoise and white chairs around the hotel pool.

But our clout began to grow. In 1979, Hillman was elected national president. I would become president of my local, the chairwoman of AFTRA's Equal Employment Opportunity Committee, and ultimately, a national AFTRA vice president. Some of the issues I engaged were in my own backyard. In 1981—a decade after New York station WABC-TV threatened the job of reporter Melba Tolliver for wearing an Afro to cover the wedding of then president Nixon's daughter, Tricia—KGO-TV in San Francisco suspended reporter Dorothy Reed for wearing her hair in beaded cornrows. The station called it "inappropriate and distracting." But after our union and the NAACP took up her cause, KGO repaid her two weeks of lost salary and struck a compromise: she lost the beads but kept the cornrows.

On the national stage, our Equal Employment Opportunity Committee was learning to challenge assumptions, generate news, and draft and win adoption of resolutions, including one requiring management executives to meet with us at least once a year.

Our pitch was simple and reasonable. We had statistical ammunition— and we had our own experiences. Sumi Haru, a Filipino member of our delegation, told network executives that she had been a cheerleader, as had her sister and her two daughters. A Latino member had served in the military. And around the country, minority candidates were winning public office. But we noted that we had never seen a minority cheerleader, soldier, or politician on TV soaps or comedies.

"Do you encounter minorities in your lives?" I asked one panel of network executives.

"Yes, of course," one of them replied dismissively. "I see them at the supermarket and even in my own home. My housekeeper is Hispanic."

These network executives would sit across from us and insist that inequities had absolutely, positively nothing to do with prejudice. Besides, they would add, it wasn't their fault. "Perhaps you should meet with the shows' producers."

So we would schedule a meeting with the producers, who would insist it wasn't their fault either. "Perhaps you should meet with the shows' writers."

Then, "Perhaps you should meet with the casting agents." And so on and so on.

When anyone asserted there were no qualified minorities to hire, we countered, "Oh yes, there are"—and developed union-sponsored showcases of talented applicants.

In New York, we pushed for more substantial and representative roles for minorities in broadcast commercials, comedies, and daytime dramas. Too many great performers of color were being penalized by the unofficial "five lines or less" rule: actors who had so few lines were considered bit players, earning a lower rate of pay. The union's EEO committees invited these artists to a daylong conference focused on these injustices and how to reverse them.

We couldn't help noticing one white man who sat in the back of the room all day, listening patiently and taking notes on complaint after complaint. None of us knew who he was or why he was attending. But days later, the union received something in the mail that resolved the riddle. Our uninvited, silent observer was Jim Cochran, an executive representing Procter & Gamble—at that time, the biggest sponsor of daytime soap operas. Inspired by what he heard at the conference, he wrote his ad agency a letter saying he wanted to see a more accurate reflection of minorities in product commercials and on the entertainment programs his company sponsored. He sent AFTRA a copy of that letter.

We used Los Angeles as our lab to study local TV news, and we found bosses guilty of reporter profiling. A grisly murder in a poorer neighborhood? They would dispatch a black reporter. A consumer story at a suburban mall? They would assign a white reporter. One African American reporter told us, "If I'm doing the news and I mention your friend, it means your friend is dead." Among television anchors, we found no Asian men and only one African American. And if a city as racially and ethnically variegated as Los Angeles was profiling reporters, other local broadcast markets around the country were doing so even more.

We went to Washington, D.C., to fight for federal regulations requiring companies using the "public airwaves" to collect and publicly release data on the hiring of women and minorities. When lawmakers suggested we could simply file a grievance with the Civil Rights Commission, we argued that most cases would languish unless we could provide statistical evidence that minorities were, in fact, being systematically excluded from jobs. Our battle with lawmakers was ongoing, with federal judges and regulators inclined to rescind our advances, and us struggling to reclaim lost ground yet again.

At one point in 2000, an AFTRA delegation was concluding a private meeting with a skeptical Federal Communications Commission chairman Michael Powell, son of former secretary of state Colin Powell. I took him aside and told him I had been good friends with his aunt Margo Hicks, one of the founders of the Black Filmmakers Hall of Fame.

"And if you know your auntie Margo," I said, "then you know how much she gave for this cause. Now you really should do your best to make sure these rules are put back on the books." He agreed and kept his word, scheduling a hearing in the summer of 2002 to consider reinstating federal regulations requiring that TV and radio stations keep records of their hiring of women and minorities. I testified at that hearing:

> You see, it's very difficult to tell how your team is doing if no one keeps score. That is why it is so difficult for me to support the broadcast industry's position that it no longer needs the EEO rules, especially when they expect us to believe that, in their words, "discrimination no longer exists." It is present in every industry, even ours. Let me tell you as an African American woman, I know it exists in my life . . . and I am not alone.
>
> The television industry is notorious for keeping detailed and accurate records on topics of interest to it. Stations know how every second of the day is used, how many dollars each second brings. They measure the audience, dissecting them into minute groups and surveying their thoughts on everything from consumer items to views on world affairs. Why shouldn't the stations want to know more about the people who work for them?

The FCC decided to once again require that stations collect data on minority employment, although it refused to require stations to release those numbers to the public. The struggle would continue throughout the next decade.

By 2010 the Minority Media and Telecom Council—the industry's leading civil rights organization—had grown so exasperated with the FCC's lackluster enforcement of equal opportunity rules that it told the FCC to call the whole thing off. Noting that EEO enforcement had plummeted to 1 percent of what it once was, and labeling it "a meaningless exercise in paperwork and postage," the council demanded that the entire system be reformed so that it would actually hold stations and networks accountable for lack of diversity. The fact that thus far the FCC remains "missing in action"—under the nation's first African American president—is disheartening.

But even in my moments of utter frustration, I know that our work has made a difference. AFTRA is now headed by Kim Roberts Hedgpeth, the first African American woman to serve as chief executive of a major media industry union. She and union president Roberta Reardon have made a dynamic team. The union also appointed as national director of its EEO efforts a Puerto Rican actor named Ray Bradford, a tireless advocate who has spent years cajoling employers and supporting minorities, seniors, and disabled performers in the ongoing fight to gain more employment.

Over the past two decades, the picture has improved. Television looks more like America.

Pamm Fair, who headed AFTRA's equal employment efforts before becoming deputy national executive editor of the Screen Actors Guild, calls our historic effort "the first viral campaign." By continually shining a spotlight on diversity issues, by securing minority safeguards in collective bargaining agreements, and even by shaming executives into doing the right thing, we helped shape the makeup of the workforce and the kinds of news and entertainment it produces.

Today, my union represents some seventy thousand performers, journalists, and other artists in the entertainment and news media, in thirty-two locals from coast to coast. Our once-reluctant partner moved to the vanguard of the fight for minority representation. AFTRA created the American Scene Awards, which recognize excellence in programming that "portrays diversity in a positive and realistic light."

One of those awards goes to the station in America that most demonstrates an unwavering commitment to the communities it serves. I was profoundly gratified when the union christened this the "Belva Davis Crystal Award."

As critical as hiring, casting, and programming are, I believe we also must pay our respects to the performers themselves for their vital role—in particular those pioneers who faced the most virulent stereotyping. Often, to get work, they had to accept roles that required them to speak in Pidgin English and feign ignorance—cast only as maids, mammies, servants, and shiftless bums.

In 1974, I was invited to the debut of an annual awards ceremony in which some of these artists were inducted into what would be called the Black Filmmakers Hall of Fame. Sponsored by the Cultural and Ethnic Affairs Guild of the Oakland Museum Association, the ceremony took place in Oakland's stately art deco Paramount Theater. As moving as the tributes were, the house was only half full, and the static presentations all took place in front of drawn curtains. I believe that a ceremony celebrating visual entertainment ought to be both visual and entertaining—so I, along with local ABC assignment editor Paul Hall, offered to produce future awards ceremonies.

I continued as awards producer for almost two decades, determined each year to step up the production values. We hired crack theater producer Ron Thompson, brought in a live orchestra, incorporated film clips into each presentation, and persuaded both the San Francisco Ballet and the San Francisco Opera to lend us sets. My unofficial motto was, "Ask and ye shall receive."

Fans—hoping to catch glimpses of their favorite stars—would ring the streets for hours before the ceremony. The black actors, producers, and directors who attended spoke of how affirming it was to receive accolades from their fellow black citizens.

Tracking the recipients down was like a treasure hunt. One challenge was Butterfly McQueen, the piccolo-pitched actress who played the maid Prissy in 1939's *Gone with the Wind*, hysterically squeaking, "Lawdy, Miss Scarlett, I don't know nothin' bout birthin' babies!" Like other black performers on the set, she had chafed at the racism coursing through Margaret Mitchell's novel—its description of Mammy looking "sad with the uncomprehending sadness of a monkey's face" and of aggressive Negroes as "black apes." The African American cast members resisted any use of the word *nigger* in the script and any depiction of the Ku Klux Klan as a "tragic necessity" against the excesses of Reconstruction.

"I complained so much," McQueen recalled, that her fellow black actresses warned her that producer David Selznick "would never give me another job."

At the film's splashy premiere in Atlanta, only the white actors were featured, given that the Loew's Grand Theatre was a whites-only theater. And the reception from blacks was decidedly mixed: some appreciated the film and the fact that it enabled Hattie McDaniel to become the first black actress to win an Academy Award, but others saw it as glorifying slavery.

Eventually McQueen became discouraged with the parts she was offered as well as with her critics calling her "an Uncle Thomasina." For a while, she quit acting.

We tracked her down to a basement apartment in Harlem in 1975 and told her we wanted to induct her into the Black Filmmakers Hall of Fame. She sounded ecstatic, saying she would be honored to attend. But when we tried to reconnect with her to provide details, she had vanished.

After days of unsuccessful attempts by the organization's president, Mary Perry Smith, to reach her, we were ready to strike her as a no-show. Then she called, saying, "I'm here!" We discovered that McQueen hadn't understood that we were prepared to pay her airfare from New York to Oakland. She had boarded a Greyhound Bus instead. That sixty-four-year-old woman spent the previous week riding buses across the country, arriving just in time for the ceremony.

We also located Allen Hoskins, who from the age of one-and-a-half to eleven years old played Farina in the *Our Gang* films. The part was designed to be a stereotypical "pickaninny"—with the slur carried to the extent that Farina always appeared in short braids and was variously referred to as a boy or a girl.

When an emotional Hoskins accepted his award, he looked out over the applauding audience with a humble smile. "Well, it's been a long time. I just want to thank each and every one of you," he said, adding poignantly, "I'm sure glad you did forgive me."

Then there was Lincoln Perry, who worked in Vaudeville's "Chitlin' Circuit" before being cast in the most racist of roles, Stepin Fetchit. The character was a lazy, bumbling fool—although his defenders would later suggest that the role had a subversive redemption to it, given that he really outsmarted his white bosses by never actually getting around to fetching anything. Perry became a millionaire in the 1930s, but he never received equal pay or billing with his white co-stars. Eventually he left Hollywood, went broke, and seemed destined never to be heard from again.

But the Black Filmmakers Hall of Fame sought him out to honor him. Perry was, by that time, an old man in a wheelchair. He was introduced and embraced by comedian Richard Pryor, who made a living satirizing the foibles of racism. A lump rose in my throat when Pryor told Perry, "Man, you did what you had to do."

The Black Filmmakers Hall of Fame gave Spike Lee its young film-maker's award when he was a virtual unknown. Later the organization was chosen to stage one of the few benefit screenings of his biopic *Malcolm X*. We hosted virtually the entire cast of *Glory*, a Civil War film starring Denzel Washington and Morgan Freeman about one of the first army units composed of African American soldiers. And when we saluted Cicely Tyson, star of films such as *Sounder* and *Roots*, she wept.

Such prestigious stars came, perhaps in part, because none other than Sidney Poitier had blazed the trail. The first year I produced the program, in 1975, I was determined to persuade the man who was then the most famous and bankable black actor to attend. But I knew I couldn't easily lure him to an Oakland program with no track record.

So I went to work on Vincent Tubbs, the first African American to head a Hollywood film union, the Publicists Guild. Not only had he done publicity for Poitier's films, but he also was his friend and tennis partner. Our request went right down to the wire: Tubbs suggested we call on the Sunday morning of the ceremony, right after his tennis match with Poitier.

Paul Hall and I both made our pitch to the actor, still a little out of breath from his game. We promised him a car waiting at the Oakland Airport, lunch, a dressing room to change for the afternoon ceremony, and a car back to catch his return flight. When he said OK, we whooped for joy.

And a few hours later, the elegant Poitier glided onstage at the Paramount Theater. The actor—addressing the rapt, standing-room-only crowd—was so overcome with emotion that he spoke even more slowly and deliberately than usual:

When I started in this business, on my first job, I was in concert with one other black man. He was the shoeshine boy on the lot. I stand before you today the product . . . of all the black artists whose lives and creativity were frustrated by those studios. It takes a group of awfully strong men to persevere.

The door has only recently opened, you know. But I'm glad to say that stepping through it are some awfully strong men and women. I got an award once; it was called the Academy Award. This, [he paused for several seconds] this is *the* Academy Award.

I was handed one more opportunity to reposition the image of black people when, in 2002, Willie Brown, then the mayor of San Francisco, asked me to help launch the Museum of the African Diaspora. I fell in love with the concept: a 20,000-square-foot museum devoted to the interconnectivity of all humanity, based on scientific evidence that we all can trace our roots back to Africa. This museum, known as MoAD, would explore the history, culture, and art of people of African descent, within the United States and around the world.

My first reaction, nonetheless, was to say no. The mayor had the astounding notion that I would be able to privately raise $5 million in two years to fund the project. I thought he was delusional.

Granted, I had served on the building committee for the de Young, the city's prime art museum, and the experience introduced me to an upper echelon of wealthy arts patrons. But I had never done any fund-raising in my life. I watched and cheered as board president Diane Wilsey raised a record $200 million. I also helped develop the exhibition concept for a modern, more artistically and demographically inclusive new facility championed by director Harry Parker—a concept carried out with amazing success by his successor, John Buchanan.

Willie Brown, however, doesn't exactly take no for an answer; and ultimately I couldn't resist. In merely a few months, I wound up as president of MoAD's board of directors. Then I had to persuade my fellow board members to contribute a total of $1 million. It was a standard that I, as a semiretired broadcaster on a fixed income, couldn't personally meet—making me all the more grateful when board member Dr. Ernest Bates, a neurosurgeon, donated half a million dollars to ensure the board reached its goal.

That left $4 million to be culled from outside sources. I selected as my first "ask" a no-nonsense philanthropist named Alvin Baum. When I nervously concluded my rookie pitch for a donation, he shook his head and bluntly told me I had failed. "Don't show me a hint of hesitation," he advised. "You have to present your request as if you believe I'm going to say yes—that you *know* I'm going to say yes."

And then, despite my ineptitude, he graciously gave me a donation. I took his advice to heart and sharpened my appeals. I tried to master the fine art of unabashedly asking somebody for half a million dollars. And it worked. We met our targets and MoAD opened in 2005, sharing a building with the St. Regis Hotel as part of a massive redevelopment of the city's SOMA neighborhood.

Today MoAD is a cutting-edge, multimedia museum with a permanent collection, as well as lectures, films, symposiums, and special exhibits. To celebrate our opening, the British Museum consented to lend MoAD some of the oldest man-made objects in the world: nearly two-million-year-old stone tools uncovered in Tanzania's Olduvai Gorge. These tools had never before left England.

I served as executive producer of a series of films on topics such as the Haitian revolution and the triumph of Nelson Mandela, featuring artists such as actor Danny Glover and hip-hop performer Wyclef Jean. But most dear to me was our documentary about my personal spiritual mentor, Howard Thurman, who had dared to envision a church open to "seekers of all colors and creeds." In 1944, Thurman established the first multiracial interfaith congregation in the United States, the Church for the Fellowship of All Peoples, in San Francisco. Throughout a lifetime in which he met Mahatma Gandhi, counseled Martin Luther King, and inspired millions of people like me, Thurman continued to urge that we focus not on what divides us, but on what unites us.

Whenever I become tired in the trenches of the battle for racial equality, I remember Thurman's assurance that oppressed people will overcome persecution via a love rooted in the "deep river of faith. It may twist and turn, fall back on itself and start again, stumble over an infinite series of hindering rocks," he said, "but at last the river must answer the call to the sea."

eighteen

...

Going Global

In the world of television news, nothing is more tantalizing than the big "get"—an interview with a source that everyone else wants but only you have. In 1977, few "gets" were as elusive or desirable as Fidel Castro. Cuba's enigmatic communist dictator was the archenemy of the United States—in fact, the CIA had been out to "get" Castro as well, secretly targeting him in hundreds of assassination plots that contemplated everything from an exploding cigar to a fungus-tainted scuba-diving suit. Demonized by the right and romanticized by the left, the cigar-chomping guerrilla was based only ninety miles off our shores.

And he hadn't given a TV journalist an interview in sixteen years.

I can't say I had any aspirations to land Castro—to do so seemed beyond the wildest of possibilities. After all, I worked as a junior reporter at a local station on the West Coast; I spoke no Spanish; I never had covered any overseas story; and I was well aware that only a network's chief foreign correspondent or primetime anchor could ever hope to garner such a coveted assignment. But at a social gathering in the East Bay, I was chatting with Barbara Lee, who would eventually be elected to Congress herself but in those days was an aide to then representative Ron Dellums.

"We're going on a fact-finding trip to Cuba, and Ron is going to meet one-on-one with Castro," she was explaining. And then she added, almost as an afterthought, "You should come along."

My neurons began firing on all circuits: I was electrified by the potential. Immediately I contacted my news director, got Spanish-speaking cameraman Dave Ambriz to sign on, and lobbied all the way up the chain of station owner Westinghouse. I encountered a lot of resistance—the trip would be costly and politically risky. The United States had waged a full economic embargo against Cuba since 1962, and only weeks before our proposed trip had the first U.S. cruise ship secured permission to dock in Havana. Some executives worried that the expedition by Dellums, one of the most left-leaning members of Congress, would be a propaganda coup for Castro. Others feared that a local reporter would be too unsophisticated to handle such an assignment.

But I was tenacious—and I was the only reporter the Dellums party had invited. Recognizing this chance as too newsworthy to pass up, Westinghouse opted to fund our trip. In truth, I knew little about Cuba; but I crammed like crazy, enlisting Rose Mary's reference librarian skills to help cull the maximum background information I could absorb on short notice.

On the May morning of our departure, Dave, producer Susan Anderson, and I caught a commercial flight to Miami and then boarded a tiny chartered plane destined for Havana. We aimed to land a day ahead of the Dellums contingent. We were soaring high over the Atlantic Ocean when the pilot began grumbling to himself, and I overheard him snap, "I've got the wrong coordinates."

I was no aviation expert, but this didn't sound good. We had heard that Cuban Americans in Miami got wind of our journey and many were furious, suspecting that Castro would use us to whitewash his abysmal human rights record. Were these faulty coordinates truly a careless mistake? Or would someone try to sabotage our mission to prevent us from setting foot in Cuba?

We would never know for sure. Our pilot made some quick recalculations, veered the plane off its wrong course, and anxiously headed for Havana—where we touched down with only a few drops of fuel to spare. Our next order of business was protracted negotiations with Cuban airport officials to acquire sufficient fuel for our pilot to return to the States. When we finally arrived at our hotel, an unexpected face greeted us: there on the grand staircase stood a beaming Huey Newton, who had fled to Cuba to escape U.S. prosecution but was then anxious to return to the Bay Area.

"Welcome to Cuba!" he said. "Can we talk?"

Before leaving the island, I would film an interview with Newton; but my producer was adamant that Newton was ancillary to the main story. Our goal was to craft a documentary to give KPIX viewers, and those of all the Westinghouse stations, their first look inside Cuba in fifteen years. Castro had once dispatched U.S. landholders and visitors with the admonition

"Yankee Go Home." But at the time, with newly elected president Jimmy Carter in office and Cuba longing for an infusion of revenue, a new era seemed at hand. Our program would be titled "Yankee Come Back."

As we were unpacking, we picked up rumors that a Russian Aeroflot plane had just crashed near a Havana landing strip. Gathering gear and scrambling downstairs to capture this breaking story, we urgently asked our Cuban escorts for a lift back to the airport.

"What's your hurry?" they asked.

"We hear there's been a plane crash," we said.

"If that's true, why would you want to go see such a thing?"

"Because it's news," we responded impatiently.

They gave us puzzled stares. "What do you mean by *news*? Why would anyone want to watch something so tragic? No one wants to see that." And they refused to transport us—giving us our first insight into how differently the Cubans regarded the role of the press.

The atmosphere draped over Havana like an oppressive blanket, smothering us in heat and humidity day and night. The streets pulsated with a staccato Latin rhythm and shimmered in the sun, colors bursting forth from building murals and clingy tropical clothing. Many everyday sights seemed almost surreal: The Cubans, unable to obtain repair parts for U.S.-made vehicles, drove decades-old contraptions strung together with mismatched parts. My narration observed "an almost comic parade of clanking, puffing cars."

I also noted the long line snaking around a department store an hour before it opened, demonstrating the country's shortage of durable goods. I reported that the Cuban government allowed citizens to purchase only one pound of meat per person every nine days, and that many Cubans evaded this restriction by eating out in restaurants—although securing a table required waiting in another long line. I acknowledged that we saw no beggars on the streets and no unemployment. As I said, "everyone who wants a job has one. Probably even people who don't want a job have one."

We toured schools, hospitals, factories, and nightclubs. I interviewed people on the street, and I was invited to the home of one couple we had randomly encountered. I queried everyone about daily life: what they did for entertainment, how they felt about the schools, what kind of food they enjoyed, and how much power women had at work and at home.

Fidel's elder brother, Ramon—the Castro who spent the revolution on the sidelines—gave us a tour of the countryside in his jeep, the excursion culminating in a visit to his cattle-breeding farm outside Havana. We also flew in a small Aeroflot craft across the island to Santiago de Cuba, near where Castro's revolution started. Gripping our armrests as a Caribbean thunderstorm tossed the plane, we had flashbacks of the earlier Aeroflot crash. Another night, after we returned to our hotel and took an elevator up to our rooms, we were startled when the doors opened and Fidel Castro himself was waiting to greet us in full military fatigues, his body poised in parade rest position.

But it was pure theater: El Commandante, as he was known, would meet with Dellums, but he was not yet ready to give the rest of us a private audience.

At the same time, I became aware that Barbara Walters was jaunting about the island, enjoying exclusive interview time with the dictator. She didn't know me, but I certainly knew of her. At the time, Walters was the most famous woman in TV news, having become the first female co-anchor of ABC's *Evening News* and earning a reported—and controversial—million-dollar salary. I was told she was traveling with a producer, assistant producer, cameraman, lighting person, sound person, and makeup artist, and that they had the use of a helicopter and boat. I would later learn that Castro had even taken her to his former hideout in the Sierra Maestre Mountains for a barbecue one night; and on another night he permitted her to interview him more than five hours before grilling cheese sandwiches for her and her entire entourage. In fact, years later she would still be forced to contradict gossip of a torrid tropical affair.

As for me, I was intimidated enough from being on my first global assignment. Now I couldn't help feeling outgunned at every turn by a network star with lavish resources at her disposal.

Nonetheless, those of us in the Dellums delegation kept up a week's worth of frenetic ping-ponging around the island. Aside from aides, the members of the Dellums delegation were all African American, each with a distinct field of expertise. Among them were Harvard psychiatrist Alvin Poussaint, Oakland Public Schools superintendent Ruth Love, banker Louis Barnett, and attorney and future legislator and Oakland mayor Elihu Harris. Late one evening, when we all returned exhausted from yet another packed day of exploration, word swept through our party that Castro at last was ready to see us.

Our instructions: Rendezvous in the hotel lobby in one hour.

Dave dashed to put his spent camera batteries on charge and to hunt for spares—the last thing we wanted was to run out of power during the most important interview of the expedition. I made my way to my room and grimaced into the mirror: my skin was parched and sunburned, my hair frizzled, my dress so damp and wrinkled it looked as though I'd slept in it. But I had no time to freshen up. I needed to help my cameraman test the mike cords, pack extra bulbs for the lights, and haul his gear down to the lobby.

We were the last to arrive, and Barbara Lee directed us to a caravan of black, Russian-made sedans. We piled in and were whisked off, racing through the quiet streets of Havana. We had been told that Castro was waiting at an undisclosed location, and that as a security measure, he slept in a different spot each night.

No one spoke. Twenty minutes passed before the car came to a halt and we clambered out in front of a nondescript building. Guards searched our equipment. Then we entered one by one through a receiving line. Fidel Castro—in his salt-and-pepper beard and formal military suit—doled out embraces, handshakes, and words of welcome in Spanish. As we milled around for a few minutes before our formal meeting began, I felt myself light-headed from fatigue and heat, and seized by panic.

My spasms of self-doubt must have been apparent, because suddenly El Commandante himself was standing before me, his translator at his side.

"What is wrong?" he asked in a tone surprisingly gentle.

"Well, it's just that . . ." my voice broke, and I blinked furiously to keep tears from dripping over the rims of my eyelids. *Don't cry,* I instructed myself. *Do. Not. Cry.* I blurted out, "I'm just such a mess, and it's really important that I not blow this interview, and now Barbara Walters has been all over Cuba, and she's got this whole staff with her, and—"

I stopped, realizing that whatever professionalism I once possessed had just spilled into a puddle at my feet. My reputation as the perpetually poised newswoman swirled down the drain. The rest of the Dellums party studied the floor, cringing on my behalf.

Castro reached out and patted my shoulder. "Everything will be fine, don't worry," he said. Then he leaned over and whispered something in Spanish, with a sly wink. The translation: "I'll give you an even better interview than I gave Barbara."

He was every iota as charming as I had heard he could be. I almost didn't mind that he knew and I knew that his words of comfort might not even be true—I appreciated them nonetheless and promptly pulled myself together.

For the next several hours, while we all gathered around him on couches and chairs, Castro puffed cigars, cracked jokes, and verbally volleyed with his U.S. visitors. We felt free to ask him about everything, from the presence of Cuban military advisors in Africa to the effects of the U.S. economic embargo.

Past one in the morning, the big meeting broke up, and I got my chance to interview Castro individually. My questions focused on his country's lack of free press and his intolerance of dissidents, including the twenty thousand people he admitted to imprisoning and others who were reportedly executed. He readily agreed that he regarded the news media as a tool of the government, and that serious dissent was not permitted, although he stressed that he punished only those bent on unraveling the revolution. As I would later say in my "Yankee Come Back" narration, "The power he uses with charm, he won with bullets."

As proud as I ultimately was of my Castro interview, I was crushed to discover that my producer didn't want to include any footage of it in the documentary. Susan Anderson was an excellent, experienced producer—she contended, though, that my voice was all over the piece anyway, and that viewers should hear questions from the U.S. experts rather than from me.

I fought, but the decision was hers to make. Unwilling to appear as though my ego were stuck in overdrive, I kept my mouth shut. Decades later, I still think back on her editing call with regret.

Yet I could hardly complain: "Yankee Come Back" won two Emmys.

But journalists can never satisfy everyone. Some Cuban Americans, rejecting anything that didn't vilify Fidel Castro, complained that I was duped by the wily dictator. One woman wrote, "I hope your face falls off!"

My career would soon bear other passport stamps. In 1980, KQED-TV dispatched me and producer Roxanne Russell to Israel, where we crafted a documentary focused in part on the aliyah, the migration of Jews from locales such as California to a new life in Israel. I couldn't help thinking how proud my aunt Pearline would be to know that I had reached the real Jordan River. I also made a pilgrimage to Bethlehem, only to be disheartened by the tacky tourism that marred the site. We ate tuna fish and cucumbers for breakfast, interviewed Arabs in the occupied territories, and took in scenes of Bedouins with their camels—sights that transported us straight back to biblical times.

We were naively and fearlessly strolling through the Old City of Jerusalem when all the doors suddenly were drawn shut and an Israeli army patrol hurried down the street with guns drawn. A young soldier stopped us and said, "I saw you yesterday at the Wailing Wall. What are you doing here?"

We explained, and he ordered us to get into the Jewish Quarter right away because a sniper was loose.

So we retreated to that quarter for a cool drink in a lovely café, and then we blithely wandered back through the Arab section to our hotel.

A few years later, I was off to the Côte d'Ivoire. The city of San Francisco adopted its first African sister city, Abidjan, the capital city known as the "Paris of Africa." San Francisco's mayor, Dianne Feinstein, took along a small contingent of city officials and reporters—including me representing my station KRON-TV—to what was billed an African success story. But I think we all could sense that we were actually witnessing the beginning of that country's decline, driven by the decadence of the wealthy and the poverty of most of the rest of the populace.

Côte d'Ivoire president Félix Houphouët-Boigny was ensconced on a gold throne in a palace with a moat patrolled by crocodiles. He was then in the process of doubling his country's national debt by constructing the largest church in the world, Our Lady of Peace Brasilia. Jarringly located in middle of bush country—in a nation where only one out of five citizens are even Christian—the megachurch was created to usurp the massive St. Peter's Basilica in the Vatican. Intending it to be a monument to himself, Houphouët-Boigny ordered construction of a stained-glass window of Jesus and a second one of himself, to be worshiped side by side.

I returned from my first foray to Africa saddened that such an extravagance existed in a country where most homes even lacked running water.

My next trip to Africa was vastly more uplifting. And although I did not go as a reporter, I believe I made an important contribution to journalism.

The year was 1994. The country was South Africa. The mood was taut. Nobel Peace Prize winner Nelson Mandela had only recently emerged from twenty-seven years in prison to become his country's first black president. His government had finally replaced the cruel system of apartheid, which artificially kept minority whites in charge and the black African majority as second-class citizens. Now determined to unite his fractured country, Mandela sought advice from those of us in the United States who had built our own bridges to interracial harmony.

The AFL-CIO sponsored one such trip, aimed at helping the all-white South African Broadcasting Corporation and all-black local radio and TV stations figure out how to work together. Our U.S. labor federation decided that my husband and I were perfect for the job and offered to pay our airfare and hotel expenses.

Because we were among the first blacks to integrate mainstream U.S. media, Bill and I were happy to share our experiences. We traveled through South Africa speaking to broadcasters and journalists, white and black. One of my messages focused on speech and the importance of eliminating the derogatory racial terms that were then pervasive throughout the nation. "If you can rid your language of insulting labels," I said, "you'll go a long way toward defusing explosive racial tensions."

Both sides asked thoughtful questions and seemed willing to at least try to get along. It wouldn't be easy—it never is—but it was a start.

Shortly before we headed home, we witnessed an unforgettable demonstration of South Africa's problems and its promise. We were outside a shopping mall when a white South African woman parked in a fashion that blocked in another driver. The other driver's white skin flushed scarlet with furor as he stomped out of his car and proceeded to smash in her driver's-side window with his bare fist. Shattered glass flew, and she fled into a nearby store.

Several South Africans were standing nearby watching the scene unfold—this vivid demonstration of the nation's raw nerves. And then suddenly, wordlessly, several of these onlookers—black and white—surrounded the woman's parked car, lifted it off the ground, and carried it out of the path of the enraged driver's car so he could be on his way. *Well,* I thought to myself, *if these people can maintain that level of cooperation, there is hope for this country after all.*

While anchoring the evening news live for KRON-TV in August 1998, I delivered a horrific breaking story on two terrorist suicide bombs targeting U.S. embassies in East Africa. Inexplicably, the script mentioned the small number of Americans believed dead or injured, but it made no mention of the many more killed and wounded Africans. I hadn't had a chance to proof the news copy in advance, but as soon as we were off the air, I tracked down the responsible news writer and unloaded my outrage.

"Why do you regard the lives of Africans as so inconsequential that they don't even deserve a mention?" I demanded. "Does the loss of human life matter only if the victims are U.S. citizens?"

The flustered news writer struggled in search of a suitable justification before shrugging and offering that it was merely an oversight.

"A big oversight," I agreed. "Don't do that again."

I was aware that we as Americans care most about our own citizens, and that of course the news would emphasize U.S. casualties. But the explosives that had ripped through Nairobi, Kenya, and Dar es Salaam, Tanzania—although directed at U.S. embassies—killed eighteen times as many Africans as Americans. In Kenya, 212 people were killed and some 4,000 wounded; in Tanzania, 11 people were killed and 85 wounded. Among the dead were 12 Americans.

Reporting next turned to the question of why. The answers were murky. Investigators initially established that the bombers were Islamic militants, perhaps seeking revenge because the United States had aided the extradition to Egypt, and alleged torture, of Egyptian Islamic Jihad terrorism suspects. But as authorities deepened their inquiry, they began to focus on the believed chief funder and mastermind of the attacks: He was a disaffected Saudi Arabian who had been building a worldwide network of jihadist cells. In 1998, average Americans didn't recognize his name. Soon they would know it all too well—Osama bin Laden.

The embassy attacks in East Africa put bin Laden on the FBI's "Ten Most Wanted Fugitives" list, and prompted then president Bill Clinton two weeks later to order missile strikes on terrorist training camps in Afghanistan—missing bin Laden himself by only a few hours.

Meanwhile, I was watching, with mounting frustration, as U.S. media coverage of the aftermath of Kenya and Tanzania dwindled to nothing. The State Department didn't seem to be doing much, either. I couldn't stop thinking about the thousands of Africans injured because terrorists were targeting us. They were being left behind to suffer while the United States and the rest of the world moved on.

Then I learned that Oakland doctor Ramona Tascoe not only shared my concern, but was actually doing something about it. As international committee chair of the National Medical Association, a black medical organization, she had collected $250,000 worth of medical supplies from Kaiser Permanente and other donors—and she intended to deliver them to Kenya and Tanzania.

I walked into news director Dan Rosenheim's office, explained the story, and took a shot. "I want to go along," I told him. "We should cover this."

And bless him, he said, "Yes, go."

Our own government discouraged the expedition and warned that it would not take responsibility for our safety. We went anyway, arriving in Nairobi just before the one-month anniversary of the blast: cameraman Joe Reardon, my husband Bill, and I joining Dr. Tascoe and forensic psychiatrist George Woods.

As I interviewed witnesses and other Kenyans, the true horror of the bombings sank in to us. Kenyans still were wide-eyed, asking "Why this?" and "Why us?" They were shell-shocked, but the survivors were pulling together to respond to the tragedy. I chose for my angle the resilience of the African people—and I also covered heroes such as Kenyan psychiatrist Frank Njenga, who soothed nerves by counseling via the radio waves and by letting callers vent their anger and anguish for hours after the attack.

Hospitals were overflowing with patients needing blood transfusions, antibiotics, and prosthetics. Local doctors were thrilled to learn that a plane-load of medical supplies collected by Dr. Tascoe had landed at the Nairobi airport. But obtaining them would be trickier.

Air France, having transported the supplies at no charge, notified us that the cargo was being stored in a hangar at the airport. But when we arrived, armed Kenyan guards turned us away. We returned the next day, convening a "press conference" aimed at pressuring Kenyan officials to surrender the goods. Rebuffing us again, they insisted no one knew where these supplies were.

I tried an old bluff, having my cameraman tape me doing mock stand-ups designed to shame Kenyan officials into doing the right thing. "Although we know these critically needed medical supplies are stored somewhere inside the airport," I ominously intoned, "the Kenyan government appears to be refusing to release them." That didn't work either.

Finally someone pointed out a man they said was the son of Daniel arap Moi, the president of Kenya at that time. I didn't know whether he really was, but he certainly had an aura of authority. And I was at the end of my rope.

"We have a big problem," I said. "I have videotape of crates of medical supplies being loaded onto an Air France plane. I have video of the plane taking off. I have a piece of paper here from Air France certifying that the plane landed, and that the supplies were unloaded. I have video of thousands of your citizens waiting for the supplies.

"But what I don't have," I continued, narrowing my eyes, "are those supplies. And if you prevent us from getting them, the whole world is going to know about it!"

A hush fell over our corner of the airport. My husband didn't move a muscle. Everyone else gazed upon me in shock. I kept staring at the Kenyan official, and he kept staring right back.

I began to realize that I may have just endangered myself and the rest of our delegation.

"Madame," the official said with a tight smile, "I can see you are upset. We do not want you to be upset. Let me see what we can do."

He disappeared for about twenty minutes and then returned with a retinue of military guards. Everyone in our group presumed I was about to be arrested. But the man motioned us to follow him to a separate building on airport grounds, where our supplies awaited. Dr. Tascoe was so relieved that she burst into tears.

The showdown would not make it into our news reports or our documentary, "After the Blast." We had no proof that officials intended to steal the valuable medical supplies, only suspicions—reinforced when we learned our second planeload of supplies, which was waylaid in Nairobi on its way to Tanzania, never arrived.

We didn't know the shipment was missing when we went on to Dar es Salaam, the Tanzanian port town, site of the other bombing. Unease permeated the streets. Our hotel was patrolled by white men in khaki shorts armed with submachine guns. We hired a guard, and then another guard to watch the first guard, and then a savvy street kid to keep an eye on them both.

Arriving at the incinerated remains of the U.S. embassy, I made no headway trying to convince a U.S. military public information officer to grant us entry to the skeletal structure. The embassy still was considered a crime scene, he said, and not a very stable one either. Capturing the scene on camera was important—but how to do it?

We located John DiCarlo, the U.S. State Department's regional security officer, who had arrived in Tanzania only fifteen days before the detonation. The bomb blew up the embassy with him inside—yet, miraculously, he didn't suffer a scratch. Fortunately for us, DiCarlo had grown up in Marin County, north of San Francisco, and he recognized me from the news there. As a result, he agreed to escort us inside, himself.

The devastation was astonishing. He showed us the spot where his secretary's car was parked: it was vaporized. He described how rescuers searched the rubble for victims, explaining, "You look for clothing first." All of those killed in Tanzania were African.

We left as both countries were grappling with how to deter future terrorist attacks. One East African doctor told me, "Realize that we can only be safer—not absolutely safe."

His wise advice would echo into the next decade, when al Qaeda's explosives would take their toll on U.S. soil.

nineteen

...

Special Reports

In the beginning, almost no one noticed the ominous oddity. But in the early 1980s the clues were laced through San Francisco's obituary pages, where week after week reports told of young men dying of pneumonia, skin cancer, or a vague "prolonged illness." These men were seldom survived by spouses or children. Many of them called the city's Castro District home.

My friend Randy Shilts was the first to draw my attention to an unnamed plague surreptitiously sweeping through the gay community. The two of us had worked at PBS station KQED—in fact, I anchored the election season panel there at which conservative state senator John Briggs publicly "outed" Randy, scorning his questions by declaring he expected as much from "a homosexual like you." We fumbled our way through the rest of the newscast without addressing the subject again, but the minute we were off the air, Randy, who talked in rapid-fire spurts, uncorked a barrage against Briggs. Most of the rest of us didn't know quite what was appropriate to say.

In 1981, the year I moved to NBC station KRON, Randy went to work for the *San Francisco Chronicle*, becoming the first openly gay reporter hired by a metropolitan daily. I felt like a protective mother to Randy, a brash and buoyant young man with a tousled mop of curly hair. He worked as hard to avoid being relegated to "gay only" stories as I once had to prevent being relegated to "black only" stories. But he became the chief advocate inside the *Chronicle* to get the story of this disease on its front pages. He fought indifference among straights and resistance among gays, many of whom feared an antigay backlash and what one opponent predicted would trigger "barbed-wire fences around the Castro."

In December of that year, the gay newspaper the *Sentinel* ran an article containing the declaration, "I'm Bobbi Campbell and I have 'gay cancer.' Although I say that, I also want to say that I'm the luckiest man in the world." The appearance of purple splotches on this nurse's feet led to the diagnosis of Kaposi's sarcoma—which in turn led him, the sixteenth case of 'gay cancer' in San Francisco, to declare himself the KS poster boy: "The purpose of the poster boy is to raise interest and money in a particular cause, and I do have aspirations of doing that regarding gay cancer. I'm writing because I have a determination to live. You do too—don't you?"

But determination wasn't enough: in those days, "gay cancer" proved 100 percent fatal.

Nor would it remain a "gay only" story for long—soon hemophiliacs and others receiving contaminated blood transfusions were stricken with the disease. In 1982, the Centers for Disease Control and Prevention gave it an official name: acquired immunodeficiency syndrome, or AIDS. In the coming years, AIDS would arguably become the most significant news story in the Bay Area and America.

At KRON I learned more about the disease from our medical reporter, Toni Casal, a registered nurse. We were the first station to interview the team of medical experts who would soon become internationally renowned for their pioneering AIDS work, including doctors Marcus Conant, Paul Volberding, and Selma Dritz. At the time, so much was a mystery that even these heroic doctors had to overcome private trepidation—as Conant would later say, "Anybody treating AIDS in the early eighties that was not afraid that they were going to catch the disease from treating their patients would have to have been brain-dead."

Panic had begun to outpace the epidemic. People wondered aloud— "Could it be spread by kissing? mosquitos? the common cold?"

When experts concluded that it spread not by casual contact but via the exchange of bodily fluids, the public remained skeptical and nervous. AIDS patient Andrew Small had to resign from a jury after fellow jurors objected to being in the same room with him. I was embarrassed to discover a similar aversion within our own newsroom.

As co-anchor of the ninety-minute Sunday news program *Weekend Extra*, I championed Toni's desire to bring Bobbi Campbell into our studio for an on-air conversation. But when Campbell arrived, all our studio technicians balked at putting a mike on him—they even refused to get close to him—creating an awkward standoff: Union rules barred anyone else from doing a technician's job. Finally, exasperated producer Beverly Hayon gave the OK for Toni to mike our guest. We were the first station in California to feature a studio interview of someone with AIDS.

To my knowledge, the union never filed a grievance over the incident. And while Campbell must have felt hurt and humiliated by such treatment, he never complained. Later, when technicians at ABC affiliate KGO refused to mike AIDS sufferer Paul Castro on its *AM San Francisco* show in 1983, he was forced to vacate the set.

I also was the first reporter allowed on Ward 5B, the first AIDS ward in America. This unorthodox unit at the county hospital, San Francisco General, was filled to capacity with dying patients, yet it reverberated with camaraderie and compassion. AIDS nursing coordinator Cliff Morrison had rewritten hospital procedures, rejecting the "next-of-kin only" rules and allowing patients to determine whom they most wanted as visitors in their final weeks. A flow of volunteers ensured that patients frequently received joyful, flamboyant, top-notch entertainment and gourmet food. The prognosis was dire, but the vibe in Ward 5B was defiant vitality.

Bill and I had talked over whether I should chase this compelling story—there could be unknown risks. We agreed I should be attentive to precautions given by medical experts but that I should continue reporting.

When the segment aired on KRON, some viewers called to complain about my having donned a surgical mask while on Ward 5B. We had to explain that the mask was not to protect me, but the other way around: because of the weakened immune systems of these patients, I was required to wear the mask to protect them from any cold, virus, or other infection I might carry.

I also reported from San Francisco's gay bathhouses, the nexus of hot debate over whether they should be shut down to protect public health. But we decided I didn't need to venture back into the cells where sex with strangers was the lure—I went in the early afternoon and interviewed in the reception area only.

When many of the single young men with AIDS found themselves without family support, an AIDS homeless shelter was established. It opened first in a motel, but threats of public protest drove organizers to relocate the shelter to a large Victorian near the Haight-Ashbury district. The success of the shelter depended on two things: donations and a covert address. Cameraman Craig Franklin and I were the TV journalists invited into the shelter's new home, where residents shared heartbreaking stories about their illness and the poverty and isolation that the shelter helped them escape. Our report garnered an Emmy.

When specialists decided that a new test was a way to halt the spread of AIDS, Dr. Volberding asked me to appear with him in a video to be shown at testing centers. In the video, we talked about behavioral changes that could arrest the epidemic, including safe sex and the use of condoms. We also encouraged that anyone who might have been exposed get tested so that the person could avoid unknowingly transmitting the virus to someone else. Apparently, that video really got around. I continue to meet people who were inspired by it. Recently, one robust man in the supermarket introduced himself and thanked me for helping him save his life. I considered our AIDS reporting to be the best use of the tools of our trade: We delivered lifesaving information and evoked empathy for those suffering the ravages of the disease.

I had my own personal scare when the safety of San Francisco's blood supply was called into question: while battling anemia, I was given a transfusion. So I privately took an AIDS test, the same one I had recently promoted in the video. It came back negative.

Randy was not so fortunate. I remember him stopping by our house and ecstatically yelling for me to come admire his new car, an Acura purchased with his advance to write an opus about AIDS. The book, *And the Band Played On*, would become an international bestseller and finalist for the National Book Critics Circle Award, prompting an Emmy-winning HBO film. To ensure journalistic objectivity, he waited to learn the results of his own AIDS test until the very day in 1987 that he finished the book: the test came out positive. With the help of an improved drug regimen, he lived seven more years.

The last time I was in the room of an AIDS patient, I was there to say good-bye to John Roszak, whom I had first met in the KQED newsroom and who served as my producer when I returned to that station after KRON. A gay man who had escaped the first wave of AIDS infections, John was terribly lonely. He often introduced me to the latest in a line of men he invited into the control room as his guests. After encountering a well-tanned trio of young men in the Green Room—all at least twenty-five years younger than John and more interested in partying than the news because it was "too depressing"—I asked to speak to him alone.

"What do you think you're doing, John?" I fumed. "I know you're not being safe—don't you see you're risking your life with all these strangers? Your luck is bound to run out. Get help. Do something! Do something before you wind up killing yourself."

He teared up, acknowledging the risks. But he made no promise to change.

When I noticed him growing gaunt, we avoided discussing the obvious. I was so furious that I selfishly let it show in my harsh treatment. We were arguing heatedly over something unimportant about the show when John confessed to me how sick he was.

It was not my finest hour. I started to cry and felt myself getting angrier—the irrational anger you feel at being powerless to stop self-destructive behavior in someone you care about is devastating. I said things I could never take back, no matter how hard I wished that I could. When my rage subsided, I was wracked with regret and remorse. Our work together had always been based as much on mutual affection as professional partnership.

So I tried my best to make it up to him and to do a better job of demonstrating what he meant to me. In his final days, I visited him in the hospital and we swapped old stories, shared some laughs, and reached through the pain to embrace one another. The KQED show he produced, *This Week in Northern California*, thrives as a testament to the news values he built and sustained for so many years.

Rollin Post and I were the true TV News "Odd Couple." Yet at every TV station I worked at, Rollin was by my side; we talked politics incessantly and co-anchored an in-depth news program at KRON for sixteen years; and we became favorite friends.

Rollin was a gentleman's gentleman—a blond, fair-skinned patrician from New York City. His grandfather had been a Pulitzer Prize–winning political cartoonist, his father a state legislator, his mother a model for *Vogue*. He graduated from UC Berkeley and got to know everybody in the political establishment. He was, in short, everything I was not.

"She's type A; I'm the type who likes to take naps. It keeps the relationship interesting," he told *Chronicle* profile writer Sylvia Rubin. "She came from a very poor family. Belva always seemed to have self-doubts about whether she was qualified to do this or that. But she's never walked away from her past. She wants to prove, more to herself than to anybody else, that she cannot, and will not, let down the African American community."

Rollin and I co-anchored *Weekend Extra* and later *California This Week* at KRON—we teamed up on public affairs and political reporting, and did tag-team coverage of state and national political conventions. "We had nothing in common," he would say, "except that it turned out we had everything in common."

I respected Rollin for his evenhanded coverage and his superhuman, encyclopedic knowledge of all things political. He could rattle off the name of the winner and loser of a congressional race in South Dakota, and probably the campaign managers as well. One reason he was such a beloved figure in politics is because he knew so much—other reporters who were frenzied on deadline would call him for facts and figures.

But expertise was not Rollin's only virtue. He was generous—sharing sources and news tips with me, vouching for me and helping me cultivate sources, and saving me, particularly at Republican conventions where people who looked remotely like me were few and far between.

Rarely did I have the edge over him, although I did when civil rights leader the Reverend Jesse Jackson twice ran for the Democratic presidential nomination. After playing a meaningful role at the 1984 convention in San Francisco, which nominated Walter Mondale, Jackson emerged a true power broker at the 1988 convention in Atlanta. Having won seven million votes in the primaries, he went to Atlanta not yet conceding the nomination nor control of his delegates—and he dominated the convention news cycle with its will-he-or-won't-he coverage. He was playing a very shrewd game, which I was keyed into because of my sources in the Jackson camp and because of Atlanta's vibrant African American power structure. This time, I was the source of firsthand information.

Usually Rollin was the one who had the inside track. If I was having trouble lining up an interview, he'd say, "Oh, I know that person a little better than you—why don't I give him a call for you?" If an editor was favoring him with better assignments, he'd say, "Why don't you give that one to Belva? She can handle that." And if I was feeling insecure about an upcoming interview and mentioned that I intended to study up, he would reassure me by joshing, "What do you mean 'study up'? You don't have to study up for that guy. You know way more than he does."

I observed his ability to schmooze and squeeze sources and tried to master the "minuet"—the give and take, the bluff and call. Rollin was the maestro.

In the late 1990s, I began to pick up on little things: he would be unable to recall a politician's name, or he would nod off at his desk in the middle of the day, or his slight stutter would be more noticeable. We at the station all adored him, so we worked around his small impediments. But for a man who was a master of details, his loss of them was telltale. One day he told me he was going to retire, and so together we ended *California This Week*.

We were feted with a "retirement" bash in the City Hall Rotunda in May of 1999, planned also as a fundraiser by his daughter Lauren and my daughter Darolyn. Part of the proceeds from the event went to San Francisco State University for an archive of TV film and video, and the rest went to MoAD to help underwrite the videos I produced there.

When I visit Rollin now, I realize that Alzheimer's disease is a cruel thief, stealing in slow motion those whom we cherish.

I had missed witnessing firsthand the crescendos of the civil rights movement—I was a single working mother struggling to make a better life for myself and my children, while the movement's heroes were waging a broader battle to make life better for all of us. Nor had I retained any desire to revisit the Deep South of my birth. My relatives had told me too many stories.

But in the winter of 1987, I was to get a second chance to watch racism rear its hideous head when I found myself in a crowd of thousands of marchers in the cold, foreboding town of Cummings, Georgia.

As the county seat of Forsythe County in northern Georgia, Cummings never recovered from the racial cleansing that took place there in 1912. An eighteen-year-old white woman had been beaten and raped, and on her deathbed she identified as her attackers three local blacks, one of whom was lynched and two of whom were hanged before a cheering mob. Then the remaining population of a thousand blacks were terrorized and permanently driven out of the county. In the 1980s, the county remained all-white.

A local man tried to sponsor a march to prove that Cummings had rid itself of racism, but he was harassed and cancelled the event. Some ninety Georgians, including Atlanta city councilman Hosea Williams, journeyed there to march instead, but they ran into Ku Klux Klan–agitated counter-demonstrators who pummeled them with bottles and rocks.

The call went out coast-to-coast for Americans not to leave the travesty in Forsythe County unanswered. From San Francisco, Glide church's Reverend Cecil Williams chartered a private plane to transport hundreds of participants to a massive march of solidarity. Among his passengers were Reverend Amos Brown, liberal grand dame Vivian Hallinan, KRON cameraman Ken Swartz, and me. Arriving bleary-eyed in Atlanta, we boarded buses bound north.

On the outskirts of Cummings, we faced a fleet of honking pickups, their Confederate flags flapping in the wind. "Git out, niggers!" the drivers shouted. "KKK—here to stay!"

Not since the GOP convention of 1964 had I felt such hatred. Our Northern California group eyed each other warily. "Can you even believe this?" we asked ourselves. "Welcome to 1955," someone said.

Soon we were beginning our odyssey, joining almost twenty thousand others, including Dr. King's widow, Coretta Scott King. The multiracial marchers bore signs reading "Brotherhood for All." The booing all-white crowd lining the roadway, who were mostly women, waved signs with different messages: "Martin Luther King Jr. was a pinko commie faggot" and "Kill 'em all. Let God sort them out."

Because I was there as a reporter, I knew I had an obligation to query not only the California marchers but also the "other side."

"Not a good idea," said Ken. "No really, not a good idea."

"Just stay with me and let's make this as quick as we can," I said tersely, aiming myself toward a group of attractive women in their thirties who were hissing and catcalling racial slurs. As they warily watched a petite black woman holding a TV microphone approach, they grew silent, their glares like bullets. I made eye contact with one blonde and asked as levelly as I could, "Could you tell me why you are so angry?"

The woman rocked back and then lurched in my direction, a fat glob of spit flying from her mouth onto my face.

I have no clear memory of what she did after that. I only know that Ken instantly shut off the camera, handed me his handkerchief to wipe my cheek, and headed us back into the throng of "brotherhood" marchers.

I trekked numbly along the mile-long route, seeking comfort in the music of people all around me singing "We Shall Overcome." I tried to regain my bearings and erase from my mind the visual image of the woman who spat on me. Easier said than done—her face has stuck with me ever since.

When we reached the end of the route, we saw why most of the hecklers were white women: Their men had gone ahead to prepare a ghastly exhibition. And those men now awaited us, clad in their white sheets and combat fatigues and hunting clothes, dangling crude black mannequins from gallows and setting one aflame in effigy.

I decided that I would never tell viewers about my personal mortification. I didn't want to the story to be "Belva goes to Georgia and gets spat on." I wanted the scope of the story to be bigger, to capture the broad swath of bigotry that stretched before us. I witnessed plenty of horrors to focus on besides my own.

As my close friend the writer Maya Angelou says, you have to tell the truth—but you don't have to tell everything.

Some of the same stories follow me wherever I go.

In the decade of the 2000s, I scaled back my workaholic ways, centering my career back at PBS station KQED, where I've been hosting a weekly half-hour show called *This Week in Northern California*. I moderate a panel of reporters dissecting the week's news, and I also occasionally report in-depth stories of special interest to me.

"Greetings Ms. Davis. I hope to God someone will let you read this letter," began a cursive note that inspired one such segment in 2009. The writer's return address was Soledad Prison. "It is intended to provide you with typically overlooked points of view regarding exorbitant costs for keeping nonviolent 'Third Strikers' in California prisons for the rest of their natural lives."

I have reported countless prison stories over the decades, and I've received thousands of letters from inmates. I'm unable to follow up on most of them, but I sensed that the appeal of this "Third Striker" merited a closer look.

In 1994, following the kidnap and murder of fourteen-year-old Polly Klaas from Petaluma, a whopping 72 percent of California voters passed an initiative to enact the toughest "Three Strikes" law in the country.

California's law mandated that for a third "strike," a lawbreaker be sentenced to twenty-five years to life. In most "Three Strikes" states, the third offense must be serious or violent. In California, although one of the prior offenses must be serious or violent, the third strike can be for anything—although four years later the state supreme court granted judges more sentencing discretion.

By 2010, the state had incarcerated more than eight thousand Three Strikers, the majority for nonviolent third offenses. African Americans made up a significantly disproportionate share of those prosecuted under the Three Strikes law.

We contacted Soledad and were invited to make a date for a general visit, to simply show up at the prison and see whether any Three Strikers wished to speak with us. A public information officer led us to an exercise yard where hundreds of inmates were playing ball, pumping iron, or participating in an outdoor church service. Prison officials announced I was there, and soon dozens and dozens of inmates lined up to share their stories.

One Three Strikes inmate's third offense was stealing a pair of socks. Another had stolen quarters from a parked van. Their experiences had led to the creation of Stanford Law School's Three Strikes Clinic, where attorneys worked on their behalf.

I also interviewed Jerry Brown, California's attorney general at the time, and Solano County district attorney David Paulson, both of whom defended California's law and maintained that Three Strikes sentencing had reduced crime overall.

Like many of my journalism colleagues, I am frustrated by the limits of time and space to tell complicated, provocative stories. I had hoped for more, envisioning an hour-long show with a panel of live guests—but a lack of resources prevented that from happening. Still, I remain resolved to advocate for overlooked and even unpopular stories.

"[We] all diligently pay weekly attention to your *Northern California* program. It has become our own civics lesson since we continue the conversations you bring into the front," one of the Soledad prisoners wrote me recently. "Your visit here was a blessing which still has its effect on many. The idea that you cared enough to cover our story is a comfort and even an encouragement to many."

twenty

...

Never in My Wildest . . .

One day it was gone. I dug into the crevices of my address book searching for my folded piece of paper, and I realized it must have fallen out when I was distracted. How many years had I carried it everywhere with me? How many times had I reread the words I wrote to myself back when I was a young single mother caring for two children and juggling three part-time jobs to pay the rent? How many times did it sustain me when I felt lost in a gaping chasm between my means and my desires?

And suddenly I realized that the paper was no longer necessary. I knew its words by heart: "Don't be afraid of the space between your dreams and reality. If you can dream it, you can make it so."

Today the Internet has breathed fresh oxygen into my mantra—it shows up on sixty thousand Google hits, and counting. Why is it that we Americans, and in particular African Americans, are so often invigorated and empowered by the motif of dreams? Perhaps because historically our dreams were the only things we could call our own? Perhaps because we've seen the glory of dreams come true?

"Hold fast to dreams," the poet Langston Hughes admonished, "if dreams die, life is a broken-winged bird that cannot fly."

"Give birth again to the dream," the poet Maya Angelou encouraged, "Take it into the palms of your hands. . . . Sculpt it into the image of your most public self. . . . The horizon leans forward, offering you space to place new steps of change."

And, most familiar of all, Dr. King—the man who crafted the most elegant speech in U.S. history around this simple declaration: *I have a dream.*

Bill and I made a pilgrimage to the Deep South together in 2000, visiting the sacred spaces of the civil rights movement and paying our respects to Dr. King and Rosa Parks for the Montgomery bus boycott that started it all.

As we pulled our rental car up in front of Dr. King's old wooden house, the house that was bombed in 1956, we met Martin Luther King III. He had no personal memory of the bombing—he was only two at the time—but soon we were chatting like old friends.

"I just want to tell you it's really a coincidence and a pleasure to meet you here in front of your family home," I said. I appreciated the blessing of getting to tell him some of what I would have loved to say to his father. "We're some of the fruits of what your dad did. We are the desegregation people. We were among the first-hired people in our business."

A KRON cameraman had unexpectedly joined us on what we'd planned to be a private vacation. I had mentioned our plans to news director Stacy Owen at a party, and she had the brainstorm to send a photographer.

"But Stacy, you don't understand—we're leaving tomorrow morning," I told her.

"Let me worry about that," she replied.

"OK," I said with a sigh, "but he has to keep up with our schedule."

Which is why Craig Franklin was videotaping from the backseat as we headed down the Alabama highway. "Keep it on cruise control," I warned Bill, my mind flashing back to movie scenes where a white sheriff with wraparound sunglasses pulls someone over and everything goes disastrously wrong.

And then, before we knew it, the slope of a bridge loomed straight ahead of us. "Welcome to Selma," Bill said, and we both grew still. Selma was, of course, the site of "Bloody Sunday." On March 7, 1965, some six hundred civil rights marchers heading to Montgomery in support of voting rights made it only six blocks. There, at the Edmund Pettus Bridge, state and local lawmen lashed into them with billy clubs and tear gas. Two weeks later, under federal protection and led by Dr. King, a throng of marchers set out to complete the aborted journey. They arrived at the state capitol in Montgomery five days after that, their number having swelled to twenty-five thousand. Before the year was over, then president Johnson would sign the Voting Rights Act.

As I traversed the windy bridge, surrounded by visiting school children from Detroit, I was overpowered by the pain and promise of the place. I couldn't help wondering whether I would have had the stuff inside me to do what those marchers did, and I felt humbled and profoundly grateful for their sacrifice.

"Lord," I said aloud, "I hope there's something I can do to make sure their spirit is never lost."

I've witnessed so many changes in my lifetime—in the world, and in me. My Louisiana parents could not have imagined that the baby they named Belvagene would have such a full and fascinating life in front of her.

As an adult, I have reached a better understanding of my parents—my quiet mother, who worked herself to the bone and never had a boss who wasn't white; my brilliant father, who chafed under the constraints of prejudice and never had the chance to make full use of his talents. They were so young when they had me, and their lives were so fraught with difficulties. If my upbringing left me desperately striving to win love and respect, well . . . striving has served me well in life.

My father later kept scrapbooks of my successes on his coffee table, and I heard that he sometimes bragged to friends and coworkers that his daughter was on TV. My mother enjoyed the occasions when I invited her and Rose Mary's mother, Miss Anna, to major events at which I was the master of ceremonies. I would help her pick out a beautiful gown and arrange a limousine service for them. And I made sure to acknowledge both women from the podium.

Often Bill and I would take the children to my mother's Southern Baptist church for Sunday services. She served as the pastor's aide, making sure his silver pitcher and cup were in place, with a freshly starched napkin around the base of both, and ice in the water. She gave what she could to the church and the NAACP.

We also frequently stopped by my father's house for Sunday dinners of roast beef, string beans, and rice. Bill and I wanted the children to see him in action—he displayed a great grasp of politics and current events and a determination to win every argument he entered. He was a Methodist, and he donated many hours of carpentry to Oakland's Taylor Memorial church.

Both of my parents and their mates came to my home for most holidays, and we all got along well. We learned late in life how to piece together a family.

When my mother suffered kidney failure and chose death over dialysis, I felt guilt: I wondered whether she might have made another choice had our past been different. And when my father died a long and painful death after complications of diabetes—he suffered through four surgeries that left him legless to the hip—I felt guilty again, regretting my decision to insert a feeding tube, because it seemed only to prolong the agony.

I learned to forgive them for everything and pray to God that they forgave me. I hope that I have lived my life in a way that made them feel proud of me. Because they never said those words, I will never know for sure.

Adulthood and parenthood helped me to understand, appreciate, and absolve my parents for their imperfections. And I think that same miracle of generational forgiveness is beginning to repeat itself with my own children. With lots of help from one of the most wonderful husbands in the world, I think I've done a very good job by many standards in raising two wonderful children. They are both caring adults who are defining success in their own terms and contributing to the world following their own natures.

Steven is a chef who owns a catering company and once had his own Cajun restaurant. He also was a culinary instructor for the Job Corps, and he now benefits others through his appreciation of food and simplicity in life: he gains pleasure in doing volunteer outreach work, teaching underprivileged children how to make simple, healthy meals from fresh ingredients. I am proud of the values that guide his life.

Darolyn remains the go-getter. Having been second finalist to Vanna White for a job on *Wheel of Fortune*, she went on to become the first African American press secretary to the second most powerful politician in California, then speaker of the assembly Willie Brown. Later she established her own downtown San Francisco public relations firm, with an emphasis in community relations, and she employs staffs in two states. Her husband, Dave, is a successful engineer, a graduate of West Point. I am proud of Darolyn's tenacity and leadership.

And I am overjoyed that she has made me a grandmother, twice. Her stepdaughter Dava, now fourteen, is inquisitive, delightful, and a great luncheon companion. And Sterling, now three, looks so much like Darolyn and exhibits her take-charge attitude—the resemblance is stunning considering they are not genetically linked.

Like me, Sterling was born to an unskilled teenage mother in Louisiana who was too overwhelmed by circumstances to care for a new baby. But, by adopting her, Darolyn guaranteed Sterling would be blessed with advantages I never had—two loving, financially stable parents; her own bedroom; the finest preschool; swimming and gymnastics classes; and doting grandparents. Bill and I cherish our time with her, despite her being the epitome of the term *handful*. Darolyn does a double take whenever she sees me get down on the floor to play with Sterling, something I didn't do with my daughter when she was that age.

My greatest regret as a mother is that I may have failed to sufficiently communicate my feelings for my children—to say "I love you" enough, to hug and hold them, to open myself up more fully to them, and most of all, to teach the art of intimacy through example. I simply had no idea how, having never experienced it growing up.

To the contrary, I've spent years scrubbing my memory of fresh hurts, walling off my emotions, never slowing down enough to feel too deeply. At one time, I was the girl too afraid of losing my best friend to confide the secrets of my own family, and then the young woman too guarded to speak of my humiliation after racists drove me from a presidential nominating convention. I have become the mature woman who still resists revealing any vulnerability. Rather than pondering the past, I propel myself forward. My union colleague Pamm Fair once described me as a duck gliding serenely across the water while, unseen beneath the surface, my feet are going a hundred miles a minute. Her depiction is true in more ways than one—it feels both difficult and dangerous for me to stop moving long enough to just think and feel. An old proverb says, "You cannot see your reflection in running water—it is only in the still water that you can see."

People closest to me, including my own children, no doubt will read much of this book and be left thinking, "I never knew that."

What an amazing ride it has been. I've been privileged to receive Lifetime Achievement Awards from the National Association of Black Journalists and the Northern California Television Academy; to share the Jefferson-Lincoln Award from the Panetta Institute for Public Policy with legendary reporters Judy Woodruff and David Broder; and to be one of the journalists featured in the Newseum, the interactive museum of journalistic milestones and icons in Washington, D.C.

After I received the Lifetime Achievement Award from the International Women's Media Foundation, I was talking with Judy Woodruff and other TV newswomen including Connie Chung and Paula Zahn about my experiences as the first black woman reporter and anchor in the western United States. You should write a book, they advised, because the next generation needs to know this history and how you did it. The complication is that I'm not sure I know how I did it!

My beleaguered husband has learned to accommodate the two different women who live inside his petite wife: the confident, overachieving dreamer; and the insecure, critical self-doubter. I am a dichotomy personified.

Even now I scrutinize every broadcast I do, anxiously reviewing the tapes and replaying the moments when I failed to ask the right question or to sound as intelligent as I should have. Even now I am self-conscious about my lack of a college education. Even now the slightest social error can provoke in me feelings of unworthiness. And even now, whenever some organization showers me with another award or accolade, I inwardly question whether I truly deserve it.

But I have spent my life plunging into new worlds—without any compass in my hand. When you don't grow up middle class, you don't know the rules when you've broken them. And the more successful I've become, the steeper the social and professional challenges. I agreed to become the only member of the San Francisco Fine Arts Museum board's Building Committee who was not a multimillionaire, and found myself flying around the world in search of the right architect, marble, glass, wood, and copper panes for construction of the museum's new home in Golden Gate Park. I volunteered to throw a dinner party in my Nob Hill apartment for the British consul general, prompting Bill to ask, "What consultant are we hiring to pull this one off?" My roster of friends now includes U.S. senators and the director of the CIA. And my journalistic goal is one more interview with a sitting U.S. president.

Television demands a kinship with viewers who invite us into their homes. I cannot help but be thrilled when newspaper profiles refer to me as "the Walter Cronkite of the Bay Area"—who wouldn't want to be compared to the journalist long known as the most trusted man in America? I cannot help but be awed and honored when I meet young people who tell me I've inspired them to journalism or public service. I've heard it said that I was the first woman of color many would come to know and trust to deliver the news of their home, their state, their nation, and their world. Having earned that trust gives me great satisfaction. And the belief that I could have been better keeps edging me forward.

With the clarity of age, I now see that everything is a temporary condition, and that I remain a work in progress—forever striving, forever doubting, forever changing. Change means placing one foot in front of the other as I cross that space from where I am to where I aspire to be. Change means no more than the turning of another page in a book still unfinished.

I recognize that there is, of course, a certain ego required to believe that anyone will want to read the story of my life. Sometimes I've told myself I should jettison the whole idea and simply retire to my small Sonoma County home, tending a "Southern garden" of greens, tomatoes, corn, and okra. Not that I could ever really retire.

This memoir is a gamble that has left my two opposite "selves" locked in a continual battle. But here it is, nonetheless. The self-doubter may cause me perpetual grief, but the dreamer in me seems always to prevail. What holds most of us back is not that our dreams are too big—it's that they are too small.

Gratitudes

My life has been filled with thanks—
given and received.

Writing a book is the most collaborative activity one can undertake. Putting words to paper may seem like a solitary venture, but that feat was possible for me only because many other people shared their knowledge, vision, talent, experiences, and love.

Never in My Wildest Dreams would be merely a dream without the scores of people who helped make far-fetched ideas and projects come to life. A few of them are noted here with gratitude:

Thank you, Norman Solomon, for your introduction to the terrific team at PoliPointPress. Without the faith of publisher Scott Jordan and the support and help of editorial director Peter Richardson we would not be sharing this moment. Thanks also to Melissa Edeburn and Darcy Cohan at PoliPoint, and I'm grateful to David Peattie at BookMatters and to Netty Kahan for the care and precision of the copyediting.

Maya Angelou has been with me since I started this project and has guided me in its completion. She has showed me that a black woman can write a book—or be queen—if that is her desire.

Bill Cosby, I thank you dearly for contributing the foreword. You continue to lead us in provocative conversations, while never losing your ability to make us laugh.

Author Lalita Tademy helped me understand the workings of the literary world.

Willie L. Brown continues to amaze me with his knowledge of almost everything, which he has shared generously with me over the years.

My thanks to Phil Bronstein and my anchorwomen pals Barbara Rodgers and Pam Moore for always offering a listening ear. And to M.J. (Bo) Bogatin for sage legal advice.

Alex Cherian at the Bay Area Television Archives found 16 millimeter film reports of stories from the mid-1960s to refresh my memory. Tom Splitz of KPIX readily gave permission for their use. Fred Zehnder was my first assignment editor, and Darryl Compton of the Television Academy took my many calls for help.

I was inspired by Louis Freeman, the news director for KDIA radio, who was the first intellectual to befriend me and tolerate my ambitions. I owe you so much.

Producers Roxanne Russell, George Osterkamp, and my first prime time television co-anchor, Ron Magers—who still owns the Chicago news market—have been friends and helpers since 1968.

My thanks to all of the photographers and editors who complete the team that creates a good television story, among them Craig Franklin, Karyne Holmes, and Ken Swartz.

News directors Don Brice, Ron Mires, Mike Ferring, Dan Rosenheim, and Stacy Owen often said yes to my wild requests. Thank you.

Designer LaVetta Forbes created practical and glamorous clothes that have lifted my spirit and served the purposes of a woman in media.

Tech wizards Terry King and David Bellard saved the day after my computer crashed just as *Never in My Wildest Dreams* was nearing completion.

Morrie Turner, thanks for immortalizing the book in your pioneering work as a cartoonist.

My parents passed on some rugged genes that have helped me withstand storms and treasure joys.

I am thankful to my immediate family: my husband William Moore, children Steven and Darolyn Davis, my son-in-law David and granddaughter Dava Wilkins, and especially the three-year-old wonder Sterling.

My aunt Pearline and mentor Anna Dean guided me through childhood, and Miss Anna gave me the gift of my lifelong best friend, Rose Mary Towns.

Edith Austin, Aileen Hernandez, Ruth Beckford, Ollie Nash Smith, and Louis Barnett mentored me as I started to mature.

I am grateful for lifelong friends Norma Barnes, Gloria Watkins, Margie Alexander, Wilma Johnson, Betty Desmuke, Wilma Vincent, Rose Mary Towns, and Freddie Howard. All are living members of Les Girls—a name we selected when we were too young to know better.

Nancy Wilson, a gifted musician and friend, pointed out the obvious years ago—that Bill and I should get married.

When the mysteries of life overwhelmed me, the Reverend Doctor Howard Thurman reminded me of the saving concept of the oneness of the human species.

Thousands of people have shared their life stories with me—Native Americans, new immigrants, the poor trapped in drug-infested pockets of cities. I thank them for allowing me to share their gripping and often heartbreaking narratives.

College for me has been the tutoring from friends in high places. Former San Francisco Fine Arts Museum Director Harry Parker and his successor John Buchanan opened the doors to the high arts. Diane Wilsey and Dr. Ernest Bates demonstrated how wealth can be wisely used.

My thanks go to Kim Roberts Hedgpeth, Lois Davis Stewart, and Ray Bradford of AFTRA for years of support, and to CEO Bruce Bodaken and Dr. Ezra Davidson of Blue Shield of California for demonstrating what it takes to be real leaders.

At the beginning of this process, Bill Carney and Sally Anderson were my readers. Anette Harris, Brenda Wade, Mauree Jane Perry, Gwen Mazer, Francee Covington, and Arnita Fermin were my boosters. Writer Carol Pogash suggested that Vicki Haddock and I would be the perfect match, and she was right.

Thanks, Vicki, for always reminding me of the value of an excellent editor and talented writer.

My sincere gratitude to all who have lent a helping hand.

Belva Davis

Acknowledgments

Belva Davis gave me the opportunity to experience a panorama of history and humanity through her eyes, and I'm honored that she trusted me to help tell her story. My thanks also go to *New York Times* contributing writer Carol Pogash, who recruited me to this project and then generously shared all the critical work she had done to help launch it; to Jayne Garrison, a fine journalist who moonlights as my de facto agent and helped bring Belva and me together; to my journalist friends Dick Rogers and Martin Snapp, who graciously read parts of the manuscript and shared insights and feedback; and to Monroe, Louisiana, research librarian Larry Foreman, University of Louisiana historian Jeff Anderson, and the Jonestown Project at San Diego State University for key assistance.

My most profound gratitude goes to my family: to my daughter Lesley for her enthusiasm, essential research, and sharp editing eye; to my daughter Sierra for her patience and for keeping me grounded in life beyond work; and to my husband, David, who remains the absolute love of my life, for everything.

Vicki Haddock

Index

About the Authors

Belva Davis is an award-winning journalist who has covered politics for four decades. She was the first African American woman hired to work on television in the western United States and is profiled in the NEWSEUM, the world's first interactive museum of news.

She has anchored at three major network affiliates—CBS, NBC, and PBS—and currently hosts a highly respected political affairs program on KQED-TV in San Francisco, the most watched public station in the country. Davis has earned eight local Emmys for her reporting. She has been awarded Certificates of Excellence from the Northern California Radio and Television News Directors Association and the Associated Press News Service, and she has garnered national recognition from the Corporation for Public Broadcasting and the National Educational Writers Association. She received the Panetta Institute award for Public Service as well as the Lifetime Achievement Award from the International Women's Media Foundation. She has been inducted into the National Association of Black Journalists Hall of Fame and is the recipient of three honorary doctorates. For more than a decade she served as the National Equal Employment Opportunities chair of AFTRA, the television union for which she has advocated for women, minorities, and the disabled.

Belva Davis is a trustee of the Fine Arts Museum of San Francisco, the Museum of the African Diaspora, the War Memorial Center for the Performing Arts, and the Institute on Aging. She is a member of the San Francisco Chapter of the Links Inc. and an honorary member of Alpha Kappa Sorority.

Vicki Haddock has spent three decades in Bay Area journalism, working as a reporter, editor, and occasional columnist for the *San Francisco Chronicle* and *San Francisco Examiner*, and before that, as a political editor and writer at the *Oakland Tribune*. A journalism graduate of the University of Missouri, Columbia, she has covered presidential and California state campaigns— and reported on an array of subjects from juvenile justice to biological warfare research. Her writing has garnered numerous citations, including journalism's prestigious Best of the West award. As an editor, she oversaw Sunday enterprise packages and supervised a team of reporters covering minority issues, education, and politics.

Now a freelance writer, her work has appeared in magazines and newspapers throughout the United States, as well as in Canada, Africa, and Europe.

Other Books from PoliPointPress

The Blue Pages: A Directory of Companies Rated by Their Politics and Practices, 2nd edition
Helps consumers match their buying decisions with their political values by listing the political contributions and business practices of over 1,000 companies. $12.95, PAPERBACK.

Sasha Abramsky, *Breadline USA: The Hidden Scandal of American Hunger and How to Fix It*
Treats the increasing food insecurity crisis in America not only as a matter of failed policies, but also as an issue of real human suffering. $23.95, CLOTH.

Rose Aguilar, *Red Highways: A Liberal's Journey into the Heartland*
Challenges red state stereotypes to reveal new strategies for progressives. $15.95, PAPERBACK.

John Amato and David Neiwert, *Over the Cliff: How Obama's Election Drove the American Right Insane*
A witty look at—and an explanation of—the far-right craziness that overtook the conservative movement after Obama became president. $16.95, PAPERBACK.

Dean Baker, *False Profits: Recovering from the Bubble Economy*
Recounts the causes of the economic meltdown and offers a progressive program for rebuilding the economy and reforming the financial system and stimulus programs. $15.95, PAPERBACK.

Dean Baker, *Plunder and Blunder: The Rise and Fall of the Bubble Economy*
Chronicles the growth and collapse of the stock and housing bubbles and explains how policy blunders and greed led to the catastrophic—but completely predictable—market meltdowns. $15.95, PAPERBACK.

Jeff Cohen, *Cable News Confidential: My Misadventures in Corporate Media*
Offers a fast-paced romp through the three major cable news channels—Fox, CNN, and MSNBC—and delivers a serious message about their failure to cover the most urgent issues of the day. $14.95, PAPERBACK.

Marjorie Cohn, *Cowboy Republic: Six Ways the Bush Gang Has Defied the Law*
Shows how the executive branch under President Bush has systematically defied the law instead of enforcing it. $14.95, PAPERBACK.

Marjorie Cohn and Kathleen Gilberd, *Rules of Disengagement: The Politics and Honor of Military Dissent*
Examines what U.S. military men and women have done—and what their families and others can do—to resist illegal wars, as well as military racism, sexual harassment, and denial of proper medical care. $14.95, PAPERBACK.

Joe Conason, *The Raw Deal: How the Bush Republicans Plan to Destroy Social Security and the Legacy of the New Deal*
Reveals the well-financed and determined effort to undo the Social Security Act and other New Deal programs. $11.00, PAPERBACK.

Kevin Danaher, Shannon Biggs, and Jason Mark, *Building the Green Economy: Success Stories from the Grassroots*
Shows how community groups, families, and individual citizens have protected their food and water, cleaned up their neighborhoods, and strengthened their local economies. $16.00, PAPERBACK.

Kevin Danaher and Alisa Gravitz, *The Green Festival Reader: Fresh Ideas from Agents of Change*
Collects the best ideas and commentary from some of the most forward green thinkers of our time. $15.95, PAPERBACK.

Reese Erlich, *Conversations with Terrorists: Middle East Leaders on Politics, Violence, and Empire*
Offers critical portraits of six Middle Eastern leaders, usually vilified as terrorists, to probe the U.S. war on terror and its media reception. $14.95, PAPERBACK.

Reese Erlich, *Dateline Havana: The Real Story of U.S. Policy and the Future of Cuba*
Explores Cuba's strained relationship with the United States, the island nation's evolving culture and politics, and prospects for U.S. Cuba policy with the departure of Fidel Castro. $22.95, HARDCOVER.

Reese Erlich, *The Iran Agenda: The Real Story of U.S. Policy and the Middle East Crisis*
Explores the turbulent recent history between the two countries and how it has led to a showdown over nuclear technology. $14.95, PAPERBACK.

Todd Farley, *Making the Grades: My Misadventures in the Standardized Testing Industry*
Exposes the folly of many large-scale educational assessments through an alternately edifying and hilarious firsthand account of life in the testing business. $16.95, PAPERBACK.

John Geluardi, *Cannabiz: The Explosive Rise of the Medical Marijuana Industry*
Reveals how a counterculture movement created a lucrative medical marijuana industry with a political wing devoted to full legalization. $15.95, PAPERBACK.

Steven Hill, *10 Steps to Repair American Democracy*
Identifies the key problems with American democracy, especially election practices, and proposes ten specific reforms to reinvigorate it. $11.00, PAPERBACK.

Jim Hunt, *They Said What? Astonishing Quotes on American Power, Democracy, and Dissent*

Covering everything from squashing domestic dissent to stymieing equal representation, these quotes remind progressives exactly what they're up against. $12.95, PAPERBACK.

Michael Huttner and Jason Salzman, *50 Ways You Can Help Obama Change America*

Describes actions citizens can take to clean up the mess from the last administration, enact Obama's core campaign promises, and move the country forward. $12.95, PAPERBACK.

Helene Jorgensen, *Sick and Tired: How America's Health Care System Fails Its Patients*

Recounts the author's struggle to receive proper treatment for Lyme disease and examines the inefficiencies and irrationalities that she discovered in America's health care system during that five-year odyssey. $16.95, PAPERBACK.

Markos Kounalakis and Peter Laufer, *Hope Is a Tattered Flag: Voices of Reason and Change for the Post-Bush Era*

Gathers together the most listened-to politicos and pundits, activists and thinkers, to answer the question: what happens after Bush leaves office? $29.95, HARD-COVER; $16.95 PAPERBACK.

Yvonne Latty, *In Conflict: Iraq War Veterans Speak Out on Duty, Loss, and the Fight to Stay Alive*

Features the unheard voices, extraordinary experiences, and personal photographs of a broad mix of Iraq War veterans, including Congressman Patrick Murphy, Tammy Duckworth, Kelly Daugherty, and Camilo Mejia. $24.00, HARDCOVER.

Phillip Longman, *Best Care Anywhere: Why VA Health Care Is Better Than Yours,* 2nd edition

Shows how the turnaround at the long-maligned VA hospitals provides a blueprint for salvaging America's expensive but troubled health care system. $15.95, PAPERBACK.

Phillip Longman and Ray Boshara, *The Next Progressive Era*

Provides a blueprint for a reempowered progressive movement and describes its implications for families, work, health, food, and savings. $22.95, HARDCOVER.

Marcia and Thomas Mitchell, *The Spy Who Tried to Stop a War: Katharine Gun and the Secret Plot to Sanction the Iraq Invasion*

Describes a covert operation to secure UN authorization for the Iraq war and the furor that erupted when a young British spy leaked it. $23.95, HARDCOVER.

Markos Moulitsas, *American Taliban: How War, Sex, Sin, and Power Bind Jihadists and the Radical Right*

Highlights how American conservatives are indistinguishable from Islamic radicals except in the name of their god. $15.95, PAPERBACK.

Susan Mulcahy, ed., *Why I'm a Democrat*

Explores the values and passions that make a diverse group of Americans proud to be Democrats. $14.95, PAPERBACK.

David Neiwert, *The Eliminationists: How Hate Talk Radicalized the American Right*

Argues that the conservative movement's alliances with far-right extremists have not only pushed the movement's agenda to the right, but also have become a malignant influence increasingly reflected in political discourse. $16.95, PAPERBACK.

Christine Pelosi, *Campaign Boot Camp: Basic Training for Future Leaders*

Offers a seven-step guide for successful campaigns and causes at all levels of government. $15.95, PAPERBACK.

William Rivers Pitt, *House of Ill Repute: Reflections on War, Lies, and America's Ravaged Reputation*

Skewers the Bush administration for its reckless invasions, warrantless wiretaps, lethally incompetent response to Hurricane Katrina, and other scandals and blunders. $16.00, PAPERBACK.

Sarah Posner, *God's Profits: Faith, Fraud, and the Republican Crusade for Values Voters*

Examines corrupt televangelists' ties to the Republican Party and unprecedented access to the Bush White House. $19.95, HARDCOVER.

Nomi Prins, *Jacked: How "Conservatives" Are Picking Your Pocket—Whether You Voted for Them or Not*

Describes how the "conservative" agenda has affected your wallet, skewed national priorities, and diminished America—but not the American spirit. $12.00, PAPERBACK.

Cliff Schecter, *The Real McCain: Why Conservatives Don't Trust Him—And Why Independents Shouldn't*

Explores the gap between the public persona of John McCain and the reality of this would-be president. $14.95, HARDCOVER.

Norman Solomon, *Made Love, Got War: Close Encounters with America's Warfare State*

Traces five decades of American militarism and the media's all-too-frequent failure to challenge it. $24.95, HARDCOVER.

John Sperling et al., *The Great Divide: Retro vs. Metro America*
Explains how and why our nation is so bitterly divided into what the authors call Retro and Metro America. $19.95, PAPERBACK.

Mark Sumner, *The Evolution of Everything: How Selection Shapes Culture, Commerce, and Nature*
Shows how Darwin's theory of evolution has been misapplied—and why a more nuanced reading of that work helps us understand a wide range of social and economic activity as well as the natural world. $15.95, PAPERBACK.

Daniel Weintraub, *Party of One: Arnold Schwarzenegger and the Rise of the Independent Voter*
Explains how Schwarzenegger found favor with independent voters, whose support has been critical to his success, and suggests that his bipartisan approach represents the future of American politics. $19.95, HARDCOVER.

Curtis White, *The Barbaric Heart: Faith, Money, and the Crisis of Nature*
Argues that the solution to the present environmental crisis may come from an unexpected quarter: the arts, religion, and the realm of the moral imagination. $16.95, PAPERBACK.

Curtis White, *The Spirit of Disobedience: Resisting the Charms of Fake Politics, Mindless Consumption, and the Culture of Total Work*
Debunks the notion that liberalism has no need for spirituality and describes a "middle way" through our red state/blue state political impasse. Includes powerful interviews with John DeGraaf, James Howard Kunstler, and Michael Ableman. $24.00, HARDCOVER.

For more information, please visit www.p3books.com.